MW01609209

Margaret Slachta

by
Ilona Mona, SSS

Translated by Anne E. Lehner, SSS
Edited by Damaris Bradish, Ph. D.

Sisters of Social Service
296 Summit Avenue
Buffalo, NY 14214

ISBN: 978-164633202-1

CONTENTS

5   Roots and Background

17   From National Catholic Women's Organization to Social Mission Society

33   A Social Mission Sister

65   Leading the Hungarian Catholic Women's Movement

103   First Woman in Hungarian Parliament

175   From Social Mission Society to Society of Sisters of Social Service

205   A Superior Created by Whip

247   Free From Public Opinion

303   The Only Man In Parliament

365   Emigration

375   Margaret Slachta, the Person

407   APPENDIX

     407   The Christian Women's Corps Now

     415   Recognitions After Death

     417   Chronology

429   ABOUT THE AUTHOR

Abbreviations Used in Footnotes

SZTTI - Sisters of Social Service Archives, Budapest, Hungary.
SSSA - B = Sisters of Social Service Archives, Buffalo, N.Y.
SSSA - H = Sisters of Social Service Archives, Hamilton, Ont. Canada
SSSA - L = Sisters of Social Service Archives, Los Angeles, California

MARGARET SLACHTA

Roots and Background [1]

Margaret Slachta was born in Kassa (Kosice today) on 18 September 1884. Her parents, Zadjeli Kálmán Slachta and Borbála Sárosi Saárossy, both came from landowner families and were descendants of Hungarian nobility reaching back to the 14th Century. [...] Liberalism was the cultural theme at the time of Margaret's birth. It expressed itself in personal, societal and political freedoms. Liberalism without regulation in the economic sphere caused great poverty for the majority of the people. Wealth was concentrated in the hands of the nobility, the church, and industrialists. Serfs received freedom of movement, but remained landless and lived in great poverty. The country lost many individuals and families migrating to create a better life for themselves and their children. Since liberalism did not embrace its faith-roots the well educated and the impoverished people stopped practicing their religion. [...]

The parents began their married life in good economic conditions. Kálmán was the president of a bank in Kosice, but because of his careless

---

[1] This chapter has been abbreviated. Only those parts have been translated that are applicable to Sister Margaret's life (Translator's note.)

character their condition soon changed. The family became bankrupt and, in 1908, immigrated to New York.

Migration to America did not help them. [...] The mother earned money by cooking for unmarried immigrants, and the father washed dishes at Ellis Island but lost his job. For a while he washed floors in the school of the Jesuits on 84th Street. Later he opened a travel agency but after a few years it had to be closed down. [...] The family experienced all the difficulties emigrants face. The mother returned to Hungary with two of her daughters in 1912 and the father returned after the beginning of World War I in 1914.

Margaret was the second among six girls. [...] Of their religious formation, there is little information. We know what Margaret shared from the diary of her younger sister, Iren. Before she started school, she passed with her mother before a store where a picture of the Holy Trinity could be seen. She asked her mother "whose picture is it?" The mother explained, "It is God's." Margaret asked, "Is God not a mother?" [...]

Sister Margaret shared in one of her teachings that her mother taught them not to shun any work. At the age of four she got a small board and rolling pin, and together with her mother she rolled out a little dough. They were also expected to participate in house cleaning. [...]

Like each of her siblings Margaret attended four years of grade school in Kosice and six grades in the middle or high school. The school gave good education and offered languages (German and French) and music. [...] By the time Margaret started higher education, the family could not afford the cost. She depended on gaining scholarships. Moreover, her father [...] offered her some copying work, as her handwriting was very neat. From her earning of five Korona[2] she put aside four for her education. She earned a teacher's degree in 1903 in Kosice, and another degree for higher education (Comparable to a Master's degree) in 1906 in Kalocsa. [...]

As Margaret began her studies for teaching in higher education, she joined the Marian Congregation. This was a favored organization for students and adults intended to deepen faith and to lead to a conscious devotion to Mary. Admission into the congregation required a year of preparation, some required prayers, and living a more conscious spiritual life. By the time Margaret reached her last year, she became the facilitator, preparing new applicants. The preparation was very thorough for the degree of teaching in higher education. The curriculum contained religion, psychology, rhetoric, aesthetics, poetry, general history and geography and pedagogy. It also included Hungarian history and Constitution and some law, Hungarian geography, German and French litera-

---

[2] Hungarian money of the time.

ture and grammar. It also required speaking knowledge of both German and French. After three years of studies with concentration on German and French language and history, Margaret left the college with a degree qualifying her to teach in high schools.

In 1906, an important event took place in the life of the college. On 18 March, Edith Farkas[3] gave a talk of the Patronage (the protection of workingwomen) to the students of the teacher's college, both those prepared for grade school teaching and those for high school teaching. Later Farkas talked to a smaller group of women and finally for the general public. The following Sunday 25 women and 120 girls gathered, with whom the Patronage was founded. Several of the students, among them Margaret, helped the ladies. Unfortunately she could help only for a short while, because at the end of the school year Margaret and those in the third year class earned their degree and left Kalocsa.

Margaret spent vacation time at home, and at the beginning of fall she taught in the high school of the Ursuline Sisters in Györ. One can read in the school's bulletin "Miss Margaret Slachta, a high school teacher with diploma,

---

[3] Edith Farkas, 1877-1942, pedagogue, organizer of women's movements; secretary of the National Catholic Women's Protective Organization and foundress of the Social Mission Society.

teaches German and French 16 hours weekly to the children in the I-IV classes." On 19 November 1906, the school organized a celebration to honor Queen Elizabeth. Margaret Slachta gave the address for the occasion. On 8 December during the admission into the Marian Congregation, Margaret was again the speaker and explained,, with great enthusiasm, how wonderful it is to be daughters of Mary and inspired them to make great efforts to struggle against weaknesses in order to be worthy daughters of Mary.[4] During the school year, because Margaret had the time, she joined the work of the Patronage that was just beginning. During the year 1906-7, according to the Bulletin of the National Catholic Women's protective organization, Margaret became the leader of the group. She submitted a study with the title: "What Are the Prerequisites of Founding and Maintaining a Patronage?" The study helps us to get a glimpse into the spirit of young patroness, Margaret. What we can notice is her motivation urging her to action and how she wants to work. Founding a Patronage had two requisites: a subjective and an objective. The subjective was the spiritual and ethica characteristics of the patroness. The patroness needed to be led by love and compassion; when she recognizes a person clothed in rags and is dirty, she sees herself as a sister who is equal with her. She must be conscious that she herself could have been born into misery, as no one can choose

---

[4] From the Bulletin of the Ursuline Sisters' high school and boarding facility of Győr, of the school year, 1906-1907.

into which social class to be born. She must possess gratitude that she offers to God through the persons she helps. The first condition of initiating a Patronage is the soul that understands what the other feels and has the strength to create that which she knows. One who has a call to be a patroness feels the pain that hurts the other and does not seek glory for the work she does. Such persons have to be discovered; therefore, many women must be invited to a lecture giving information on the movement. The speakers must be gifted to inspire for the cause; and those who volunteer must be instructed. They are to participate in the courses about Patronage and come to know the institutions of the movement. When they have prepared patronesses, the phase of inviting girls can begin. The recruiting can be held where there is opportunity for it. In some instances they might speak to mothers who are gathered in a religious organization asking them to inform and send their daughters. Another opportunity may be where a cottage industry is functioning; the patronage may take the form of an association that develops such industry. (Margaret points to the possibility of selling the products within the organization.) Among the industrial workers of Györ (in 1907) Patronage can be organized through the health care cashier desk; and even a nursery could be established where the children could spend the day and receive meals for a small fee. If a Patronage is organized for household workers, the workers themselves could propagate the organization among their friends. She found that the simplest way to start a Patronage was to organize those girls who leave the so-called School of Repetition[5]. Those girls could be attracted to the organization through their teacher. She explained that experience proves that this age group is grateful if they receive attention: they love studying - that is, to use their brains. It is important that the patroness work separately with the younger and the older girls. Their inner world is different and, therefore, they need a different approach. If the older and the younger girls are together, it is difficult to respond to their unique needs.

Maintaining a Patronage had economic requirements and the supporting members paid a yearly fee to meet them. Renting meetings rooms was not necessary since classrooms were present everywhere and the owners allowed their use without a fee for the purposes of the Patronage. Money however was needed for embroidery materials for the poorest among them. Providing a musical instrument one had to think of a small instrument, but singing could be taught without an instrument. The modest lunch for the participants was covered from the membership fee of the patronesses. Establishing a library required serious monetary investment, but the girls participating needed a library very much. The zealous patron-

---

[5] After the six years of grade school, three years of so called repetition had to be embraced by the students in Hungary by those who did or could not attend high school. (Translator's note.)

esses would have to respond to this need according to the possibilities of the place.

She explained that when a Patronage was established, maintaining it is the next challenge. The subjective condition for a well-functioning Patronage is that the patronesses prepare themselves under the guidance of the leader. If there is no central direction, no spiritual preparation and a work-plan, continuity is endangered. The leaders must be made conscious that in the Patronage everything happens for the benefit of the girls and the organization lives through them. The leader can use two methods relating to the girls: one, as with a group existing of several individuals, the other, singly to one or another girl. Developing groups begins with developing individuals. One has to work with the girls as an artist works with his art. She contemplates her art from a distance in order to preserve in it harmony; at other times she works close to it to develop its shade of color, because the artwork's harmony depends on that.

The sequence of a meeting is approximately the following: 3 to 4, embroidery - this is also a time for gathering and the opportunity to talk with the girls. From 4-4:30, religion; 4:30-5:45, a small agape and singing. Following pray together until 6:30, play; and from 6:30 to 7, library. Activities in the library are to be conducted by a patroness who knows the books and is able to suggest readings to the girls and is able to teach those who need to learn the art of reading.

The Patronage needs such patronesses whose hearts are wide open, who are selfless and willing to use their energies for the good of others. It needs women who are intelligent enough to recognize that they can succeed only in harmony with the central leadership. An important question is faced at this point: how can the patroness gain authority or respect from the girls? With some persons gaining respect is natural; others may have to acquire it, and it is possible to learn it. One method for it is not to overcome noise with shouting; in disciplining, strength becomes invisible that way. She should start talking only when attention has been gained. Silencing is easiest by simply looking at them. Upholding authority happens only through faithful consistency. The patronesses must give the example of it.

Gaining the love of the participants follows gaining authority. The love from the girls is a reflection of her love for them. Even if the girls are limited in understanding but have feelings, they can distinguish between a condescending smile and a truly Christ like love that radiates joy. Girls have to be loved as God loves us: in a divine manner. The treasure of a compassionate love needs to be prayed for, and maintaining it demands self-denial. For value one must offer value, for power self-denial.

If the fruit of a life's work is the salvation of one soul, this in itself is a rich reward because even the simplest soul has an absolute value. It is such a value for which God found it worthwhile to create her; and for which our Redeemer found it worthwhile to shed his blood. Would a person not find it important to give one or two hours, a week, or a month, or a year, or even an entire life?

Even in this small treatise we can find those principles that later directed the life and activities of Margaret Slachta: the internalization of the Gospel sense of sister/brotherhood; the value of a human being measured as high as Christ's death on the cross. This theory, however, needs to be translated into practice. The essence is love; the patronesses must love the girls in a "divine" manner, and then the girls will love the patronesses in return and do what they teach them. In her concluding words Margaret Slachta gives a glimpse of the vision living in her soul: to give an entire life for the service of God and human beings.

Most likely her well-done work in Kalocsa and Győr drew the attention of the leadership of the National Catholic Women's Organization, because Margaret spent only one year in the school of the Ursuline Sisters in Győr. In 1907, she embraced work as an educator in the teachers' training institute at Csalogány St. in Budapest. The director of that institute at the time was Sarolta Geőcze, a great personality in Hungarian women's education. During vacation in 1907, the "scandal" of the savings bank of Kosice happened. The Slachta family became bankrupt and decided to emigrate. Margaret did not go with them and her older sister, Maria Antonia, who suffered with epilepsy, was entrusted to Margaret's care. Being ill, the family did not dare to take her along. Margaret accepted responsibility for her sister and temporarily employed Rozika[6] as a caregiver.

The yearbook of the Csalogány St. School notes that Margaret took the students to the botanical gardens and, in November, to the cemetery where the nation's great personalities were placed to rest. However, Margaret worked only three months at the institute. She left 31 December 1907.[7]

As mentioned before, the National Catholic Women Protection organization took notice of her, and in the beginning of 1908 she was sent with Sarolta Korányi to Berlin to a workshop of secretaries for the workingwomen's organization. She was in Berlin approximately 8 or 10 weeks and by 23-28 March 1908 she was a speaker at the social workshop of the Women's Protective organization. At that time, Margaret thought that she would begin to organize the workingwomen with Sarolta Koranyi on a Catholic basis, but when she learned about the plans of the Social Mission, she did not continue with Sarolta Koranyi, but with Edith

---

[6] She became later Sister Rose Kathleen, SSS, She was a fervent collaborator of Sister Margaret in hiding Jews in the home of Sr. Margaret's family. Báthory St. 10, in Budapest. (Translator's note.)
[7] From the yearbook of the teacher training school at Csalogany St., 1908.

Farkas.

From National Catholic Women's Organization to The Social Mission Society

At the turn of the century, during the period of "individual initiatives" the wife of Count Paul Pálffy, born Countess Geraldine Károlyi (1836-1915) put forth an initiative of great importance, out of which grew the National Catholic Women's Protective Organization that worked with great enthusiasm and effectiveness. Countess Geraldine Karolyi was married in 1855 to Count Paul Pálffy, and from their happy marriage seven children were born. Unfortunately her husband died very early in1866. As a widow she dedicated her life to the education of her children. She made a long trip abroad and came to know, in the West, social-charity works. From 1874, she no longer lived on their family property (Malaczka, county of Pozsony), but lived continuously in Budapest and participated in social life. She became seriously ill in 1881 and, during her recuperation, she decided to dedicate her life to serve God and the people. Her first action was to embrace the direction of the Knézits Street Elizabeth Hospital, founded in 1870 by the wife of Count John Zichy for the sick poor. In 1890 Countess Zichy moved to Vienna.

Countess Pálffy transformed the small six-bed hospital into a well-functioning hospital with

200 beds. She invited the Daughters of Charity to be the nurses.

From this hospital's small chapel charity work started and gave birth to the Hungarian Catholic women's movement. In 1893, a few women workers from the tobacco industry asked to join May devotions in the chapel. The superior asked them why they did not go to the larger parish church. They responded because their clothing was filled with the smell of tobacco and the people moved away from them disgusted by the smell. The sister allowed them to enter and began conversing with them. She reported this conversation to the Countess. In the fall of 1896 the first unit of Protective Association was founded with these workingwomen. Apart from Countess Pálffy, the Rev. Michael Bunda, spiritual director of the Seminary of Budapest and later a Canon of Oradea, very fervently attended them spiritually. At the beginning of 1897, under the patronage of Countess Maria Josefa (later the mother of King Charles IV) the Catholic Women Workers' Protective Association was founded with the aim to "promote the spiritual and material welfare of workingwomen." Actually their vision was to create a workingwomen's organization, but times were not yet ready. The purposes of the workers' protective association were: spiritual assistance; religious education; providing inspiring and recreational presentations; establishing libraries; introducing homemaking and housework skills that a good Catholic working woman or mother of family needs to know. The members were helped materially when, without their fault, they did not find a job or became disabled. Members were assisted with legal protection in cases of unjust treatment as an employee.

As president of the association, Countess Pálffy opened a home with 74 beds for working-women at 10 Bakáts Square, Budapest during this year. Canon Bundala contributed financially not only to this home, but offered his summer house at Rákoskeresztur to be at the disposal of the association so that the members could have rest and the ill a place for recuperation. In 1904 Canon Bundala left for Oradea; this group was fused with the National Catholic Women's Protective Association, and the home was transferred in 1906 to 3 Bokréta St. in the 9th district of Budapest.

Having learned of their needs, Countess Pálffy with women of the nobility organized programs on Sunday afternoons for women under protection, and they opened another home with 32 beds on Hermina St. Soon other workingwomen sought connection with the protective association [...]

The by-laws of the Catholic Women Protective Association defined the goals of the Association: "...to maintain and further develop in feminine members of society, who are breadwinners, the spirit of faith and morality and assist them intellectually and materially." These goals may be attained through:

- Regular group meetings, counseling and instructions focused both on religion and morality, and practical knowledge needed for everyday life.
- Creating specialized patronages and homes, not only in Budapest, but also other areas of the country."

The Countess worked first with ladies of the nobility, but soon began working predominantly with educated women, particularly with pedagogues. The Protective Association for working-women was soon called Patronage, and such patronages started to develop in Budapest. By 1904 there were five such patronages in Budapest, and two in other cities. The development was slow. Women to be protected were plentiful but leaders, patronesses, were missing, and the Countess did not want to involve persons who educationally and spiritually were unprepared for such an important service.

She found in 1902 a co-worker, Edith Farkas, on whom this responsible service of instructing and preparing patronesses was entrusted. She was an excellent leader of a patronage in the Castle district. Edith understood the ideas of the Countess, and moreover had personal initiative to lead and further develop the great service. From 1903, under the presidency of Edith Farkas, the patronesses gathered time and again to hold conferences. In 1904, at the suggestion of Edith, the

Countess invited Ottokár Prohászka, the new spiritual director of the central seminary, to give monthly conferences to the ladies. From these developed his famous conferences. For preparation of the patronesses, Edith gave courses twice a month, in which she enlarged their spiritual, pedagogical and social knowledge. By 1906 nine patronages functioned in Budapest, and that many in other cities outside of the capital. The Women's Protective Association adopted the name: National Catholic Women's Protective Organization. Appointed by the Countess, Edith Farkas traveled the entire country, primarily to the Catholic Teacher and Professor training institutions to give information on the Patronage and to inspire new co-workers for it. Moreover, she was to prepare the stage necessary for visible public service in feudal Hungary. Countess Pálffy, who was the Lady-in-waiting for Queen Elizabeth, obtained for Edith Farkas membership in the Noble Ladies' Foundation of Graz and, with it, finances and Ladyship title.

Countess Pálffy still kept in her hands the direction of the Patronage's spirit, but she no longer could participate physically in leadership. She continued to enrich its spirit even during her last years. She studied works on social justice, particularly those on women issues. She maintained wide-ranging correspondence with directors of similar Swiss and French organizations. Unfortunately, her correspondence was destroyed for reasons of safety during the communist period of

1919. In 1908 she handed over leadership to Edith Farkas.

Sarolta Korányi wrote about her in 1921. "The Catholic Women's Protection Organization attended to workingwomen, and from educated women developed groups, who after a few years founded wide ranging social works done by Catholic women. These works can be seen directly or indirectly as the initiatives of Countess Pálffy. It was admirable how she identified as a high-ranking lady with that world to which the workingwomen belonged and she did not encounter personally, only through the patronesses. Her age and health did not allow her to leave her palace."

Countess Pálffy recognized that excessive centralization does not serve development. For an organization to flourish, specific, independent goals are needed. She desired to maintain only a unified vision and sisterly relationships among them. It seemed natural that the Patronage organize workingwomen groups. However, it did not happen that way. Independent from the Patronage, organizing workingwomen was begun by Sarolta Korányi. She received much help though from the Patronage, so that workingwomen over 17 years of age could move to the independent workingwomen's organization. In this manner the Catholic Workingwomen Organization was begun in 1912. Countess Pálffy died on 15 March 1915 after a long illness. Ottokár Prohászka said in appreciation of her, "She recognized social work as a strict obligation, but not as a volunteer. She took her part in it as one obliged to do it. This social responsibility is the Countess's outstanding characteristic and greatest honor."

Let us look in broad strokes at the wide ranging branches of social work of the Women's Protective Association: The Catholic Workingwomen organization was founded by Michael Bunda in 1897. This was merged in 1899 with the Catholic Women Organization led by Countess Pálffy. This organization had six branches:

1. Workingwomen Protective Organization, actually the so-called Patronage functioned under a leader and her assistant who on Sunday afternoons had meetings with workingwomen. The content of the meeting consisted of spiritual, intellectual, and recreational material. This kind of activity by the Patronage was extended in 1907 to prison ministry for both sexes.

2. Sales women and store employees protective organization. The countess understood that different working branches have different problems; the workingwomen need different consideration and help.

3. Establishing hostels or homes for workingwomen. Among these outstanding is the one at Bakats Square, that later was transferred to 3 Bokréta St. because this was the home functioning the longest

among the homes of the Women Protective Organization. Moreover, it was this place from which the last director, Sister Sara Salkaházi, a Sister of Social Service, went to her place of martyrdom on 27 December 1944, together with some of those she protected from the Nazi insanity. There existed a second home on Hermina St. The Franciscan Missionary Sisters led it especially for educated women and for students of the nearby Elizabeth school for women.

4. Protecting women working in households. This protected girls flocking from rural areas in great numbers into the city. Ladies went to train stations meeting the girls, accompanying them to homes and tried to find safe working places for them. With this, the railway mission was initiated. On Sundays these girls were gathered and the activities of the Patronage were offered to them.

5. The fifth branch was the Women Protective Association founded by Canon Bundala.

6. The Saint Elizabeth Charitable Organization of Ujpest-Rákospalota. Training of Patronesses began there in 1904. Ottokár Prohászka, the spiritual director of the Central Seminary, gave monthly conferences to the ladies, and for the sake of an identical

preparation, Edith Farkas gave twice monthly conferences to the patronesses and patroness-candidates. "We hope, these meetings will be prelude to greater workshops on social work that will be beneficial to all those ladies who are engaged in Christian charity works", was written in the 1905 yearbook.[8] This desire was later fulfilled. The yearbook states that a home embroidery and flower decoration workshop took place and the patrons not only received instruction but the knowledge/skill secured income for them. The Patronage was a branch for protecting women and in Budapest there were eight well-functioning Patronages, in rural areas three and Edith Farkas was the vice president of this branch.

In 1906 a week-long course for patronesses was held in Saint Stephen Hall, where "the most outstanding sociologists gave lectures on themes of social work" giving a shining witness to the interest in and attraction to our communities and organizational efforts for social services."[9] This course was opened by Bishop Ottokár Prohászka, and closed by the Archbishop Gyula Városy of Kalocsa. Groups of patronages multiplied outside of Budapest, in Kolozsvár, Nyitra, Kassa (3) and in

---

[8] The Catholic Women Protective Association.
[9] The report of the National Catholic Women Protective Organization, 1906/7.

Kalocsa. In the patronage of Kalocsa, Margaret Slachta joined from March 1906 to June, finishing her training as teacher. In the fall she participated in the work of the patronage in Györ.

Edith Farkas opened a new ministry for the Women Protective Organization that on 4 April 1906 went, for the first time, into a prison working with women prisoners. During the same year six women were working in this service under the leadership of the initiator. One year later a similar organization was started under the leadership of Count Sándor Pállfy.

Edith Farkas must have decided earlier to dedicate her life to serve God and people. The yearbook of 1905 prints one of her teachings stating: "the ill society has a burning need for souls who by vocation will dedicate freely their time and energies for the well-being of suffering people." She chose to dedicate herself to this, and as a sign she wore a ring with an engraving, IHS. When Edith explained the patronage organization in Kalocsa, Margaret Slachta asked her what that means. Edith responded: "You, too, will have such a thing." This response gives the impression that Edith carried in her heart the idea of the Social Mission Society.[10]

The work in prison ministry drew her attention to juvenile delinquents. In 1906 the Patronage

---

[10] According to the memory of Sister Paula Rónai.

rented the first floor and basement of Elnök Street in the 9th district of Budapest to establish a transitory home for girls needing corrective education.

In this widespread work as the Executive Secretary of the National Catholic Women Protective Organization, Edith Farkas frequently became discouraged. Her self-giving volunteers worked with heart and soul but their life-circumstances did not free them for this work alone and they were not sufficiently trained. This did not satisfy Edith. She needed persons like soldiers whom she could command. She needed women free to embrace the great task to organize, who desired to dedicate themselves to it and to be led. When in her soul a plan developed, she shared it with Bishop Ottokár Prohászka, who listened with great amazement and admiration. Her plan was to create an organization to serve the greatest need of the times, to serve saving souls. This called for persons whose status stood between religious and lay people. They would function under her leadership. Thus, the Social Mission Society came into existence, wrote Maria Stoffer, her first collaborator and friend.[11]

An additional factor played a role in the creation of the Social Mission Society. Edith Farkas came to know a Swiss moral pedagogue and sociologist, Friedrich W. Foerster, whose ideas and methods were included in her plan and activities

---

[11] Stoffer Maria recollection - manuscript, SZTTI 1226/7

Later, after 1910, the Literal Commission of the Social Mission ordered the translation of two of Foerster's books: <u>The Lebenskunde</u>, (Art of Living), and <u>Lebensfürung</u> (Life and Character), and they were promoted until 1950.

A third thread contributing to the creation of the spirit of the Social Mission Society connects Countess and Mrs. Pálffy Pál, who supported religious located on her estate. With her help the Franciscan reform movement was established in the county of Pozsony. She had a part in building the church of the Jesuits in Pest and gave support to the Carmelite initiative of P. Leo, who in Győr was one of the most popular spiritual leaders of that time. He wanted to organize women as Third Order Carmelites to care for the poor and to nursing service in homes. Among those who went regularly to him for confession, he gathered 12 -14 volunteers for this, but there was no one among them with leadership talent. In 1905 in the Cathedral, at a May service, a worldly woman who went there only out of courtesy, accompanying someone who had converted, asked her relative to take her to a good priest for confession. The relative sent her to P. Leo. P. Leo soon recognized her abilities and asked her whether she would be willing to enter in his organization. Etelka Tóth said yes. She came to know only afterward that the organization would be realized later. The idea of P. Leo was very much opposed by his provincial, P. Soós. That period in the life of the Hungarian Carmelite's was very difficult. "At the time of my entry (1917) - wrote P. Szeghy Ernő - the Hungarian Carmel suffered through a very serious childhood illness, and could not be considered as recuperating. It was only fourteen years ago that it separated from the Austrian Carmel and became an independent province. There were few members; there was much work; formation was poor and spirituality even worse. When I entered half of the members left the Hungarian Carmel."[12] P. Leo found a supporter in Countess Pálffy Pál, and on 1 January 1906 he sent Etelka Tóth to Budapest, to the Hospital of the Red Cross, to receive training in health care. He called her back to Győr, gathered together the members of the future community, and in the "dark chapel" honoring Mary of Loretto, had them make their vows. "From then on he could exercise authority over us," wrote Etelka Tóth. In September 1906 he sent the whole group of the Third Order Carmelite Sisters of the Holy Spirit to Budapest to nurse in the Countess's hospital at Knézits St. The hospital most likely could not make much use of them therefore the National Catholic Women Protection organization placed them in 1907 into the home at 11 Elnök Street to care for delinquent girls needing reforming education. However, P. Soós was still not at peace with this initiative. During the summer of 1907 he was in Rome at the general chapter of their order. Next to Rome at Rocca de Papa, P. Soós came to know a Third Order Carmelites of the Sacred Heart of Jesus and their foundress, Terezia of St. Joseph.

---

[12] Szeghy Ernő, i.m.339.lp

whom he invited right away to Hungary to take over the foundation of P. Leo. The foundress came to Elnök Street in Budapest 2 August 1907 with several sisters. She saw the poor situation and that the ministry of sustaining orphanages was not their mission. Moreover, she saw the persons involved. She wrote in her autobiography that she looked immediately for another solution. She found in Újpest a house that fit her goals and she bought it. From those in Elnök Street, she chose those she felt were promising and took them to Újpest. The rest she left at Elnök Street. Terezia of St. Joseph did not know Hungarian nor did the sisters who came with her; and the group from Győr did not know German. They could communicate only with the help of a translator. Etelka Tóth describes how shocked they were to learn that the greater part of their companions disappeared together with the sisters who came. Only five of them were left there. Terezia of St. Joseph expressed sadness in her biography that neither the pastor of the Castle Hill's church (Charles Kanter) nor P. Soós prepared those left behind.[13] The founding superior was a very agile woman; soon she bought a house on Maglódi Street. The pastor of the parish got in contact with the bishop, wanting to find out who these sisters were, because officially he had no information on them. The chancery turned to P. Soós who wrote in a letter, found in the archives of the Archbishopric of Esztergom,

---

[13] The servant of God, Mother Tereza of St. Joseph … An Autobiography, tr. Bittle, B.Wauwatose WN, 1953. 158-175.

3015/1908. V. 18, "I have not written so far because the superior, when I asked from her the necessary information she responded that on account of a new situation the thing is no longer actual. Since then she did not mention to me anything. From the Maglódi Street foundation I have no knowledge, and I have the impression that the superior wants to communicate with ecclesial authorities directly." In the Bethany House of Charity, (IX, 11 Elnök Street), Etelka Tóth remained with five Third Order Carmelites from Győr, with the role of matrons, supervising the girls. The others most likely left for home because, apart from Etelka Tóth, no word was heard of them.

For Margaret Slachta 1907 was a defining year. In June she finished her work in Győr, and most likely on the advice of National Catholic Women Protection Organization, she left for Budapest, and was employed in the Teacher College on Csalogány St. as an educator beside Sarolta Geőcze. In this new job Margaret worked for three months. In January-February 1908 the Patronage sent her to Berlin into "Sozialen Frauenschule" (Social Work School for Ladies) where she took a course for executive secretaries for workingwomen. In March 1908 she taught in the workshop of the National Catholic Women Protective Organization.[14]

---

[14] Only Margaret Slachta's and Edith Farkas' talks are listed here. Others also gave talks.

The lectures:
23 March: Margaret Slachta, Social Problems
24 March: Margaret Slachta, Efforts Toward Solutions
25 March: Margaret Slachta, Guidelines for Social Problems
27 March: Margaret Slachta, Christian Vision of Work.
28 March: Edith Farkas, Christianity in Practice.

We presume that Margaret Slachta worked in the Women's Protective Organization during the rest of the year. In August she took a vacation in Parád and she wrote of it to her mother. "My dear Mami, in the end I came quite unexpectedly to Parád, because Countess Pálffy wrote a kind letter that I may come. This is a beautiful place, extremely pleasant and quiet."[15]

Sarolta Korányi wrote an article in the calendar of the 1909 <u>Catholic People's Alliance</u> entitled "Is It Necessary to Organize Workingwomen?" In it she gives a report on the preparatory work and she concludes that those who want to become members or are interested in the issue are to turn to Margaret Slachta, secretary at the hostel of workingwomen 3 Bokréta Street. This gives the impression that Margaret Slachta joined as a worker of Sarolta Korányi. However, it did not happen that way. Edith Farkas most likely mentioned to Margaret the idea of "her soldiers" and Margaret must have seen this as a vocation that

---

[15] SZTT 1180/2.

could fill her life. She said she would join. Edith Farkas talked with those who remained from the group of Győr. Etelka Tóth responded that they made a vow to P. Leo; only he can make the decision. In the meantime P. Leo left the Carmelite order and became a diocesan priest. Edith Farkas contacted him and got P. Leo's permission. On the feast of Saint Elizabeth of Hungary, 19 November 1908, Etelka Tóth joined with Anna Edit Csehál, Mária Csehál, Margaret Slachta, Patronesses. Another patroness, Elizabeth Bokor joined In December. With this, the Social Mission Society was founded as a section of the National Catholic Women's Protection Organization. This is how they appear in the yearbook of 1908. The Csehál sisters soon left. The founding members of the Social Mission Society therefore are: Elizabeth Bokor, age 22; Margaret Slachta, age 24; Etelka Tóth, age 27; and Edith Farkas, age 31.

A Social Mission Sister

The cradle of the Social Mission Society was IX, 11 Elnök Street, where those entering joined the remnants of the group from Gyor. Their situation was not easy, since as a "novitiate" apart from their own training they had to take care of 20-25 girls needing correctional education. Margaret Slachta, at her entrance, asked for the Constitution. Edith Farkas gave some typed pages with the title: "The Plan of the Organization and Basic Rules of the Catholic Feminine Social Mission Society." Edith Farkas herself most likely wrote it. (It can be seen that not even the name of the organization was stated correctly.) In this draft she emphasized that the necessity of this organization "springs exclusively from the specific needs of modern life." The necessity and the importance of the lay segment of society for the tasks in the areas of faith, life and justice were emphasized:

> We need such dedicated women who in the sight of lay people are not religious and, in the view of the Church, not laity. We embrace everything that the saints found to be necessary for salvation; however in our services and external form we tread new paths together with lay people. We were guided to this by the experiences we had with the protection of women. I am trying, for the glory of God to see whether we can succeed with our tested patronage spirit to realize a new Society. The goal of the Society is to

unite in community-life women who want to live for saving souls, regardless of working in offices or employed in areas that explicitly and directly serve this goal (like educators in institutions, probation officers, factory supervisors, administrators in care facilities, etc.) or in worldly offices (like teachers, clerks), but live by the spirit of the Society and participate in its activities as much as is possible.

The plan speaks furthermore of the inner organization of the Society, of obedience, areas of ministry, spiritual direction, daily schedule, clothing and the upkeep of the Society. We must remark that making known the Social Mission Society is not the aim of this book; we mention it only to shed light on the life-path of Margaret Slachta.

The leader of the small institution on Elnök Street was Anna Edith Csehál and her secretary was Margaret Slachta. Of this endeavor the National Catholic Women's Protection organization writes under the title, "Prison Ministry at the Bethany Home of Charity is the Cradle of a New Society." They provided a few pictures of its life: the small chapel with a dove symbolizing the Holy Spirit; the girls' bedrooms, dining area and workroom; and the office. In the office, the directress and her secretary are seen in a dark, ankle-long dress, they have nothing on their heads; their hair is combed in a simple fashion. The article makes known that this institution will be closed, because out of the goodness of the bishop of Kassa

(Kosice), the saintly and justice-promoting Agustin Fisher-Colbrie would give them the house of the Hunyadi Foundation in Szikszó (with 26 rooms and 82 acres of land, including garden and vineyard. The 1909 yearbook reported the function of the Feminine Social Mission Society, how they moved to Szikszó; and what kind of services they offered. They moved during spring of 1909. Their task was to care for girls who needed corrective education as prescribed by the law of 1910 in lieu of imprisonment. The capacity of the institute was for 60 and they started with 58 young offenders. At the same time, the communal religious life had to be organized. Of this time, Margaret Slachta wrote in 1942, "The Social Mission Society had not yet developed its own life-form, it only searched how."[16] The development task fell to Margaret since the foundress did not live with the community. She moved in 1913 into her apartment on Krisztina Square in Buda.

The typewritten Constitution stated: "All Sisters do not have to make the year-long formation; those who are considered to be capable may be accepted right away among the members." The first six sisters were judged to be capable and at Pentecost of 1909 they took vows. The preparation for vows was led by Edith Farkas with great impact, because Margaret Slachta opined in 1937 in this way: "I did not ever forget those times and the teachings we got." (It is interesting that Edith

---

[16] Voice of the Spirit 1942/5, pp 44-45

Farkas never made vows in the presence of the sisters, nor did she renew them with the sisters.) We know the text of the vows from the typewritten record.

> My dear Redeemer, Lord Jesus, in love for you and Holy Mother Church I vow now obedience in the spirit of the Rule of the Social Mission Society, to do everything punctually what the spirit of our Society requires for the salvation of my soul and in the service of my neighbors. I offer joyfully and with great enthusiasm all my energies, and my gifts for the sanctification of my soul and the souls of others, and to serve with all my ability in all kinds of social work. Kindly accept my vows, and Lord Jesus, bless it with your grace that I may be faithful to my vocation and gain the crown of eternal life. In the name of the Father, and the Son and the Holy Spirit. Amen.

This Society responded to contemporary needs, and it flourished very rapidly. The sisters in Szikszó were not very happy that "all the bad girls of the country" were sent to them, but they came to love them rather quickly. The girls were of help to the people of the town in various ways (caring for the poor and the ill), and once, they even helped to extinguish fire in the kindergarten. The village did not have firefighters. The spiritual and practical guidance of the sisters was in the hands of Sister Margaret. In 1909 help came from a priest, Engelbert Mázy, OSB, the supervisor of the royal district of education in Kassa, (now Kosice). He came to

Szikszó to visit one of the women who entered, and who made her confession regularly to Fr. Mazy. He conversed with the sisters and began to visit them regularly, giving them spiritual guidance in the spirit of the ancient Benedictine tradition. Later, with the permission of the Bishop of Kassa, he revised the Rule of Saint Benedict for the use of the Social Mission Society. In a pamphlet published in 1911 about the Social Mission Society, written by Edith Farkas, the foreword, signed by Bishop Prohászka, wrote of appreciation for the service of Mazy: 'I have great respect for the merits of Dr. Engelbert Mázy OSB, Director of Kassa for creating the constitution of the Society and for the spiritual guidance given to the members."

Accordingly, the spiritual life of the sisters was based on the revised Benedictine rule. Organizationally they had two groups: those who were educated, and those who were not. The educated sisters did not wear veils, they wore a black dress with a white apron; the non-educated wore a headdress, black dress and blue apron. The sisters lived community life, sharing the same daily schedule, but slept with the girls. Sisters rose at 5 AM, prayed together, meditated, attended Mass. and after breakfast went with girls to work in the farm. They made a note that Sister Margaret was an expert in hoeing. (She loved gardening all her life.) After the midday meal the sisters had recreation, during summer with summer games, in winter those of winter. Sister Margaret emphasized doing exercises and required that, after noon meal, sisters take rest for a half hour. Whoever wanted could read or sleep, but silence was required.

Sister Margaret told the following of the life in Szikszó, "No one was a more passionate, 100 % Social Mission Sister than I was. I still cannot remember how the following event could happen: during those days, I could not share or experience concerns. The cash drawer of Szikszó became completely empty, and this was for me funny! The Mother Superior felt hurt that I found this to be funny."

One of the great events of the Social Mission Society happened in Szeged, in 1909, at the Catholic Conference. Edith Farkas assigned Sister Margaret to be the main speaker. Rozika, who was mentioned before, told that Edith asked Margaret to appear according to the fashion of the days and with hat. Her talk had a great impact on the people, as Sr. Margaret spoke of the conditions of workingwomen, the importance that women unite for helping, and employing secretariats for workingwomen. Forty years later Sister Paula shared her recollection of that event, (since Sr. Margaret stayed with them) but even more of her "brilliantly shining eyes as she spoke of a love-relationship with God that does not demand separation from the world." By that time Margaret's vocation had become certain. In 1924 she said in one of her teachings, "I know of myself how I entered into the Society, but I became conscious of the certitude of this vocation only about a year later."[17] With the development of the Society, it became necessary to have a center in Budapest. For this, Edith Farkas bought, in 1911, the house on Krisztina Square 125, (now 61/a). She moved the novitiate, called Seminary, from Szikszó into this house. Sister Margaret had to come, as she was by assignment the vice-president of the Society and the superior of the Seminary. She wrote of the changes in a letter to her parents who were still in America, "I shall leave tomorrow for Budapest. I sent my belongings already and, with this, the happy 2 1/2 years of my life ends. A new period is beginning with a greater sphere of activities in the public, but I hope it will be just as happy as previously. Ultimately, we spread happiness into life and not the reverse. Of course, within the conditions I am living, this is very easy because I have it so good that I can't express it."

The task of the seminary was to prepare future life for those who desired to enter into the Society as intern members. The formation was threefold: spiritual, theoretical, and practical. In the seminary the indispensable sacrificial spirit had to develop into joy, "because only happy, harmonious persons are able to show true sisterly interest in the pain and problems of others; only in this manner can they become selfless," reported Sister Margaret in 1913. This assignment did not last long. In a letter of spiritual confidence she wrote in 1933, "In the beginning, being the Vicar of Mother

---

[17] In Sr. Margaret's teaching on February 3, 1924

Superior, I guided the sisters' spirituality; but she felt that I bound the sisters excessively to myself, and she wanted that I orient myself to outside ministry and not keep any contact with the sisters." Sister Etelka Tóth, who was the Vicar of the Mother Superior between the years of 1915-1922, recalled the situation in this way, "One of my main responsibilities was to keep Sister Margaret away from the sisters. The seeds of conflict between the two personalities started to come to the surface."

The outside ministry was to protect and promote women's interests, which was very important for Edith Farkas right from the beginning. "The Social Mission Society was called into existence from the conviction that permanence and planned services on behalf of protecting women's interest and well-being demands an independent organization." This was Edith Farkas' repeatedly expressed idea, and was so well known that Bishop Prohászka used it on his greeting card 18 March 1911: "I do not forget the great work on protecting women, and want to help. In Ss Corde, P.O." (In the Sacred Heart, Greetings.)

In 1912, at the end of the yearly retreat Edith Farkas taught the sisters, asking them to stand up: "I want to share the following thoughts with you standing. Let us converse and listen standing because it is more festive, more beautiful and more respectful. Our goal is to protect women's interests and this directs our soul in a specific direction. I would like that you place everything under this goal; this means to fight for this goal, overcome within ourselves all obstacles to it, develop our gifts for this, assign our studies for this, and make our connections in view of this. It means to eradicate everything that does not serve this aim and to develop everything that will promote it."[18]

Sister Margaret naturally worked in this field all along. It is enough to mention the big Catholic Conference of 1909 or that of 1911, when the Society organized on 21 April a "Social Meeting" in the former State house, (today it is the Italian Institute on the Bródy Sándor Str.). Sister Margaret gave a talk titled "Societal Symptoms and the Social Mission." The importance of that meeting is manifested by the fact the newly appointed Prince Primate, John Csernoch, presided.

Edith Farkas also gave a talk to the co-workers in the National Catholic Women's Protection Organization. Social Mission became sufficiently developed by 1912 to include teaching social work in its ministry. In November the same year, it organized a social work course for the volunteers who joined them. The field of service was immense; there were not enough sisters; volunteers had to be trained. The volunteers had two categories: associated ladies and members of the Charity Organization. The associated ladies continued to live in their secular environment (family),

---

[18] SZTTI 1180/11

living the spirituality of Social Mission and joining in some way in their ministries. They had a specific emblem and after a specified time – later after a year of formation – they took a vow for one year to remain faithful to the Society, keep the associate regulations and continue to serve the interests of the Social Mission. Admission was held once a year in very festive manner. They received a monthly circular letter from September to June, and, as compensation, they also received the bulletin.

In the Charity Organization anybody could be a member, including men. Their responsibility was to contribute 1 Korona monthly to support the works of Social Mission and to participate in the work as they chose.

The Circular Letter: Bishop Prohászka, at the suggestion of Sister Margaret, wrote monthly a full-page letter with some spiritual and social theme for the members of the Charity Organization.

The first Circular Letter, dated 19 March 1912, began this way, "We start out from God alone, but we cannot return to God alone only together with others." The bulletin was the paper of the Social Mission and all the women's organizations that collaborated with her. In the beginning only 4 -5 issues were prepared yearly, and the first issue was published in March 1912. It recounted the visit of the great Swiss pedagogue, Foerster.

In 1912 a great event impacted Sister Margaret. Her mother, Mrs. Kálmán Slachta returned from America with her two daughters, Barbara and Elizabeth, (their father remained in America with Iren). Temporarily they stayed with friends, but their financial situation was completely insecure. Later Mrs. Slachta moved to Budapest to search for some way to survive. Sister Margaret most likely tried to find several ways to help her family, but we know of only one letter in this regard, written 13 May 1913 to her mother. She thought her mother could start, in a small way, a hostel for women replacing the Margaret hostel. She would need to rent a larger house and rent out rooms for university students; they could also have their meals. However,

> ...our Mother Superior does not want it the way I thought; rather she would like that you embrace the household responsibilities in the Seminary. The Society would give to you room and board, a room and kitchen, heat and light, (the kitchen could be Elizabeth's bedroom). Your responsibility, mother, would be everything that is necessary in a kitchen; that is, preparing the menu, shopping, instructing the novices who are assigned to the kitchen and keeping them orderly. For the meal of Elizabeth and Betti's you would pay to the kitchen's cashier as much as the Society defines for the sisters' meals. But our (dear) Mother Superior says that she would agree to this arrangement only if you would state, that you would not be hurt because she

would keep the "enclosure" toward you as any other secular persons. This means, that you free her from all those obligations that would be required by the customs of society. She does not mean anything specific, only that you would come and go without being considered a guest.[19]

The sources we know so far do not give information whether this happened or not. Most likely yes, because in Iren's recollections she stated when their father arrived in Budapest in 1914, no one expected him. He went alone to 125 Krisztina Square, before his daughters arrived at the East Train Station. Other sources inform us that later on Mrs. Slachta was the accountant of the Society, followed by Kálmán Slachta.

In 1913 Edith Farkas, without breaking relationship with Engelbert Mazy, OSB, the spiritual director, transferred spiritual direction of the Social Mission to the religion teacher, Oszkár Szilágyi, who was once a Benedictine monk from Pannonhalma, but transferred to the Trappists with permission. He joined the Marienhill Abbey in South Africa that combined contemplation with missionary work. With this, the Trappist era began in the Society. Thus the idea that the Society "in public view are not religious" became distant, because

---

[19] The remark of Edith Farkas means that according to customs of those times Edith would not consider her to be a Lady. That is the reason why Sr. Margaret tries to verbalize it in such a refined manner. Author's note. SZTTI 1180/27.

they now practiced enclosed, strictly religious customs. For example, they made their vows prostrate, laying on the floor. Sister Teréz Schwartz wrote that she was always afraid during the ceremony that she would kick the sister behind her. Naturally fasting, keeping vigil, self-flagellation was not absent from the life of the sisters. Oszkár Szilágyi expressed, right from the beginning of his service, his antipathy toward Sister Margaret, whom he obliged to make penances all the time. She had to lie down at the chapel door, and the sisters stepped over her; or as a penance she was not allowed to sleep in bed. She had to take her mattress each night and make her bed on the floor before the door of Mother Superior. The sisters, who were engaged in social charitable works and organized women in the entire nation, had to flagellate themselves even on their organizational trips. The clap of the whip could be heard from the room where they were housed, wrote Sister Petra Rónai.

In 1913 Sister Margaret worked fulltime in outside ministry. She lectured in the whole country on social issue themes. The following gives a small insight into what that meant in her travel schedule:

5 February 1913, Kőszeg;
6 February, Sopron;
8 February, Budapest;
17 February, she sends a post card from Basel (Switzerland);
9-10 March, Szombathely;

12-13 Esztergom;
26 Vác;
31 Eperjes;
10-12 April, Pozsony;
13 Pápa, 14 Budapest,
21-22 Rákosliget;
and three days without a given date in Szikszó
where she gave a course for those who desired to
enter into the Society.[20] During summer fifteen
sisters, Sister Margaret among them, gave a series of lectures in Hungarian and German during
their vacation. The year's outstanding event undoubtedly was the three-day course on social issues held in Székesfehérvár. Presenters were:
Edith Farkas; Philip Rottenbiller, Judge of the Cu-
ria; Oszkár Szilágyi, Matilda Kreisler and Margaret
Slachta, Social Mission Sister. Margaret was re-
viewed in the Diary of the County Fejer (19 No-
vember1913). "Margaret Slachta fired up the audience with her magnificent talk. We need to work
together particularly in the future when the great
issues of women will be under consideration and
the defense of the Christian women's vision work
and bonding will be necessary. If we will not do
the work, others with a different vision will." The
editor of the newspaper closes describing the
course, "These ladies, nearly without exception,
can speak beautifully; some are so enthusiastic,
they can fire up the entire audience. We laughed,
we cried, we rejoiced the way they inspired; during
these three evenings a picture of the world was

---

[20] Értesitő (Bulletin) 1913/4, 35.

drawn before us that we never knew, but was important to come to know."

The year closed on 12 December with the trip to Transylvania. Margaret Slachta traveled with the novice, Petra Rónai, to the great cities of Transylvania: Cluj, Brassov, Fogaras, Nagyszeben, and Arad. They spoke to ladies and to students about social work and of the Society. They gave information on ethical issues, based on the book by Foerster, The Art of Living.

The year 1914 began with lectures. In April (15-19) they organized the 2nd Austrian Catholic Women's Day in Vienna. "On this occasion Margaret Slachta represented the Social Mission Society; the Patronage Organization, and the Catholic Girls Association" and Hannay Brentano gave a talk with the title, "Socialis Frauenberufe," (Women's Social Calling). Connected to this she spoke on the Social Mission Society, whose members "represent a type of women in Hungary who dedicate their life completely to social service activities." This idea had not been realized in Austria or in Germany. As the general interest showed, the growing need for social service and the lack of it was being felt more and more. Not until 20 July 1919 was "Caritas Socialis," an organization with similar goal founded in Vienna.[21] Following this talk the Social Mission Society received a request

---

[21] Hildegard Burjan, a lady of social action founded this organization.

to administer a home for workingwomen with 200 beds in Vienna. Unfortunately this invitation could not be accepted for lack of sufficient members.

Sister Margaret began preparations for a School of Social Service in 1914. The beginning of war hindered regular activities, but she worked with great determination on this important non-war related project. Systematic classes in the evenings for adults and for young people were held.

In 1915 the Bulletin received a new name with the title, The Christian Woman and a new sub-title, "Catholic Associations' paper. Editor: Sister Margaret Slachta."

The first leading article was signed by Bishop Ottokár Prohászka, but was written by Sister Margaret.[22] The short article tells the Bulletin was started three years earlier; during the first year it was published only twice, in 1913 four times, and in 1914 for five times. During these years she looked around in the world and recognized it had another vocation, not only giving information. She saw that each movement carries ideas, convictions, worldviews and a desire began to grow in her to be the carrier of those ideas that *"will begin among us a specifically Hungarian Catholic women's movement* that is signified by contemporary charity activity." In this, the idea of a unified

---

[22] SZTTI 1212a, p 21
[23] Bulletin, 1913/3. Leading article.

Catholic women's movement was emerging.

During 1915 Edith Farkas chose a different spiritual director, Antal Schütz, and she placed Oszkár Szilágyi as professor of religion. For the sisters, Piarist spirituality was a great relief. The Trappist customs were ended.

The idea of a unified Catholic Women's Movement had a history before Sister Margaret wrote the sentence. During summer of 1913 the Worldwide Organization of Women Fighting for the Right to Vote held its Congress in Budapest.[23] Sister Margaret wrote of this in the leading article of the Bulletin. "The league fighting for Women's right to vote embraces the five continents and we, within the borders of our country, do our work not only with little impact but do not even desire to associate, to organize, learn from and help each other, but instead our energies are directed toward the contrary." The article appears without a name, the responses however point to a name: "...the beginning lines speak of your pen."[24]

The co-workers loved the idea so much that preparatory work began in September under the title The Catholic Women's Council. They held the first elective meeting to develop personal relationships among the leaders of the different organizations. On 2 December the second elective meet-

---

[24] Bulletin 1913/4. P.4

ing was held and more organizations joined what was to become the Catholic Women's Association. In May 1914 the <u>Bulletin</u> brought the proclamation: "Let us form the Catholic Women's Association and all of us, who understand the call of the times and the values of Catholicism, join it."[25] It is interesting that Edith Farkas, who drew attention to the importance of the Catholic feminism, wrote the leading article of this issue.

The By-Laws of the Catholic Women's Association were completed and submitted to the Ministry of Internal Affairs for approval. All the Catholic Women's organizations, including those whose aim was faith-related, joined the Association. In September 1914 the <u>Bulletin</u> informed that the Catholic Women's Association was founded under the title Marian Congregation. As president, Countess Mrs. Ede Pallavicini was elected; however, her family obligations and the ongoing war hindered her starting to function. For this reason the Catholic Women organizations was united under Catholic Charities for the duration of the war. We know from other sources that at the meeting in June, Sister Margaret was elected to be the acting secretary. For the acceptance of this office Sister Margaret needed permission, but Edith Farkas denied permission.[26] The united Catholic Women's Association did not get launched and, in the soul of Sister Margaret, the idealization of Edith Farkas

---

[25] <u>Bulletin</u> 1914/3, p. 11
[26] From the Recollections of Sister Petra Rónai.

was destroyed. This may have become visible in her because, according to her contemporaries, the Mother Superior constantly made Sister Margaret feel her displeasure.[27] Regardless of this, Sister Margaret was free to work on the plan for the School of Social Service and it opened in January 1915 for three hours a week, primarily for co-workers and for adults who were interested in social issues. They offered a course for young adults two hours a week and for high school students - both girls and boys. The classes included Faith and Morals, Applied Household and Health, National Economy, Psychology, Organizational and Social Ethics, Rhetoric, Civil Law, and Field Work. Presenters, apart from the sisters, were professors of the different subjects, and among them were some very prominent persons: e.g. Sándor Sik, Antal Schütz.

At Pentecost, Mother Superior assigned Sarolta Korányi, Margaret Slachta, Paula and Petra Rónai to prepare a plan that would bring together all the organizations that were under the umbrella of the Catholic Women's Association, but could not begin functioning, under the Social Mission Society. They brainstormed for a long time, and in the end decided to create local organizations of Social Mission throughout the country on a religious ethical basis, but with a social-charity program. If sufficient local organizations came into existence, they could be united in a larger unit. With this, the

---

[27] SZTTI 667/d

53

organizing of local units of Social Mission began in the total historical territory of Hungary. When Sister Margaret was about to return from organizing in 1915, Edith Farkas informed her by a telegram that she assigned her to Szikszó, she may not come to Budapest. Sister Margaret at this time led the ministries of the Social Mission Society, edited the <u>Christian Women</u>, directed the School of Social Service, supervised the function of the Girls Clubs and was the acting secretary of the Social Mission Charity Association. All this she had to continue from a distance.[28]

Sister Margaret suffered very much from her deep disillusion of her ideal model. This disappointment caused conflict with the Mother Superior and Sister Margaret lost the peace of her soul. She most likely expressed her disillusion to her confidante. We can presume this from some of her letters that were kept in the bequest of the girl from the Patronage in Győr, Rozika, who was now Sister Rose Katalin.[29] The situation is well painted in a poem to "My Sister Betty" that is a paraphrase of the poem by Petőfi, "To Brother István":

Our poor sister!

---

[28] SZTTI 1180/39

[29] Sister Roza Katalin Peitl, 1890-1979. She attended the Patronage load by Margaret Slachta. From 1907 she cared for the ill Mariska at the Slachta family. She entered in 1909 into the Social Mission Society, and in 1923 into the Society of the Sisters of Social Service. She was one of the greatest helpers of Sister Margaret during the time of the Holocaust.

If she would not have struggled
with her environment,
she would not have been sent to Szikszó.
She is a heroic soul and true,
and thought that all good persons are so.
The continuation of her suffering
was that she received forty students in Szikszó.
She will receive in heaven the reward
for her perspiration in her dedicated works.[30]

We may presume the possibility that Sister Margaret shared her bitterness with Rozika and she would try to ease her pain with pious platitudes but she took everything connected with God seriously. Sister Margaret had to fight a difficult fight with her self. A letter written to Rozika on 19 July 1915 bears witness to this: "You do not have to pray anymore, but we cannot start yet thanksgiving with full meaning, since I did not yet reach complete freedom. This summer I would like to make a retreat. Perhaps that will complete it."

In another message without a date, Sister Margaret wrote: "Thank you, thank you for what you have given me and what you shall give me."[31] The following text can be read on a holy card "Wednesday in Holy Week, 1916, 3:45 PM. If at any time you had temptations against hope, think of me, and you will no longer have doubts about your redemption; it is written who teaches others to do good, will shine in eternity like stars. You have

---

[30] SZTTI 1189/39
[31] SZTTI, 1180/59

done for me much more than that. You freed me. Even in eternity grateful, your Sister Margaret."[32]

The next letter was dated 29 April 1916, written in pencil on the train between Budapest and Arad. Sister Margaret sent the biography of Saint Kathleen of Siena to Sister Kathleen, translated from German most likely by Sister Margaret. The ending lines give a perfect picture of the transformation in Sister Margaret's soul. "God's 'grafting knife' has done its work, by her sufferings she was transformed, the 'old self got annihilated' and resurrected for a supernatural life." Sister Margaret wishes this for Sister Kathleen. Here is a quotation from her letter, "You could not strive for a higher goal than what Saint Kathleen achieved, but I wish with all my heart that you do. I do not mean external successes or areas of action. That is given by the Lord, if he so wills. But I wish that you be able to be annihilated, that is to live in God as she did. This is what I wish for you on the occasion of tomorrow, and will beg with all my heart during Mass and at communion. May God bless you, protect you, lead you, form you, annihilate you and bring you to new life."[33]

We can get another glimpse into Sister Margaret's heart through a letter of 6 June. On a card she sent the message to Sister Cecilia, "I would have liked to say this still in Szikszó, that

---

[32] SZTTI, 1180/ 314
[33] STTI, 1180/59

true freedom is in obedience and true spiritual maturity in self-contempt."[34] The last letter of this kind was written after June 1916. The entire letter is submitted because it gives a perfect picture of the transformation of Sister Margaret's soul, of her ideals, and the bases of her teachings and spirituality. She lived these thoughts and shared them with those who could learn from her.

Social Mission Society Bethany House of Charity, Szikszó, County Abauj, Tel. 20.

Dear Sister Kathleen!
We had two holy Masses on the feast of Sacred Heart, the second with exposition. I offered the latter for you - I asked specially the Sacred Heart to help you, and in return for those many graces that you gained for me from God, to give you the grace to work through victoriously all your difficulties. At this point I think particularly of your relationship with Sister Etelka. I am certain I made it more difficult for you with my worldly way of thinking, by which the soul loses the sacrificial flexibility and becomes hard. This is easy to learn because this is natural, and the natural is easier for everybody than the supernatural.

During my last stay in Budapest our good God made me understand (you probably have prayed very hard for me?) that the problems of the past would have dried up in their source, had I not lacked so deeply humility, free self-

---

[34] SZTTI 1180/60

giving, and self-forgetfulness! What you have learned in this from me please forget, my dear Sister, and be for everybody who you were and are for me. For this, it is necessary never to forget what perhaps Kempis says: the superior and the members are the instruments of God's will. May there be in you a greater and more supernatural wisdom, and never analyze how God's instrument acts, how she may sear or cut you; only be attentive what kind of instrument you are. O my God, how much I see now how we do not measure up to the expectations of our Lord, when we make ourselves dependent on others how to act. More than that, I learned from you that true love does not diminish, does not get lost, does not become cold, and will not become hard, when we see failings in the loved one; rather it becomes more self-giving, more perfect. I wish you, my dear Sister, a deep self-knowledge, an all-inclusive sacrificial love, true simplicity and total self-forgetfulness.

Your grateful sister, Sister Margaret[35]

Sister Margaret was organizing the local units of Social Mission in Transylvania. The Mother Superior, at times, assigned her to work outside Transylvania as well. Thus, she arrived in Gyula in February 1916, where the young priest, Vilmos Apor, (later bishop in Győr) wrote about her visit, "Yesterday a Social Mission Sister Slachta Margaret arrived, whom my pastor requested to give a talk on the question of war-widows and orphans. She is a very sympathetic looking sister. A woman

---

[35] SZTTI 1180/57

was needed to place into our priests' mouths this theme. I became very enthusiastic seeing the sister's warm zeal; each of her words showed that the love of Christ drives her."

We have seen that Sister Margaret recognized her failings after a very difficult interior struggle, "... the great lack of heartfelt humility, free self-giving and self-forgetfulness", she looked at her superior as the embodiment of God's will and respected it. Edith Farkas, despite it, planned to send her to Turkey. The issue of 5 May 1916 of The Christian Woman had a short essay titled "Women's Issues in the East." It reported that both French and English women religious left Turkey because of the war and the women in Turkey remained without spiritual leaders. From the offer of a great field of action, the Social Mission Society will take a share and the leadership has already approached the competent authorities and made an offer." Edith Farkas had approached the Prince Primate and offered Sister Margaret to be sent to Turkey as a missionary.[36] The competent authority did not accept the offer.

On 27 August 1916 the Romanian army invaded Transylvania after Romania joined the Allied forces. The population of Transylvania fled in great disarray, and the entire territory became a war front. The central army quickly defeated this invasion and the people hoped to return. The exile

---

[36] SZTTI 12˙2, p. 28 Recollections of Sister Petra Rónai

of Sister Margaret in Szikszó ended; she was allowed to return to Budapest but was not allowed to live in the community, and on account of this she moved in with Frieda Stadler[37] and had her meals in a home for children. She asked and received permission to return to Transylvania to study the situation before the public administration returned. We read her own writing of the study she made:

> While they are here, frequently and many of them are in great need and in a bitter situation; but they still exist. But what will happen when they return? They find plundered homes or only their ruins, or an empty plot where their home stood. What will happen to them? Let us go and see the pillaged Transylvania so dear to our hearts, and tell to all who hold them dear what we have seen and ask those who have alleviated even the misery that was unseen, but is crueler than what has been seen.

> We left, Sister Paula and myself, on 11 November. We traveled on fast trains, on horse-drawn wagon, in compartments of commanding officers, on trucks, any way we could. During night, we rested in comfortable rooms or in an unheated train with frozen windows, or in army commanders' office leaning on boxes, or on the top of tables in an office, any way it was possible. Our travel led us through the only Transyl-

---

[37] Fieda Stadler 1888-1969. She was an extern member in the Social Mission Society. After 1923 she became a co-worker of the Society of the Sisters of Social Service. Author, editor, organizer of young women.

vanian road on which people fled, with felled trees, destroyed bridges, burned villages, pillaged cities, train compartments burnt black, smoky ruins of houses and empty plots. We saw the relieved Nagyszeben and Brassó that was saved. We saw Fogaras that was waiting for the Hungarians returning to empty homes, the wounded Székelyudvarhely and the silent, snow-covered Csikszereda.[38] Nobody was expected there, because there was nothing to return to. We saw the struggling situation of Hungarians squished among different nationalities; Hungary bleeds not only on the war-front. We saw all this. Afterward we discussed with those returning home, in what way could help be given to them? How was it possible to open offices for family protection? We suggested asking the ladies of the various cities, and we would travel to as many cities we are able to of those parts of the country where pillaging has not happened. To places where we cannot go we shall send circular letters, appeal in the <u>Christian Woman</u> for financial help, and send to the offices in Transylvania as much as possible. After all this, we returned home, and shared what we had seen, what we started, what we decided to do, and ask you our co-workers to help alleviating the misery you did not see, but - we can assure you - is more cruel than what you have seen

This is how we ask: If on Silvester evening or on the day of New Year you view your warm home, or kitchen or food storage, think of those

---

[38] Cities of Transylvania.

in whose rooms only broken furniture is seen, where no heat has existed for a month and in whose storage only a few broken cans can be found from all the food preserved during fall. If in your soul thanksgiving rises to heaven, because you have not lost anything, think not only a thanksgiving prayer but also on a thanksgiving sacrifice. And please take from your underwear, or fabric, the extra pillows in your guest room; the dishes piled high or your cutlery. Select some from among your furniture and say 'from a truly loving Christ-like heart, I want to give these for my sisters in Transylvania who have lost everything.' Be this your thanksgiving sacrifice and also your intercessory sacrifice. We do not know what the future holds, and perhaps this will be accepted as a protection from future suffering by Him, who directs our life's path.[39]

Sister Margaret naturally prepared an official report and submitted it to Edith Farkas. The Mother Superior re-wrote the report and submitted it under her name.[40] From the nation-wide collection, the Christian Woman gave ongoing reports: money and material donations arrived, and these - as Sister Margaret in her report called the Family Protection offices - the Women's Protective offices distributed. The groups that were organized before the Romanian army attacked and all the offices of the Women's Protective Organizations united with the title: The Association of the Social Mission

---

[39] Christian Woman 1917/1. p. 6-7.
[40] SZTTI 1212. P. 29

Society's Transylvanian Section. The founding congress was held in Gyulafehérvár, 18-21 September 1917 with the presence of Bishop Károly Count Majláth, and two months later in Budapest on 10-11 November with the name, The National Organization of the Association of the Social Mission Society. The chair was always the President of the Social Mission Society, at that time Edith Farkas. Acting Secretary was Sister Margaret Slachta.[41] With this year a chapter of Sister Margaret's life was concluded. During the past nine years we came to know not only a very successful, pioneering social worker, but something even more important, her soul, living a spiritual life, one that was transformed in the hands of God. A great obstacle to living a spiritual life is that one can mistake the person with the vision she proclaims. When one becomes disillusioned in the person, one easily rejects the vision. Sister Margaret understood early that the best persons might become untrustworthy. They seem to be great, but in reality are small. One day they seem to be firm, the next day they fall. Such is human virtue. Sister Margaret avoided this pitfall. For the difficulties she had with Mother Superior, as we have seen, she felt herself to be the cause. It is characteristic that those difficulties seemed to others the greatest. Sister Petra Rónai wrote that she cried

---

[41] The Christian Woman 1917/ 5-6 p. 17. The office-holders were the same sisters, who later founded the Sisters of Social Service, and at that time decided that the Society may not lead any organization or association under its own name.

over them, and when Sister Margaret happened to walk by and saw it she asked, "Why do you cry?" Sister Petra responded, "Because you suffer so much." "I suffer?" Margaret asked, "I did not notice." In her thinking and in her behavior the natural became supernatural, as she later explains in one of her teachings, "The cross we embrace teaches us the secret of the cross: together with suffering, we can be happy. This is the greatest miracle of a life in grace: it is possible to suffer very deeply and at the same time to be happy."[42] This inner joy steeled her for new tasks that the approaching traumatic year of 1918 carried in its womb.

---

[42] SZTTI 890, Meditation on the 14th of July, 1927

Leading the Hungarian Catholic Women's Movement

By 1918 the war was practically over. The German army won on the western front, but could no longer use that for its advantage. The Central Powers fate was already sealed. Sister Margaret did not occupy herself with the war except what she did for Transylvania. Even that was for the victims of war. On the pages of the <u>Christian Woman</u> she kept repeating and urging her coworkers, to collect food, to conserve it because shortage of food would occur, and while there still was food the opportunity should be used for collecting it to have reserve. Few persons followed her advice.

Meanwhile in Hungarian political life - as if there would be no more war - the most important topic was the right to vote, since industrial workers, the landless and women had no right to vote. During the summer of 1918 the new right to vote law was created that partially solved this problem. At the same time it rejected women's right to vote regardless that the radical feminist fought for it very hard.[43] In 1913 when the World Congress of

---

[43] The law: 918. XXVII. The right to vote included each 24 year old male, having a Hungarian citizenship, knows how to read and write; is engaged in industry or commerce; is a soldier with at least the title of minor officer; or has a hero's medal or a Charles troop cross.

Women that was fighting for the right to vote held its meeting in Budapest, Sister Margaret wrote in the Newsletter, with Edith Farkas' full agreement, that she was sad for not having a similar organization in Hungary. She called to keep alive the idea of a Christian feminism. The idea that "whoever owns the press, owns society" became ripe by 1918, and with the leadership of P. Béla Bangha, work in the press began.[44] In the beginning it publicized the existing Catholic publications, but soon the need arose for a daily paper with a Christian vision. The first step was P. Bangha SJ.'s visit to Edith Farkas at the beginning of 1918. He asked that the paper, Christian Woman, change its name and be transformed into a political paper. This happened. In March 1918 the paper appeared with the name Hungarian Woman. The subtitle read: "The Christian Feminism's Paper, the Social Mission Society's National Organization's Official Communication". The editor of the paper: Sister Margaret.

Why was the subtitle, Christian Feminism, necessary? The first issue gave the answer: It wanted a feminism that in its vision and worldview was different from the "radical feminism." Edith Farkas in her article, "Unfurling the Banner," quoted the president of the German Protestant Women's Association: "It is shameful if a nation's women's movement is directed and represented by

---

[44] P. Béla Bangha SJ. 1880 - 1940. Author, editor, church orator, organizer.

those who do not know and do not want to know Christ."[45] The Christian attribute did not want at this time, or at any time, to be focused against anybody. It wanted to signify an 'owned worldview.' The first issue made quite clear this intent as it presented a comparison of the two worldviews.

Let us see clearly!

What does radical feminism want?

What does Christian feminism want?

1. More self-determination for the woman in the family regarding her finances and children.

1.The same, but emphasizing with rights also responsibilities.

2. Influence in public affairs.

2. The same, but beside public activity it values highly and holds indispensable the hidden root-work that is the source of spiritual energies in the family.

3. The right to vote; creation of a world organization of nations; obligatory international

3. The same, but it rejects an anarchic peace and holds that giving life for the interest of the

---

[45] Hungarian Woman, 1918, March

justice system.

4. The extension of human rights.

4. It wants the extension of human rights by not upsetting the order and security of society. The specific interests of women does not eliminate from the interests of human society, since life is not a private interest.

nation is a virtue.

5. Equal occupational preparation of girls with boys, and opening all professions for girls.

5. It urges opening adequate professions for women, not forgetting their specific life-tasks, and protecting their feminine values and gifts.

6. In the economic sphere to correct the situation of breadwinning women, and equal pay for women for equal work with men.

6. The same, but separating efforts organizing for women's well being from elimination of religion and morality.

7. Elimination of child-work.

7. The same.

8. Freeing women's

8. Contrary to a mechanistic solution, to protect

time for economic advantage and the creation of common kitchen and child-care.

9. Including into public sphere women's special gifts and altruism.

10. Eliminating religion and morality to propagate liberal materialism.

the warmth of family life that alone can assure educating children for love and morality.

9. It wants this, but more than proclaiming but not realizing altruism: it wants Christianism.

10. To transcend excessive individualism and create a Christian worldview.

Following this opening article the Hungarian Woman printed one politically focused article after the other from the pen of Ottokár Prohászka, Edith Farkas, Sister Margaret, and others.[46] On 23 May 1918, at the invitation of the Pazmaneum in Vienna, Sisters Margaret and Paula gave "information on the aims and activities of the Social Mission Society, on the organizational work for Christian Feminism, and asked support by all possible means for the case of Christian feminism.[47] A few

---

[46] Edith Farkas: "Our Participation in Public Affairs". 1918. V. 11; Ottokár Prohászka: "Women into the Parliament!" 1919. X.8.
[47] Hungarian Woman. VI, 22, p.4.

days later Sister Margaret was in Timisoara informing women's organizations on the differences in feminism. Sister Margaret found the work to prepare the program for 1918 -1919 more important than working on feminism and educating on political activities. With the title, Social Guide, a sixteen-page booklet was provided for the coworkers in September 1918. The booklet had two parts: Earlier Goals and New Tasks. Among the earlier goals she mentions easing economic misery and struggling against sin. This must continue, but charity work should to be transformed into social work.[48] "That means we do not think only of assuaging misery and suffering, but on ending the causes of poverty and misery." She explained in great detail how this work could be pursued within the social organizations of the times. The second point was among the earlier goals: "to make preparations for women's civic activities." "So far we hardly worked for this." wrote Sister Margaret, "Those who raised their voices were radical feminists; therefore their words carried a foreign spirit for realizing political involvement for women. We must grow up for practicing our civic rights, that when this issue arises again, who knows how fast

it might happen. We are to be those who give direction."

---

[48] Social work at that time in Hungary did not mean organized charity work as we know it today. It's meaning was social change, building a better world, preventing social problems from arising, etc. We call this work for social justice. (Translator's note.)

The third earlier goal was to propagate a religious mentality in order to overcome a rebellious spirit. Her argument is interesting.

The terror of revolution is not yet dead; it still tempts; the body of our society collects still harmful nourishment and we do not know when this will burst out in violence. Revolution and religion do not belong to each other. We are still inclined to place the spiritual in the other world, and are not suffused with the realization that happiness and unhappiness come from a good or evil spirit. Our serious societal malady has one cure: *Christianity nourished by grace*. We shall become victorious only if we succeed having present in all situations - in family life, in our work and profession, in literature, in the theatre, and in our government - a genuine spirituality. This is the big task of the present. If we do not work at it, we too shall be buried under the ruins of our demoralized society.

Following this she continued with the second part, new tasks. Actually it is only one, but she explains it from several angles and methods. The new task is to work saving the middle class. She states that the middle class is declining and partially submerged already. But a social class lives or dies in individuals. "The middle class needs to be saved; this challenge stands before us. To do it we must study the question as seriously as the issue deserves. We need to understand it clearly in theory, since only those can work for it well who understand the theory and the causes of the issue. We must deal with the reasons of the evolutional process unfolding before us. We need to know our own characteristics and ourselves in order to be able to transcend the seeds of death within ourselves. The death of the Hungarian Christian middle class and the spirit it represents happens through the decline of the economy. Any class that cannot assure its economic well being is not able uphold the hegemony of its spirit, its vision. It is of national interest to uphold the middle class and together with it the culture of the nation."[49] An enumeration followed of the possible solutions. In this text Sister Margaret only looked ahead to a task that in reality never came to be realized due to historical circumstances. One <u>Social Guide</u> could be published in October, and on its 32nd page two themes were treated, one by Antal Schütz:[50] "The Role of Spirit-filled Social Work in Developing a Christian Personality" and "The Tasks of Modern Social Work" from the pen of Sisters Benedicta Balázs and Margaret Slachta. The small study spoke of how works of charity can be perfected into social work. Their conclusions can be applied even today. They summarized the essence in three points:

1. Instead of helping individuals, problems can be remedied by regular and organ-

---

[49] Social Guide, 1918, September
[50] Antal Schütz, Sch .P. University professor, theology + 1953

ized charity work.

2. Efforts have to be made that govern-mental help will be complemented by society.

3. Works of charity by society must be transformed unto social work while preserving the charitable spirit.

In October 1918, before tragic events hap-pened, there was one solemn event: the birthday of Ottokár Prohászka on the 10th, and the dedica-tion of the Ottokár Orphanage in Csobánka. Sister Margaret made a film of the celebration and lent it primarily to co-workers of the Social Mission Soci-ety. After this, only sad events happened. On 17 October, István Tisza reported in the Parliament: "We have lost this war." On 30 October, Mihály Károlyi created the National Council from radical politicians and the social democrats and on 30-31, the revolution called Fall Roses broke out. With this, the historical Hungary was destroyed.

Before the revolution began, women be-longing to the Christian Socialists – who later were called Christian Women Corps – on 28 October submitted to the Ministry of Interior their plan re-garding voting rights for women.[51] Before re-sponse could be given, as a fruit of revolution, change in government occurred with the leader-ship of Mihály Károlyi and his circle. Hungarian Woman, in its issue of 9 November, communicat-

---

[51] Hungarian Woman 1920 March 20.

ed that the Catholic People's Association, the Social Mission Society in its own name and in the name of its National Organization joined the National Council. On 13 November, King Charles IV resigned. Sister Margaret edited the 23 November issue of the Hungarian Woman and on the front page she submitted the following good-bye to the royal couple:

Hungarian women line up silently! History lays down a boundary stone between our nine century long tradition marked with tears, blood and glory of the past and the present when the bearers of the Crown of Saint Stephen leave the country. Make a last honor guard; enkindle the flame of your reverence, since in whose soul this flame is extinct when it parts from the past or is not able to enter through the door of history's development by closing the gate of the past with reverence, is already betraying the new because the entrance will be burdened with the curse of infidelity. We want to serve the new Hungary in fidelity. We want to make a silent line, Hungarian women, when King Charles and Queen Zita leave the throne. Line up for honor guards; allow in your soul the flame of your reverence to wave high, Hungarian women, on the day of our last King's abdication!

The new leadership of the country, the National Council, announced a general and equal right to secret vote, women included.[52] The No-

---

[52] Males - even those who do not know to read and write - could vote and be elected from age 21. Women from age 24,

vember issue of the <u>Social Guide</u> spoke to the women who gained the right to vote on 16 November. It asked the members of the local organizations of Social Mission to declare themselves a political unit. The members were to

- Learn their rights and responsibilities as citizens.
- Create courses to teach women to read and write in order that more women could gain their right to vote. Inform members and, through members, inform the women about daily politics.
- Direct elections, and give their votes to women with a Christian vision and who work for women's interests.
- Unite all the local Christian women's organizations with the goal of collaboration.

The leader of this organizing, based on the Social Mission's local units that extended to the entire nation, was Sister Margaret. She called together during the second half of 1918 the first political meeting of women. In it, they declared themselves a women's autonomous political organization within the Christian-Socialist People's Party.[53] Work was started immediately. Ladies organized the Catholics of Budapest, assigning a person with responsibility for a house, a street or an area. The new leadership of the country announced elec-

but must know to read and write. <u>Voice of the People</u>, November 17, 1918, p.5.
[53] <u>Voice of the Spirit</u>, 1943, December 15. P.191.

tions, and the Christian Women Party could also run, and that meant that the nation's women had to support it. Sister Margaret and the leading sisters needed permission to do this work. Edith Farkas gave permission and supported it with several of her political writings. Here we quote briefly from her article published in the Hungarian Women of 31 December1918: "Serious moral reasons impelled our National Organization to enter into a new field of service caused by the revolution, into political activity - as good citizens to participate in the nation's great intellectual struggle without falling into the style of the suffragettes[54] and to have an active role without rejecting our ancient faith, our heroic Hungarian blood and our femininity." In the same issue Sister Margaret emphasized responsibility, "...are you imbued with the realization that when you received the right to direct public life *you became responsible for its direction?* It depends on you, too, whether the map of historic Hungary will be thrown onto a garbage heap, whether your children will learn anything about God in school, or some pagan moral teaching will take the place of religious education, or terror will dominate over life, or whether it will be possible to defend personal freedom or the freedom to organize."

The government established the right to vote, but was no longer able to direct the situation.

---

[54] "Suffragette" was the name at that time of those English women who fought for women's voting rights

While the Fall Roses revolution started out with high hopes, it lost its impetus and leaned ever stronger toward the extreme left. In February 1919 Edith Farkas left for Switzerland;[55] responsibility for tasks at home fell on Sister Margaret. On 21 March the Bolshevist revolution broke out. Sister Margaret did not lose her head, she acted when it became possible and she wrote down "Why and what did we do during the time of the Soviet regime?"

> When we arrived on 21 March to the consequences of that unfortunate war starting five years ago, to the *proletarian-dictatorship,* it was clear to us that the reigning materialism will destroy everything that a Christian worldview holds sacred. We looked around urgently and weighing the given situation decided that we who took vows on social mission and as being Christian *progressive women,* we shall eke out with positive, creative work for ourselves a place in this new situation.

> As far as it depends on us we shall not step aside and shall not allow ourselves to be destroyed. We shall seek such solutions with which we shall be accepted by the new world order without compromise or giving up our principles. In this way we shall enter into the system those moral values that they reject, but one day will realize that they cannot succeed without them. For this solution there was only one

---

[55] Letter of recommendation by Archbishop John Chernoch, Esztergom, no.1123

possibility: *work in production*. In every other profession, teaching, journalism public relations or organizing, a vision must be provided or sold. Only vegetables, milk, basket weaving existed in "political freedom," that is, free from politics. Besides there was fast approaching a frightening hunger. Even if we will be unable erase it in a significant way, we can ease it to the degree of our production. Moreover, we had our co-workers who in better times worked with a self-sacrificing love for the realization of our vision and suddenly lost their basis for survival. We felt we had responsibilities for them. Moreover, we were urged by a desire to keep them together in whatever manner.

The system ordered us to lay aside our uniform, and we did, but not because of the authorities order but because of self-protection from the irresponsible elements on the streets. We submitted (Sister Margaret alone), in uniform, the following proposition to the president of the government of the People's Council, Sándor Garbai.

Honored President!

We believe the greatest and most difficult task of a government is to lead the nation with the least upheaval and in the fastest manner through a time of transition; moreover to develop a just equalization between social classes in a most disciplined way and, through it, to protect better material goods. Lastly to assure those moral energies without which we will not be able to realize the noble aims facing us. In-

dividuals, and therefore the masses, will disobey their leaders and it may easily happen that
classes of means or wealth will become bankrupt without gaining better life-condition for the
working class. Consequently, in the general
upheaval the ent re nation will be destroyed.

In these dangerous times we desire to serve
the common good in the following manner: The
members of the Social Mission Society's National Organization, under my leadership, belongs in great measure to a social class who, on
account of their situation, were far from labor
unions. Together with this, they are persons for
whom it will be the hardest to adjust to the new
system because most of them will have lost the
means for survival and must search for work for
which they are unprepared; and therefore we
must help them through the initial difficulties of
breadwinning. It is in the interest of the common good that everybody enters, in the fastest
way, into productive work and no one is only a
consumer. I am asking the Governing Council:
GIVE US URGENTLY THE POSSIBILITY TO
PUT WORKS INTO OPERATION THAT WILL
GIVE SOLUTION TO THIS DOUBLE PROB-
LEM.

Before anything else, I am asking to entrust
to our National Organization, particularly in our
capital city and in its surroundings, such empty
plots and land that are not cultivated (Vérmező,
Németvõlgyi ut, parks, parts of Népliget and in
the city) on which we would start immediately
vegetable gardens, raising chickens. That could
ease the prcblems of hunger in the city if it were

to be surrounded by army or put under siege.

Moreover bring from the countryside immediately as much food as is still available and store it in the city. To preserve and maintain it would give work for a number of persons. It is true that food means more than vegetables and eggs, but these are very valuable at this time.

I would develop a detailed plan for both of these proposals as soon as the Governing Council gives a full or even a partial agreement to it in theory.

We would organize into groups those who work with vegetable gardens, those who raise chicken and those who work in food industry and attach them to our National Organization as parts of the social democratic union on condition – that as the union states – RELIGION IS CONSIDERED A PRIVATE MATTER, AND OUR MEMBERS ARE NOT HINDERED IN ITS PRACTICE AND WILL NOT BE FORCED UNDER ANY FORM TO DENY IT. My conviction is that only joint Christian and socialist organizations make possible the hope for a bearable transition. Only a union with the socialist movement will assure THOSE MORAL ENERGIES, WITHOUT WHICH THE MASSES would be lost; not understanding its magnificent vision would abuse them. Of this, we have seen many examples. They would destroy themselves and destroy all of us including those who are now leading the fight for the creation of a better world. For this reason I am asking the Governing Council to promote urgently this effort for joining. The Social Mission Society is well known as true to faith and, at the same time, is completely modern. Joining the Christian and social movements would make a decisive impact on the Christian society; and it is absolutely necessary that all classes in society work together for a better future.

Budapest, 26 March 1919
Margaret Slachta

Garbai repeatedly refrained from giving answer to the proposal (consequently neither did we enter into the Union). Would he have accepted, many tears would not have been shed during the time of dictatorship, and perhaps would not be shed now. For some, this statement might seem to be exaggerated, but those who knew the general public feeling, knew that Christianity torn apart, humiliated and divided was receiving only a small role. Would it have united, it could have worked for maintaining Christian values regardless of any governmental form. Those who know the communist-socialist reality, know and have experienced how direct communication, i.e. knowing each other, with some exception, can ease the wild aggression in them.[56]

The theoretical dimension of the Margaret Slachta proposal precedes the teaching of Vatican II; she stated in 1919 what *Gaudium et Spes* says in 1965, (Ch. I, # 21): "...while rejecting atheism, root and branch, the Church sincerely professes

---

[56] Hungarian Woman, 1919, August 23, p. 6

that all men, believers and non-believers alike ought to work for the rightful betterment of this world, in which all alike live." [57]

Garbai kept silent regarding the basic principles of the proposal but he wrote a letter of recommendation and submitted our plan for agricultural work to another authority and from there to somewhere else until finally the agricultural committee organized a conference and dealt with the proposal in great detail. It is true, however, that weeks went by before work could begin and was placed under the title of the Agricultural People's Committee No. XI Trade Union

The proposal was dated 26 March 1919 in the Newsletter of the Governing Council; the order of the Agricultural Commission of People was given on 4 April, "The unused land and plots in Budapest that are good for agricultural production must be cultivated." [58] Of the experiences in the trade union the Hungarian Woman gives, in its issue of 17 April 1920, a small taste:

> About this time a year ago we began our agricultural work. Our co-workers for many years worked selflessly for the common good, but now all had to become breadwinners: catechists in the capital, religious, a few countesses, some Daughters of Charity and we Social Mission

---

[57] Walter M. Abbott, S.J.: The Documents of Vatican II. P. 219
[58] World 1919.iv. p. 7. Red Paper 1919. Iv. 4., p. 5.

Sisters. There were about 60 of us. All possessions were confiscated. We were prevented from doing social work; we did not want to live on donations. We did not want to accept intellectual work either, because we could engage in it only by sacrificing our principles, therefore we took into our hands the hoe and the spade, even the pickaxe and in April and May broke up lawns and fallow land. More than that, we had to gather up bricks at Pasarét and clean up trash for weeks and weeks. Even though our work was very tiring and we were not accustomed to it, it gave us much consolation during those difficult months.

In the mornings we started with common prayer under the skies; during our rest one of us read from a book on spirituality, and on Saturday evenings on the way home, we picked many wild flowers for the altar of the chapel of Christina Square. We did every kind of work by ourselves: fertilization, mowing, cutting with sickle, and bringing water from the lake to the plants. We took plants with us in baskets. Once on the electric car one of us was called Grandmama. O, how much experience we gained during these times about fidelity, about appreciation; about illusions and reality! But we saw what a good impact we made on simple but good people with our determination. One time a coachman, who came to know that the woman for whom he delivered stakes for tomato plants had two diplomas, became deeply moved. He did not accept a tip from her saying,

"Daily I earn 75 Korona."[59] He came the next day again, even though not hired, working out of his good heart. We embraced our tasks with great simplicity; offered our difficulties as reparation, and considered this as training for ourselves. What a joy we had seeing our plants grow and our plot becoming more and more beautiful. Young co-workers and our faithful scouts built us a tent for rest, and on the afternoons of Saturday we could start distributing each other's produce: radishes, lettuce, peas, spinach, green beans, squash, potatoes, corn, cantaloupes and tomatoes, one after the other. We had some to give to our needy and ill acquaintances and to the poor. We worked in the fruit garden of the Capuchin fathers for half of the fruit raised, and they told us in no year had they received that much fruit as in that year. One of our co-workers - the daughter of a landowner - led a cow owned by our trade union on the street. Somebody called after her deriding, 'you led earlier a dog with you didn't you?' She replied in a good mood, 'Anyone can lead a dog, but not everybody can lead a cow.'

We grieved much losing a rabbit, or when no gosling came from the goose eggs; and we kept laughing on some situations when one of our co-workers, a teacher, was asked in marriage by a swineherd, repeating that he is a good party member; and he usually gets some extra income from robbing freight trains. At other times dehumanized workers walking by would raise their fists shaming us, 'Isn't hoeing

---

[59] Hungarian money of that time. (Translator's note.)

good for you now? For how much would you have done his work earlier?' Our consolation was that instead of hate we could respond in our hearts with compassion.

I think back with gratitude of these difficult times partially being a social day-worker of the Lord; I had to live for a while a life through which I came to know better the life of those who earn their living from this kind of work; partly because I could recognize the victory of Christian convictions and education; those educated Christians whom difficulties could not break and to whom evil could not teach class hate.[60]

We submit one more report about the function of the No. XI Trade Union. The hard work, like that of bees, struggled with the impossible, and when the overseers of the No. II. Agriculture Committee came to examine the work, one of them said, "As it turns out the garden of the XIth Trade Union is the nicest." *"Sister Margaret achieved what she wanted; the co-workers and sisters remained together; the office of the Women's Protective Organization on Váci St. was untouched; when the weekly earnings were distributed they all came together."* Sister Margaret, as a Social Mission Sister, wanted to place between the "comrades" a wedge that lived among them by Christian values and principles; that way of living was quite different from theirs. "That will weaken

---

[60] Hungarian Woman 1920.IV. 17. P. 3.

them by winning them over to the Redeemer, from whom they turned away only because they did not know him."[61]

Our report would not be complete if we do not quote Margaret Slachta's opinion on the reasons for the development of the Republic Council. This issue of the Hungarian Woman was published under the Romanian occupation and was heavily censured. She must have taken a strong stance on behalf of workers, if the text that conveyed so much good will, understanding of and promoting the interests of workers did not get deleted. (The beginning of the text was deleted.)

Even though it is not a welcome thing these days to speak of torture-chambers, outrageous deeds, embezzlements that came to light. Those are partially true, but some are fabricated. They shed a dark cloud on the past five months that in reality were dark. Still we must state there were some persons who, even though mistakenly, worked out of idealism. The leading class did not want to create a better future. The working class wanted to help itself; it created trade unions; a monetary merit system; they approached people who believed them but were misled. This road led through the hell of war and to the vengeful communist terror. The false vision of communism, the collaboration of many immature and criminal persons working

---

[61] The Political Activity of Margaret Slachta, the first woman representative. Published by the Christian Women Corps, Budapest, 1922. P. 9.

among them brought the nation very fast to a tragic break down. (Here 34 lines were erased.) [....]

We must will this development! Therefore let us be radical. Let us be concerned with the common good, and step up to lead the movement; giving the movement content and meaning and people will not get lost. Those who do nothing, who promote vengeance, who build walls around themselves, are preparing another revolution. [62]

Antal Balla described the difficult Hungarian situation after the fall of communism in the book Bolshevism. It was not a class domination of the workers, but of those poorly educated intellectuals, who were brought together during social upheavals by a secret law of blood. The victory of the Romanian army east of the Tisza sealed the fate of Hungarian communism. Béla Kun and his companions fled the country at the end of July. The power was handed over to socialist government under the leadership of Gyula Peidl. On 3 August, against the protest of the Italian Colonel Romanelli, the Romanian army occupied Budapest and on 7 August a counter-revolutionary company called White House forced Gyula Peidl and the socialist government to abdicate. Prince Count Joseph was proclaimed governor, and he appointed

---

[62] Hungarian Woman, 1919. IX. 16. P. 4

István Friedrich to be prime minister.[63]

In this new situation Edith Farkas stood whole-heartedly with the party serving by a Christian vision.[64] István Haller[65] during August 1919 urgently called Edith Farkas to ask for Sister Margaret and the sisters to continue the work organizing the party. Party organizing work began during the revolution of Mihály Károlyi. Edith Farkas recognized wisely that rebuilding a Christian Hungary was of the greatest importance and for this everything else was secondary. She allowed the sisters to do this work. More than that, she herself presided over the great conferences of women and gave inspiring talks.[66] These conferences were held in the Vigadó of Pest and Buda, where the Scouts of the Piarist Fathers maintained order. Of the mood of these conferences, Dr. Jenő Zakar wrote to Sister Margaret, "In 1919 I listened to your inspiring talks in the Vigadó of Pest, during which our Piarist Scouts offered service. The enthusiasm can never be forgotten that filled the people in the Vigadó - packing the place completely - over the joy of the nation's rebirth after the fall of the Republic Council."[67] The occupying Romanian authorities took

---

[63] Antal Balla: World History of the Newest Era. Budapest, 1937, p.505.

[64] Hungarian Woman, 1919.August. 23, p.1-3.

[65] 1stvan Haller 1880 -1964, newspaper editor, Christian socialist party, 1919 - 1920 prime minister.

[66] See: No. 62.

[67] The letter of Dr. Jeno Zakar to Sister Margaret. Archive of Sisters of Social Service, Budapest 1193/63.

away the freedom to meet. For this reason the regular meetings of Tuesdays from 19 August on were called "afternoon club" and, in these, the Christian Women Corps prepared for the elections. However, before elections could be held the Western powers functioning from Paris, decided the future of Hungary - that it would not negotiate with the government of István Friedrich but was willing to hold talks with a transitional government that included representation by all parties, including the social-democrats.[68] Sir George Clark arrived with this mission in Budapest on 24 October 1919 as representative of the Western powers. He held his talks in the Werbőczy Street palace. "The doorbell rang frequently and the porter brought in telegrams from different groups of people, from national and Christian organizations to bear witness for the government, and against any kind of democratic transformation," wrote György Ranki in 1967.[69] The Christian Women Corps found it important to show to the representative of the Western powers the true desire of the nation. Against the prohibition of meetings - it organized a huge protest by women. On leaflets and in the press the announcement was published, "A message from the leadership of the united Christian Party's Women Corps: Our ordinary Tuesday meeting is canceled again. Our afternoon Tuesday Club will

---

[68] Antal Balla: The History of the Hungarian Parliament, 1867 -1927, Budapest, 1928. P. 429.
[69] Gyorgy Ranki: To the History of Clark's Mission., Historica Review ,1967/2, p.156-187.

be held at 3:30 PM at the location of Saint George Square. Sister, we expect every one of you."[70] There did not exist a hall at Saint George Square, but the building of a ministry that opened onto Werbőczy Street and the office of Sir Clark. The members of the Women Corps brought along with them a small Hungarian flag to unfurl at an opportune moment. More than 35,000 women appeared. Sister Margaret with the help of co-workers organized the women into lines of fifteen, but first she wanted to meet with a delegation. Sir Clark did not receive them for a protest; that had consequences. For this reason his secretary received the copy of the Hungarian Woman rolled and bound by a ribbon with the flag's colors. The paper was presented in English, with illustrations and the following text:

> The enslaved women of Hungary, trampled underfoot, to the free son of England, Clark. We ask understanding, justice and freedom! The best among us bled to death during the five-year-long war. We lost everything. Our 1000-year-old nation was cut into pieces. Our food-stores are empty, overcome and miserably poor, robbed by the Bolshevik army. The remnant true Hungarians languish in the casemate of Arad, Kolozsvár (now Cluj) and Brassow; deprived of our last treasures. The free press and the freedom to assemble were constrained and forces wanted to deprive our martyr nation of a Christian government.

---

[70] National Paper, 1919. X. October 28. P. 6.

Never was a government as close to its people as it is now. Never before has evil and money worked so successfully to save from a deserved punishment those who committed treason several times, thus digging our grave.

We, the women of a small martyr nation, raise our voices to a free English nation. We know how to suffer; we know how to make reparation for our sins; we know how to die for our nation as our heroic Hungarian women did; but we can live only as Christians, as Hungarians, and as free people.

Free son of England, the cry of the enslaved women of a nation trampled underfoot is to you for Understanding! Justice! Freedom!

In the name of several million Hungarian women,

The Hungarian Women

The secretary of the mission accompanied the delegation to the street and said good-bye very politely. Sister Margaret, in response, wrote: "We esteem him for his polite gesture, but the members of the commission of five are mistaken if they believe we came as women and they satisfied us with their politeness. *We, as equal citizens with everybody of our nation, expect everybody to face the facts, even if this is manifested by a conquered nation's citizens and Christians.*"

The mission of the Western powers asked

that this huge crowd of women leave silently; the Romanian occupying army came with guns against the unarmed women. The leadership of the Women Corps assured the secretary of the mission that everything would happen in order. "At this point the women started to walk, totally silent, in closed lines of fifteen, waving the thousands of banners. We do not know how many there were but the march lasted 27 minutes. A silent cry broke through the closed windows of the mission.

Secretary Günther came down again and said the following: 'Sir Clark sends the message, that even though he could not view officially the march, in reality he is observing this protest, a kind he has never seen and could not even imagine.'"[71]

Clark's mission ended with the creation of a coalition government under the leadership of Károly Huszár, and this government was recognized by the Western powers. The Romanian army left the city on 16 November and the next day Miklós Horthy rode into Budapest. Restoration of a constitutional life began, and preparations started for the elections of a national assembly. "...with this, a stormy search began for women speakers and organizers. Most of the candidates wanted Sister

---

[71] Hungarian Woman, 1919.XI. 16. P. 3. National Paper, 1919. X. 29. Cover page; Budapest Gazette, 1919, X.30. p. 22. Bandholz Harry Hill: An Undiplomatic Diary by the Inter-Allied Mission to Hungary, 1919-1920. N.Y. 1933, p. 136.

Margaret."[72] The date for elections of the national assembly was 25 January 1920, and in this national assembly Bishop Ottokár Prohászka also accepted a role. He gave a talk about his program and Sister Margaret was the female speaker.

We heard many names mentioned in connection with the elections. However our souls did not resonate at any name as much as when we heard that your Excellency would embrace the sacrifice of accepting nomination for the elective district of Szekesfehervar. When I say we, I mean the united Christian party's independent women's region with its 50,000 women, whose reverence I am bringing. This reverence is not brought to the orator, or the author, nor the professor, the genie, not even to a church authority; it is offered to the apostle of the Gospel's message.

With the small political activity of the Christian Women Corps we looked around in the nation's life and it soon became clear that a nation could be guided toward happiness, primarily not with the intellect nor by force, but with spirituality. We women set spirituality as our first goal. When we heard of your Excellency's decision, we found our spirit in deep harmony because we knew that Christianity would not be just a password, but a lived reality. You, more than anyone among us, know that the foundation of

---

[72] Margaret Slachta the first woman representative p. 13 "She spoke at more than 600 meetings" New Generation, 1920. III.28.

every nation is pure morality.

Secondly, we offer our reverence to you, the pioneer. We women of Budapest are not simply the repeaters of men's thoughts, nor the shadow of men. We judge things through our own spirits; we have our own goals, perceptions, will, vision and programs. Participation of women in civic life is not just greater numbers; it is the addition of specific strengths of her personality. Knowing this, the Christian Women Corps does not want to participate only by election in the struggle for the Christian vision. It wants to add her feminine strengths to the service of the nation.

She recognized that equality, assured by law, exists only on paper, but not in life.

Therefore, the Women Corps stands here as a partner for struggle; it wants to attain equality in life - not uniformity, but equality. Since this era still deprives them of it, women cannot own the present, but she will own the future. We are the agents of the future.

At this point we come to offer our reverence to your Excellency for your pioneering spirit. Regardless that we do not belong in the voting district of Szekesfehervar, nor is the time here for elections; I am breaking through the formalities and ask, in the name of the Women Corps of Budapest, accept us among those whom you represent. As you were the apostle of land reform and of all true social development, take into your program to help bring into reality that which the law gave to women on paper."[73]

Bishop Prohászka reported this talk in his diary. "11 Jan. 1920. I offered my program at 11 A.M. in Saint Stephen Hall; many were present. Afterward they accompanied me home and in front of the gate they sang the Hungarian Anthem." The diary continues: "Sister Margaret was here and spoke very well. I love this refined, gentle, brilliant girl, a true refined spirit; but she is very radical. She identifies very easily with the lifestyle and customs of the lower classes; for example, she is very undemanding, she is satisfied with everything, is willing to sleep on the floor, etc."[74]

The elections of the National Assembly (19 January 1920) brought complete victory of the National Christian ideas. "We must particularly remember during this election the priceless work of the Social Mission Society (!) that took a lion's share in the success in the capital city."[75] Truly, when the sisters awakened the women to their responsibility for the fate of the nation and by the force of their numbers, they fulfilled a historic role. All newspapers reported on elections. "When the nation chose for the first time equal rights to vote extended to women, the women entered into the trenches of political life. We saw everywhere that

---

[73] National Paper (Nemzeti Ujsag,) 1920 I. 13. P. 8; Diary of County Fejer, 1920. I. 13. P. 3.
[74] SZTTI 731.
[75] National Paper, (Nemzeti Ujsag) 1920. I. 27. P. 3.

women worked harder, canvassed more enthusiastically, and with greater fire than men. In some districts women belonging to the lower classes, and in some instances the votes of the housemaids determined the outcome." The Women Corps invited the elected representatives to their festive meetings in both of the Vigadó's on 26 January. They were greeted in the name of the women, asking them to represent women's interests, since women helped them enter the Parliament. The United National Christian Party did not nominate any women for representative; therefore they could not enter the Parliament. Sister Margaret said the following to the elected, "Honored representatives, do not forget that never has so much prayer been attached to elections as to yours; never has so much expectation and hope been bound to a mandate as to yours."[76] Sister Margaret defined on 30 December 1919 what she meant by Christian politics, "Christian politics begins in the soul, it continues in personal life, and it reaches its summit in the life of the nation. Whoever emphasizes Christian politics, but has not received the Redeemer in his soul and in practical life, spreads sand against the wind."[77] About the term of this National Assembly Prohászka later offered this sad opinion, "a Christian course without Christianity and Christians;"[78] they did not fulfill the hopes placed on them.

---

[76] Margaret Slachta, the First Woman Representative….p. 14.
[77] Hungarian Woman, 1919. XII. 30. P. 2.
[78] Ottokar Prohaszka: A Modern Catholicism….p.37

The struggle before elections still went on when the alarming news of Prime Minister Károly Huszár ran through the maimed country:

Today I visited with the American Methodist Mission the places of misery in Budapest. I became convinced that in Budapest hundreds and thousands of children live without clothes, shoes, and without food, in dark, smelly, and in unheated homes. The Hungarian society may not go, even for a night, to sleep in peace if it overlooks this misery crying out to heaven and will put hundreds and thousands prematurely into graves.

I ask officially those who have some extra money, or clothing, or food, and wood for heating, urgently hurry to help those in this misery. Moreover, I call everybody in the name of Christian love for neighbors and humanness to help quickly, without fanfare wherever they can.

I saw in a room eight abandoned children. I saw an ill woman in a wagon with five children, of whom an eight-year old girl takes care. I saw a family of eight without furniture, lying over an empty straw sack in a dirty hole. I saw several hundred children barefoot, without pants and overcoat. These things may not continue this

way, or else more terrible social eruptions will happen.

I not only ask, I expect from every member of

Hungarian society, whoever has the means to quickly come to the help of those in misery while it is not too late. A greater societal committee will be called to distribute donations sent to my office.

January 16
Károly Huszár, Prime Minister[79]

The committee called was the Christian Women Corps, because this was the only uniformly organized group extending to all the districts. The Women Corps embraced the work with the criteria that help was given to all in need without distinction of religion and party affiliation, and they kept that very faithfully.[80] The work was announced:

A message from the leadership of the Christian Women Corps!

Our ordinary meeting of Tuesday 27 January at 4 P.M. will be held in the Vigado in Pest, and at 5 PM. in the Vigadó in Buda, where Prime Minister Károly Huszár will give information about the work to help the needy that was announced by him. We ask the regional leaders, those co-workers who are in charge of street and house and all our members to attend this meeting.

Having completed the electoral process, let us offer all our strength to Prime Minister Huszár for his great undertaking to help everyone irre-

---

[79] National Paper, 1920 I. 17.p. 5; The Evening, 1920. I. 18.p.
[80] Margaret Slachta: the First Woman Representative, p. 16.

spective of religious or political affiliation, only on the basis of love for neighbor. Participation in this action is to happen on an individual basis and not as a member of the party. We expect each of our co-workers to join this work in the pure and honorable spirit of Károly Huszár as he leads this action.

Work began, which the following article bears witness. The editor wrote somewhat super-ficially, because the Social Mission Sisters partici-pated in this action. The greater share of work, however, was done by the "Christian-socialist Women Corps," so opined Sisters Margaret and Elizabeth.

Day by day more and truly generous donations arrive to ease the misery of poor of Budapest. It is impossible to estimate the value of food, of bandages, clothing and medicine that make this action ever more successful. To distribute the immense collected material demands serious and dedicated organization. The indefatigable Sisters of Social Mission embraced this great work led by Sisters Margaret and Elizabeth Bokor who have already developed the program of helping. We had opportunity to receive in-formation on the manner of distribution from the organizer of this action.

The entire body of the Christian-socialist Wom-en Corps was mobilized for an honest, compas-sionate activity to ease the hunger. They told our co-worker. 'We have nearly in every house someone in charge, an inspired Christian woman, called care-giver-of-the-house who has received from us forms that serve a double purpose: they show the donations of those with means in the house and they give a report on the condition of the poor living in the same house. We expect part of the responses by the first days of February. This will make it possible to start the distribution by 3 February. The office of distribution has space in the palace of Count Karolyi, and we shall store a great part of the things donated there. We are emphatically asking all those in need not to turn to us, but to the person who is the caregiver-of-the-house. These caregivers will give us information with the greatest accuracy on the condition of the needy, and we shall see to it that the need will be alleviated according to the means available.

After the completion of easing misery, our organization, with its extended outreach, plans to try to solve another problem of no less importance: the question of work and mediation of work. With the same determination and dedication which the Social Mission used to do its tasks, we want to eliminate a belief that awakening joy for work and starting production depends on good luck. With quick and exact information on work openings and with the house caregiver's file of information of those who seek work, we believe solving oppressive poverty and hopelessness would receive impetus.[81]

The work easing poverty continued even

---

[81] New Nation (Uj Nemzedék) 1920.I. 31.p. 3 p.

when the Women Corps received a new and a very honored request. István Haller, who received three mandates to the Parliament, kept only one, that of Czegléd. "...for that of the 1st district of Budapest he recommended Sister Margaret Slachta." Of the nomination of Sister Margaret the Pesti Hirlap on 11 February 1920 wrote, "Moreover, in the name of the 22 electoral districts of Budapest a delegation of 100 women from the Christian Unification party also asked for her. The competent group promised to submit the desire of women voters. The nomination of Sister Margaret happened through a strained waiting between those in favor and those against her. Nearly 130 members of the elective commission including the president Paul Joannovits, retired secretary of state, pursued absolute legality and submitted under secret vote the three nominated names. Sister Margaret received absolute majority. Therefore party-center accepted her as an official nominee at their meeting on 26 February 1920."[82]

Sister Margaret, having a vow of obedience, asked Mother Superior's permission, and having received it, accepted the nomination. Edith Farkas understood perfectly the signs of the times and wrote an article entitled, "Sisters With Vows in Politics?" "*Work for saving a Christian Hungary is*

---

[82] Margaret Slachta: the First Woman Representative, p. 15. Nemzeti Ujsag, 1920. II. 27. P. 3, The issue of the Budapest Hirlap, 1920. II. 27. Gives the exact number of votes: Of 133 valid votes: Margaret Slachta received 69; Gy. Baranszky 40; M. Kmosko: 19; J. Anka: 3; Empty: 2.

not politics; it is a blood-stained holy work. It is understood that the Social Mission Society, as such, does not work in it as a body, only a few nominated members."[83]   Sister Margaret expressed her political Credo in the same issue of the <u>Hungarian Woman</u> this way, "What strength destroyed and intellect could not defend (the two arms of men) perhaps will be built up by the heart and the soul will bring it to life. When a woman appears among the ruins of a destroyed world and wants to spread over the burning wounds of humanity her heart and soul as a healing balm, do not reject it."

The Christian Women Corps had one month to bring to victory the case of the first Hungarian woman before the supplementary election of 25 March 1920.

---

[83] <u>Hungarian Woman,</u> 1919. IX. 16

First Woman
In the Hungarian Parliament

Before beginning this important chapter, we want to clarify an important error. All the opponents of Sister Margaret with a different vision attacked her on the basis that she represented clerical stance and that the Hungarian church assigned her to this task. Her opponents were in grave error. From what has been described so far, it is clear that the official church had nothing to do with the fact that Sister Margaret was nominated. This could not have happened. The Social Mission Society, as described in chapter three and according to canon law, was not a religious order. Edith Farkas clearly explained that such committed persons are needed "who in the eyes of the world are not religious; and in the eyes of the church are not lay." The Social Mission Society was an organization "living in the manner of religious" whose members do not take public vows - at the most, private vows - and those are not recognized by the church's canon law in force at that time. They are called societies without vows, living a common life like religious."[84] Sister Margaret could enter the scene of political life with the permission of her superior, without permission from church authorities, based only on her sense of vocation, "To involve

---

[84] Dr. John Scheffler: The Catechism of Religious life. Oradea, 1937., p. 370

women's life-giving, motherly energies into government life"[85] and to realize it in the spirit of Gospel truths. Ottokár Prohászka, who understood this idea completely, expressed his agreement, not as a bishop, but as a person in public life.

> More feminine traits are needed in our governmental life - more sense how to live. In this area great tasks are ahead for the Social Mission Society. The energies within it comprise great assets that, at this time, lie still unused for the well being of the nation. If we engage women's hearts, their feelings, and their brilliance into politics, we have found the collaboration of the entire nation, and with it the basis of its well being. This is the aim of the Social Mission Society; it wills that Hungarian women offer the richness of their soul and the warmth of their hearts to society, into social work; to unite the energies living in hearts for the well being and benefit of the nation.

Prohászka gave this talk in October 1920 at the Catholic conference. After the conference the entire National Organization of the Social Mission Society held its yearly congress. During this congress he emphasized his words even more, "We need more femininity in governmental life, more sentiments of a housewife, more ability to live. If we understand this, we shall also understand why we need women in governmental life. It is not simply for voting, not for playing politics, but to

---

[85] Hungarian Woman, 1920. IV. 17. Cover page

create, give warmth, organize, and infuse into politics a new and practical spirit."

At this time Edith Farkas spoke in the same vein. "No societal, economic and political work exists of which we can say, this is not our task - we can realize our social mission only if we approach human beings in all aspects of life, with every pertinent method."

It could have been presumed there would be little struggle between the parties for the seat, since Sister Margaret was the official nominee. However, it was not so. From within the Christian Unity party the first contender arose, Dr. András Csilléry, and eventually five more men.[86] They seemed to believe it would be easy to gain against a woman, reported the <u>Working Woman</u>.[87] Sister Margaret entered the fight with the help of the Christian Women Corps. Her program - very important for her - was the program of Hungarian women. She hardly ever spoke in her own name, always in the name of the country's women. She wanted to make conscious in her hearers that she proclaimed the principles and plans of the Christian Women Corps. She spoke for the first time on 3 March in the Vigado of Buda:

---

[86] <u>National Paper, (Nemzeti Ujsag)</u> 1920. III. 10. P. 3. Counter Nominees: Zoltán Kerkápoly, Ódön Szentirmay, Endre Török, and Franke J.

[87] A social democratic paper, representing the interests of workingwomen. 1920. III. 15.

Elector Citizens of the First District!

The political program of Hungarian women is to enter into the Parliament because the direction of the governing power is separated from the lives of individuals. For this reason the women's political goal is: human beings and the well being of human beings as individuals. I would like to treat the great political program of women on three occasions. Today I want to speak on the conditions of the well being of families. On the next occasion I shall speak on issues of education, instruction, and public morality; and on the third about protection of women and men in national life.

We are facing the grave problem of survival. We need to have general insurance for people: the retired, the ill, and the aged. We may not forget to create insurance for mothers; today it does not exist at all. Women working in industry and in commerce do not possess any assurance of giving healthy, strong children to society, no security to nourish them well, to nurture and to provide adequate health care. We demand, according to the nation's unified perspective, mediation of jobs. The government is to provide work for everybody; whoever does not accept work, should not receive aid for the jobless; those who want to work but cannot find positions are to receive aid from the government.

Closely related to the above is the question of taxation. We need a progressive taxation of property and income. It is unjust that people with small income and property pay a percentage as much as those who own and have far more income - more than they need. Excessively big properties that exceed multiple times the conditions necessary for living are to be taxed highly. We have to place, with great determination into our goals, taxing heavily articles of luxury, bars and nightclubs, better use of the state's goods, and the revision of rent for goods lent out by the state.

We must begin, with determination, a fight against high prices. *(Applause.)* Our mentality in commerce is demoralized. These days everybody drives up prices and extorts. Moreover, it is another task for women to fight against food falsification. We must demand pertinent punishment of those who fill their pockets with money at the cost of depriving others of good health and strength. To this issue belongs the fight against everything that is cheating e.g. the use of loopholes or outright law breaking that are set up to allow cheating in production and commerce. It is not possible to stop these things from one day to the other, but the most important is to stop the need of having to stand in line for hours in front of food stores. *(Applause.)* It may seem a small thing to stand in line, but if we would bring together all those poor workingwomen, the exhausted wives of low earning office workers who have to stand in line half a day long or half of the night, we would realize what a great national problem this is. It is the thousand small things that make our life unbearable. By creating production co-operatives for consumers and for commerce, the above problem could be eliminated.

One of the grave problems is housing. Today in Budapest approximately 20,000 applications are submitted for housing. Housing conditions are so bad in Budapest that 80-90 thousand persons are crowded together ten to fifteen in one room. Added to this terrible housing problem is the equally terrible situation of food distribution. We see that lack of sunlight, bread, food, and fuel comprise a true catastrophe. War did not suction away so much life-energy as this misery. Contrary to all this, our vision is: streets with small houses and gardens, small households, small economic endeavors, everything that exists to create a happy, contented family life. A section of Taban comes to my mind; we must give space to a new suburb.

Everybody makes promises presenting a program. We are practical persons even when we want to make promises. I reflected for two days whether to say, what I want to say now solemnly as a program, coming from my heart and soul, and it is the following: First, on the day when the 1st district makes possible the victory *(shouts: We shall! Applause for quite some time)* and I shall receive the mandate, I shall accept all your letters - I do not want to call them applications - describing your living conditions, especially of those who retired before 1912 and attach them to my mandate. No reason to keep them in a drawer without acting on them! Within three months from the date of receiving my mandate, I will realize this program.

Second, on that day which I shall hold sacred, each father and mother, who has difficulty raising their children, be the child small - even if only a few months old - may give to me the facts, the photo, and the description of their circumstances. From that day on, I want to be the mother of each child of the 1st district whose parents alone are unable to adequately care for that child. From that day on, I want to share the heavy burdens of the parents. The date to fulfill this promise is September.

The third point of my promise is to regulate and organize Taban. To this promise I cannot in good conscience give a date. If on the foregoing you give a questioning look at me about how I can promise such things, I respond as follows: When we had elections in Budapest the Christian Women Corps manifested that it is united and acts together. Women's hearts meet together not only within the borders of the nation but also throughout the world. In memory of those happenings, the innovations and developments the 1st district of Budapest will bear witness and all hearts will beat together - an international Christian women association.

In order that this promise will not be words flying into air, in testimony to it, I shall place on the same day a plaque on the wall of our party's office these three promises that you may hold me always accountable for fulfilling them. *(Vivat! Applause!)*

Finishing, I ask the following: I saw during the election process that Macchiavellism did not die even in the ranks of those who ran under Christian passwords. Therefore when we enter into this struggle that by all appearance will be difficult, I recommend my untarnished, clean name to the first district's Christian chivalrous men. *(Joyful applause, affirming shouts.)*[88]

The above ideas were explained in great detail in her first talk in the Parliament, and summarized in a proposal for decision. Her second political talk was given on 9 March, one week later.

Elector Citizens of the First District!

Those areas of work that are closest to our hearts and minds are assuring the well-being of people, supplying food for the inhabitants, public health and the issue of general education for all. Today we shall treat the issues of reform of education, of public education. *(Following she gave an overview on the history of the education of women in the country and showed, with contemporary data, how the people do not make use of the possibilities.)* From this, I want to draw conclusions about the condition of Hungarian public education. We must talk not only

---

[88] The three program talks of Margaret Slachta are preserved in a typed form bound in the issue of 1920-22 talks in the Parliament. Compare: Pesti Hirlap, 1920.III. 3, p.1-2. Nemzeti Ujsag, 1920, aiii.3. p. 3. Budapesti Hirlap, 1920. III. 20. P. 3

of how many kindergarten and grade-schools are missing, how many high schools would be needed, but also that our nation does not have a person to direct them. Our nation does not have anyone who would give guidance to parents about professions into which to direct children. Jews occupy all the well-paying jobs; but the modest paying schools and daycare facilities employ Christian women. Whether you like it or not, I always emphasize, that the present anti-Semitism is not Christian. Those who propagate hate are not Christian. This is the point where we say, 'Christian society! Do not hate Jews, but love more our kind!' *(Long applause, affirmation.)*

If now we ask, what needs to be done to realize reform? My response is: First we must multiply the number of schools and increase the pay of teachers. This question, however, depends on resources. As we are now faced with financial problems, allow me to sidetrack and talk about the importance of co-operatives. It is not enough to demand always and everything from the government; to regulate this or the other category of payment or old-age benefit, build schools, etc. Rather we need to work for the nation to become financially more secure, to have more income, to have the means to realize the common good; otherwise our demands have no basis.

What does it mean to improve the nation's economic condition? I refer now to the example of Dania. In 1881 they organized a milk-co-operative in a village. The first co-operative owned 400 cows, but within three years 251 plants opened to create milk-products from the cooperatives all over the country. At this time there are more than a thousand. I emphasize, we must not demand from the government all kinds of reforms through laws alone, but by creating many kinds of co-operatives for production and, with it, to raise the financial conditions and people's well being and thus the ability to pay taxes. Then we can stand up to the government to make demands. *(Yes, yes! Applause.)*

Let us return to the sad situation of day-care centers and grade schools. I state it is our vision that children should enter into grade school by the age of seven. Besides, it is an important demand that schools be like a little heaven with joy and happiness. I will not rest until, instead of the ruins either at Vérmező or in Tabán, a magnificent settlement facility will be built where children's hearts and souls can be satisfied. *(Applause, Vivat!)* I shall be concrete. If you ask me on whom shall I rely? I tell you: On a woman Minister of Education in the state of Colorado in America. I would ask the party of this excellent woman minister to help us. Death rate of babies in Hungary in 1910 was 20.7%; in 1916 it was 26.6%. However, if we examine statistics by social classes we may see that we have sisters whose children are born only to die, the percentage of death is 35%. We must do a pioneering work in this area

.

The second great problem is that we have to be conscious of the disappearance of the present middle class. Who will take the place of the disappearing middle class? In world-history it is the most rare phenomenon that such a huge group as a destroyed middle class would be able to regenerate. In contrast, there is a vital, undamaged, religious peasant group. The future of our nation depends on whether we shall succeed to lift and organize this class that is vital and strives upwards, to the point of becoming strong in their good qualities, grow in number and take the place of the demoralized middle class. More than that, to be empowered to hold onto their place successfully. For the preservation of the vitality of a nation not only blood and biceps are needed but also spiritual energies, inherited good traditions; all that is good and is present in a middle class. I see as my most important task to save in the middle class the most outstanding qualities, work to preserve their culture. The 1st District's greatest achievement will be to realize this and to manifest it to the world. *(Vivat! Applause)*

We have to work to realize obligatory eighth grade education for children and that parents may not send them at this early age to bread-winning jobs. Educational materials need to be revised and we must urgently demand taking from the children's backs the heavy burden of work that saps their vitality. Beyond that we need - if only we are able to realize - that until 18 years of age young people have opportunity two or three times a week to continue to study even if it is in the evening. We must demand differentiated schools. For us, unfortunately, schools are as abstract as the Parliament. As the Parliament is not familiar with life, the schools do not know anything about life. We must bring life into schools in order to educate for life and not for school alone.

Moreover we must strongly emphasize we want schools to educate for family life. We need schools to teach farming, gardening, etc. It is very important to revise the methods of religious education. I believe the Red government would never have gotten power in government if children in Hungary would have received a true, practical, palpable education on the love for God; if they would have been nourished with love for God.

We need now to follow up with providing summer-camps for children that, in America, are established and combined with teaching disabled children (Budapest has 1500 disabled children of whom only 70 receive proper education) and in this area many abilities could be discovered and saved.

A week from today I shall give the third talk of my program, and in two sections: on Tuesday for women and on Sunday for men. My theme will be on the reform of women's situation, the women, the men and children from the viewpoint of our nation. To place women into societal activity is a question that needs to be discussed from two contrary viewpoints: from that of the woman and the viewpoint of men. Lastly, I ask you to take that which I am saying as coming from the depth of my heart, where one works praying on a program. Because this is the most loved program of my heart, I shall arrive praying. I am asking you, even if you are unable to come at other times, come for those days. Each woman and man, do me the favor of coming and bring along whomever you can.[89]

Candidates not only spoke, they promoted their plans and vision on posters. The members of the Christian Women Corps displayed posters. When the opposing party's men tore down the posters of the Slachta party, ladies brought ladders and placed their posters higher. The strongest opponent of Sister Margaret, Dr. András Csilléry, EST wrote, "thinks that for him only Margaret Slachta is an opponent; he does not bother at all with the other two candidates. He asked only one short question: who is more needed for the country a Social Mission Sister or Dr. András Csilléry? After this he poured out a deluge of attacks. He said that a Social Mission Sister, who so far engaged in charity, did so only to succeed in politics and wants to make compromises with everybody. wants to resolve the problems of small office workers, and relieve misery through donations She sheds her femininity; projects her political maturity with aggressive brutality. The poster of Dr Csilléry said the gentle femininity on the posters denigrates the officers of the Hungarian military. Following all this he enumerated a long list of his own merits: he will 'stop the nation from sliding down the slope toward which the Christian politi-

---

[89] Compare: Pesti Naplo: 1920, III. 10. P. 2; Budapesti Hirlap, 1920, III. 10. P. 3. Nemzeti Ujság, 1920, III.10. p. 2: Uj Nemzedék, 1920, III. 9.

cians of Hungary hurdle.'"[90]

The response of the Women Corps was not slow: "Margaret Slachta, the official candidate of the Christian Unified National Party; the vice President of the National party sends this message to Dr. András Csilléry!"

Honored Candidate!
I read the latest leaflet of your party. I read it and I was glad that it was not me who wrote it. No, in a similar situation I would not have written it. Of course I would not have wanted to enter into a similar situation, because my goal would not be to gain at all costs a mandate. I **would need a moral basis.** I do not find it important to respond to the slanders and distortions of the flier. Who divided the party; who considered the mandate of the first district was owed; who gained nomination on legal or illegal grounds; who bought souls with flour, sugar or with other things? Every member of your party who thinks correctly should know. Each should know and does know. Here knowledge is not missing, but something else. Therefore, I send this message to Dr. Csilléry. A lieutenant who participated in a war told me that he has a memory he would like to erase very much from his soul. He was in Serbia during the Communists time. During his fact-finding service, he saw three children. When they saw him, they put their hands behind them and looked at him. He told them several times to put up their

---

[90] Az Est, 1920. III. 25. P. 2.

hands, but they did not move. The lieutenant thought they wanted to throw a bomb at him and shot at them. Two of the children ran away, one was shot. The lieutenant went to him to take away the bomb. The dead child had a piece of bread in his hand. By his action, Dr. András Cilléry asked me to surrender. I could not do it because if I lift up my hands the piece of bread will fall from my hands.' That bread I hold through my mandate and bring to the first district.

I ask Dr. András Csilléry: As a Minister of Health what did you give to the people? As a representative what can you and what do you want to give to the people? Do you want to make people believe through lies and deceptions that I hold a bomb in my hands and thus take away my mandate? Will you Dr. András Csilléry embrace giving economic help to all the poor children in the first district and thus raise them to be good human beings? Will you, Dr. András Csilléry, take responsibility to complement the very low social program benefits for all the first district's retired persons who have worked hard all their lives in order that they need not go begging? Will you, Dr. András Csilléry, realize a settlement for children and re-build the ragged huts of the people in Tabán? Or will you give a pompous program through newspapers to your electors, with a main theme of only criticizing the government because you and your friends were left out of governing. Are you not afraid, Dr. András Csilléry, if you take out of my hand the piece of bread meant for those who hunger, and gain the mandate, that it will be such a heavy burden on you that you will not be able to bear it? [91]

With the flyers of András Csilléry the deceptive attacks did not end opposition. It came from a direction nobody anticipated -: from the conservative women. The attack hit below the belt. There appeared a pamphlet with the title <u>Laugh Europe!</u> Its content appeared regarding a 26 March 1919 letter to Sándor Garbai. They wrote the following.

Margaret Slachta wanted to make a better Hungarian future with the communists. She imagined in her naïve lack of knowledge that fire and water will unite and merge together. Is it possible to imagine that the materialist Jewish worldview will at one time melt together with the idealistic Christian worldview! When the Hungarian farmers resisted, the office workers fled, the rail and post workers held strikes; the honest Hungarians and true Christians were hanged, and when everybody knew that the red craze could only last for days, then Sister Margaret stepped ahead, and on 26 March 1919 extended her hand to the red terror and spoke of such a Hungarian future, that the red criminals and she, Margaret Slachta, will introduce into Hungary! One, who gave witness to such political immaturity, might possess adequate gifts for charity, or might very beautifully work in small gardens, but in a Parliament, where one needs to possess some measure of political

---

[91] Sr. Petra Ronai: The history of our Society. Testvér, 1931. IV. P.5. Rev. Zadravecz secret diary, 1967. P. 264.

foresight, believe our serious warning, she is not fit! When everybody will have to give account of her collaboration under the soviet regime; when everybody was tested and many were w thout guilt imprisoned because they were suspected of work with the soviets and reported to the police, perhaps it may have been necessary for the leaders of the party to examine your activities too. Of the truth of the above everybody can be convinced through the Hungarian kincs court; the Hungarian prime-minister's press office or from the issues of the Hungarian Woman that were miraculously allowed to be published during the Romanian invasion and under its protection on 23 August 1919.

Two faithful readers
of Hungarian Woman

According to the opinion of contemporaries, the members of MANSZ published these lies. Sister Margaret responded through the press.

Honored Editor!
I take now into my hands the leaflet with the title Laugh Europe that was meant to be the last attack against me, and to which there is no longer time to respond on posters. If the authors would not have left out purposefully half of my message published in the Hungarian Woman, and if emphasis were given to some different sentences of my proposal to Gabrai, each child could note - those who can discern - recognize clearly how I extended my hand to the communist terror. However, I have not been so

naively uninformed as the contender tries to paint me, and that was evident from the text quoted. I stated on 26 March (the date of my proposal) what would happen, how our country would be destroyed if those who mislead the people who do not turn away from their materialism. More than that, I wrote to Gabrai that one always needs to count abuses, of which there are already many present. Moreover more courage was needed at that time for saying those things stated, than for not speaking out. Besides, an unnecessary energy was spent working to discover that sensational information in the press office of the prime-minister, research in museums, and asking the prosecutor's opinion in the name of the "minister of national welfare" since we ourselves published it in 10,000 issues of the Hungarian Woman after the fall of communists. Why didn't you attack me for it then?

Respectfully,

Margaret Slachta[92]

This response was published on the day of elections, 25 March 1920. Another organization published the text of Margaret Slachta's last poster proclaiming the candidate's words from the height of second floors: "I do not hate. I do not slander. Creative programs shine before my soul. There will be again a new Hungary in which the cross shall reign and in which we all shall be true sisters and brothers."[93]

---

[92] Nemzeti Ujság 1920, III. 25. P.3.
[93] Az Est, 1920. III. 26. P.3.

The third program talk was given in two parts: on 16 March for women, for men on 21 March. Only the talk to men was preserved. It is quite characteristic that in this talk Sister Margaret speaks more freely of herself and of the importance of her vocation. She did not enter Social Mission Society as one alien to life; no, she entered to be able to serve others better. She does not say clearly, only refers to the fact that vocation binds her soul with the same exclusivity as married love binds couples. According to Sister Margaret this is the "Golden Bull" of feminism:

Those who usually attend our meetings know that I always give short talks; today is an exception, I would like to talk longer. *(Hear, Hear!)* Do not take what I am going to say as a program talk. I want to speak from my soul to your souls.

When I entered the Social Mission Society I wanted to become their sister. I did not enter as alien to life. For this reason, I follow with the greatest interest and warmest love the forever present challenge of the relationship between man and woman and the many conflicts and difficulties arising from it that very often cause tragedies between them. It is my conviction there does not exist a separate interest of the man and the woman since in a family the two are one. It is not possible to neglect the interest of the woman without hurting the interest of the man. It is not possible to offend against the man's interest without causing suffering for the woman and children. The man, the woman and the child are, in one word, the family, an un-breakable whole. Therefore, I want to deal with the situation of women in economic, societal and political dimensions.

Our ideal is that women remain within the family - better said - return into the family. We Christian and convinced women are satisfied with what we think is the greatest: to form a human being, to strive for a never- ending, eternal happiness. However, tell me truthfully whether a woman can, in the midst of her family where she received the greatest vocation she could receive, live up to her vocation? Men think, that for someone to be able to create something, education and study is needed; but for the greatest thing - to bring forth new life - no education is necessary. For we Hungarians where are the greatest personalities? We have to search for them with lamp in hand until we find one. Whose responsibility would it have been to place a great person, a moral character into this world? The woman! *(Yes, yes!)* She did not realize it because she was unable to. Men misunderstand her vocation, her mission; men think, since giving and forming life cannot be learned from books, woman's job is the cradle and the stirring spoon; nothing about upholding a nation, creating new things, or bringing up men with a moral, dependable character. The situation of women in the family is misunderstood, and their interest is not represented. One of my programs is this: *to empower women in the family intellectually, spiritually and with a worldview to that level by which she will be able to serve better the interest of the family, the child and the husband without being forced to become a breadwinner.*

I shall repeat the idea: there is no separate interest for the wife; there is no separate interest for the husband, because the two are one. I shall touch on the struggle of a breadwinning woman. The burden of a breadwinning woman is three or fourfold. Most often such a woman is a wife, a breadwinner, and educator and a servant. Moreover, a breadwinning woman's condition is very bad; she is expected to do heavier work at the workplace and is paid much less. By the time a woman gains a diploma, she has become weaker. *(Yes, yes!)* If we look at women in industry, she keeps her working hours like men. When does she cook? When does she do the laundry, iron or clean house? When does she cradle or take care of her child and attend to her husband? Respected Sirs! It is impossible to carry such burden. Economically this situation is totally unfair. The woman working at both places, as a breadwinner and in the family, will seek revenge. Moreover, in this the interest of the man will suffer the greatest loss. Many among you at the age of 40-50-55, at the peak of men's life, are already disabled. You can thank for this the fact that the interest of your mother was not protected. The most urgent program facing us is to protect the interest of a working mother.

I shall treat now the moral situation of women in society. Time will come when a man and a woman meet. Men and women have an eternal vocation to each other; the eternal woman to the eternal man - the gentle, self-giving, loving woman, a feminine spirit to the strong, intelligent, man able and willing to create. The present situation, however, is while men and women have a mission to each other - to strengthen each other - in the present situation and worldview they rather weaken each other. Men will lure women by their vanity; women will attract men by sensuality. *(True, true!)* Men will bestow everything on the woman when his passion binds him to her, but, in this, he loves only himself.

Respected Sirs! The idolatry we see in our days is that, in the life of men, only one act is First, Second, Third, who temporarily has a wonderful life. However when he begins a family with lost strength, if he finds someone with whom he can settle down, roses will have become withered, and disillusionment will quickly follow. Slamming doors and other sad events will be repeated frequently. *(True, noise.)* Why? Because two persons, created for each other, got married and did not develop those traits that were given to them to bring happiness to one another. The woman was not truly a woman; neither was the man truly a man. *(So it is, so it is, applause.)* They become each other's curse, each other's burden, they who should hold hands and make each other happy; who should walk together supporting each as they travel in this sad and difficult world. It is insane to speak of making the nation happy; it is insanity and pharisaic to work to make a nation happy if primarily, in our soul and in our families, happiness and harmony are missing. That is why I make efforts, even in a political sphere, to organize women separately. I never wanted to separate women from men, since that would be a total misunderstanding of the eternal plan of the Creator; but I believe I did not make a mistake when I recognized in myself a deeper feminine consciousness. I have recognized from within myself what is the vocation of women, and the reason why I organized women separately, was to be directly connected to them and so be able to bring forth from them the eternal feminine that, in my opinion, is the creator of happiness in the eternal masculine. My ideal is to place with a highly intellectual man an equally highly intellectual woman. (*Vivat! Applause.*) Men and women meet in family life; they should also meet in civic life. So far, men and women do not meet in civic life. Now in this experienced great suffering we become awakened to the consciousness that between us there is not only a physical difference, there is also a psychological spiritual difference. The feminine is present in the psyche. [...] Therefore I say to you: in my person here standing before you, the adult daughter of the weather-battered 20th century, to ask for bonding in vision on behalf of the ruins of our nation. When we have to work together, even in government, let us place side by side that man and that woman whom life's call and occupation do not separate, but being equal, will understand each other. Be not afraid of such a Christian understanding of women's liberation. Benjamin Kidd says: 'There does not exist anything more rational than slavery, but slavery naturally will destroy that state which introduces it.' There is nothing more rational than a stronger, a more clever and higher gifted man keeping a woman in awe, but, in the measure a man empowers the woman at his side, that much more will the man become happy. *(Long applause)* I shall be happy if I succeed in bringing women even a little closer to men, calling them to an intellectual equality; these two creatures who are meant for each other, but have not yet found each other. *(Yes, yes.)* Do you remember of Madách, <u>The Tragedy of Human Beings</u> where the pharaoh lifts a slave woman to his side on throne? This slave woman did not think it an error or accuse the pharaoh from the minute she stood on the stair of the throne, but whispered into the ears of pharaoh: 'Do you hear the slaves cry, their suffering; do you hear the pain of the people, do you hear my sister's sighs?' And we know that pharaoh freed his slaves. *(Yes, yes, animated applause.)* I ask you to take home from this conference a light, small as that of a firefly, and enkindle it there. Whoever goes into an unhappy home, overcomes his manly self and asks, 'does it perhaps depend on me to make my unhappy home to be happy?' will return to a happy home. Take also the light of a firefly and decide: I want to join the work that wants to fight for many thousands of happy homes like mine.

Sirs! My program is to represent happiness in the Parliament. *(Applauses, affirmation.)* I want to take in my hands this program as one takes into the hands the Eucharist - that out of our sighs and tears come, from the Parliament, a ray of happiness for our nation. *(Long ap-*

plause, affirming shouts.)[94]

Of this conference, held the day before elections, several papers reported. <u>Nemzeti Ujság</u> wrote:

Margaret Slachta in the Vigadó of Buda, jam-packed beyond imagination, gave witness of her mandate in her fourth program talk to the gathering of the outstanding politicians of the nation. Doctor Paul Joanovich, the presider, read a letter from Ottokár Prohászka. The Bishop explained that those who know the laws of social development will not listen to the theory of 'cooking spoon' by the enemies of the mandate of a woman,[95] but consciously oppose them, thus witnessing to development. They will entrust their better future, their own and their families' happiness to one of the most outstanding women. The candidate, Margaret Slachta, had for her theme public health and public morality in her fourth program talk. He gave shocking facts of the terrible damage tuberculosis made in the life of the nation, the many sexual illnesses and alcoholism. While millions were spent to kill in war, only a million and a half is forecast to heal lung diseases. If we consider the lost days of the sick left without care is about one million working days in a year and multiply it with the daily wage we will see how many millions we lose in our nation's critical situation. Following this, the bishop ex-

---

[94] <u>Nemzeti Ujság</u>, 1920. III.20. p.2., III.21. p. 2.
[95] Women's task and place is in the kitchen, not in the Parliament. (Translator's note.)

plained the importance of fighting against alcoholism on behalf of our nation and, added in conclusion, that all of us can have only one common goal: that the entire first elective district become one great, loving and peaceful Christian family.[96]

The results of the elections were expected with great anticipation both at home and abroad. From the 10,187 cast votes Sister Margaret received 5,471 and became a representative of the National Assembly. The result of the election caused uncontested joy in the entire nation. From abroad - even from America - questions of interest arrived and the responses spread with the speed of lightening through telephone and telegraph.[97]

Two radical papers reported the impact of Sister Margaret's election.

Conversation with
Margaret Slachta, Representative

She wears a simple black dress and the cross of the Social Mission Sisters is her only jewel. Thick black hair crowns her high forehead, and on her face is a constant smile. From her gray eyes intelligence shines. She expresses thanks with happiness for congratu-

---

[96] Nemzeti Ujság, 1920. III. 24. P. 3; Budapesti Hirlap 1920. III. 24. P.4. Pesti Hirlap 1920. III. 28. P.3.
[97] Nemzeti Ujság, 1920, III. 28. P.5. Budapesti Hirlap, 1920. III. 28. P. 5; Pesti Hirlap, 1920. III. 28. P. 3.

lations and summarizes her program with concise words.

'I shall enter the Parliament on Monday and will begin working immediately. So far politics has been an abstract concept and had no contact with the family, where individuals struggle, are anxious and fight for survival could be detected. The interests of the family have to be entered into the national politics. If families wither away and individuals become bankrupt, politics itself will fall into ruins, because no one will remain for whom politics are needed. I shall do everything in my power so that people can earn a living, have a decent life; I shall fight for wage-reform, to solve the problems of retirement, and housing.

'The second focus of my efforts will be the complex reform of instruction and education.

'The third will be the reform of women's situation. I want to emphasize, this is not a question of women alone; the interest of men and of the family cannot be separated in this issue.

'Finally, I shall deal in a detailed manner with *public health issues* and with those problems that need to be addressed regarding *public morality.* '

She ended with a smile. 'This will be the context of my political work. One thing, however, we may not forget. I am primarily the representative of the 1st district. I am not a politician by vocation who shows a lovely face to the electorate only to gain their votes. I shall carry in my heart the fate of the 1st district and want to fulfill those promises I made.

'*From now on the 1st district is mine* and, even if in national politics it will be difficult to realize anything, in our own area I will do everything. Human energy in reality is limited, but with the help of God we can achieve everything.'

From each of her words unbelievable desire for work and strong will was manifested.[98] Good omen!

Among the political events in an unfavorable situation at last something happened by which one could stop with good feeling and contentment. I think of the result of the 1st district's election. The reason why we consider Margaret Slachta's becoming a representative in the 1st district an important event is because the electorate consisted of educated women and men. For Csilléry (her opponent) those electing methods did not win for Hungary any honor in the eyes of foreign countries. As for him, never before was so much political irresponsibility and immaturity present in an election. In contrast to such an irresponsible attitude, a Social Mission Sister stepped forward with pale face and simple black clothing. She was a soldier of charity and compassion who never knew compromise; moreover, she was a well-prepared leader of social movements. *She entered politics not on-*

---

[98] The Evening. 1920, III. P. 1.

ly as an outstanding person, but also as a candidate of a Christian party that instead of demagogy and hate desires to bring about consolidation and wants seriously to work and unite all the energies available. Two foci were before the electorate; the absolute majority did not elect demagogy but content. We do not agree on everything with Margaret Slachta and her party; on some points there is a great distance between us. But her election must fill even her opponent with contentment, because this is a witness to the maturity and objectivity of the electorate. And this is a good omen.[99]

Sister Margaret Slachta accepted her mandate on Palm Sunday, 28 March 1920, at the Holy Trinity Square in Buda with festive celebration. Her acceptance speech, beyond its actual political content, was an expression of a person attached to transcendent beliefs. In her life, a 14th century mystic's insight came to be realized who wrote "The higher stage of active life is so attached to the lower stage of contemplation as to become more and more intimate; living more from the depth of her being and thus becoming more and more human."[100] Let us hear now from this more human being.

---

[99] Pesti Napló, 1920. III. 28 Cover page. A similar enthusiastic report can be read in Nemzeti Ujság, p.7. In the Uj Nemzedék, p.7. and in the Uj Idők. 1920. IV. 14. 192-p3.
[100] The Cloud of Unknowing, Bp. 1987. pp 28-29

Elector Citizens of the First District!

A profound joy fills my heart at receiving the mandate. Not because the majority gave me a mandate, but because this mandate gives me to serve you. You, 160 strong men in the Parliament! You can protect the borders of this country! You can work at building a new constitution; build factories, start big industry because, in my humble person, Hungarian women line up behind you. From the hearts of millions of Hungarian women life may flow onto the great achievements of men. *(Joyful shouts, applauses.)*

I recall the spirit of our great mothers who rest here, amid the blessed and ancient walls of the Buda fortress. I recall Saint Elizabeth of Hungary; who served the nation through charity and Elizabeth Szilágyi who, from among the simple and sandaled people,[101] gave a king to the people. I recall Mrs. Perenyi, who came to bury the nation's heroes and Ilona Zrinyi and Cicella Rozgonyi, who remained woman while wielding the sword. My sisters! Following such an exalted line of women, let us all march at the side of men to serve our country. *(Shouts of agreement.)*

This mandate tells me that beside the noble inhabitants of the houses with several stories and the palaces of the first district people, thousands of caretakers and cooks, the simple peo-

---

[101] Who had no money to buy shoes. (Translator's note.)

132

ple lined up behind small groups of people with noble purpose, came from the poor shacks of Tabán, and gave into my hands this mandate. In my mandate the demand for the democratic progress, the fight for social justice and collaboration in true neighborly relationships are engraved. *(Shouts of agreement.)* I know that in this wide house there is no mandate to which so much prayer, so much profound good will, so much deep spiritual work, so much profound fidelity and self-giving effort would be attached than to this. I take this mandate into my hands like a prayer book, as a command that above my social orientation, prayer and the cross must stand guard always. *(Applause)* Otherwise, I know we shall get lost; otherwise, the Marseillaise would be the outcome of social thought. I know if we would leave this road, our program would become red. There is no redemptive thought, no true and faithful human relationship except in Christendom! I ask of you only one thing! May our meeting this Palm Sunday not be followed by a betraying infidelity. *(Shouts: Never!)* In order to have strength for the work ahead, I need your confidence, your fidelity and your perseverance. When I started this struggle I was told, 'you shall get disappointed in women; you shall be disillusioned in men.' My heart told me I shall not be disappointed, and I was not. I believe that today we are a new shoot on a land thousands of years old. We speak a new language. We know, even in politics, fidelity and love. [102]

---

[102] In: Talks in the parliament, 1920-1922.

With these words and with Palm Sunday's celebration Sister Margaret began her thorny road in the Parliament, where her male colleagues anticipated her. Most of them considered her as an intruder only because she was a woman. These colleagues, within a half year, created a new law limiting women's right to vote; while those who elected her expected that the only woman representative among 160 men would be able to make miracles. At the same time the great masses were inclined to turn away from those who hold that success and results demand sweat and blood, hard work and patience. Her opponents felt they could use any methods against her because she strove expressly for the victory of Christian principles. Apart from these difficulties, even more awaited her - that which Jesus expresses this way: "Members of her own family will be the enemies." (Mt. 10:36.) However, this would come sometime later. The day after Palm Sunday she entered into the Parliament in the company of Edith Farkas and her mother. "The representatives gathered in the corridor greeted, with great applause, the first woman representative of Hungary who also was greeted by those in the chamber. Those in the gallery participated in a spontaneous ovation" (and some women greeted her waving their scarves.) Margaret Slachta took her seat on the middle-left at the end of the second row. The presider introduced the letters of mandate of the newly elected members of the national assembly, which they handed over to the standing committee for verification.[103] This was the usual procedure. However her opponents submitted a petition attacking her mandate. They reasoned that she gained votes by bribing the electors, influencing them with promise that she would bestow on the inhabitants of the district all the goods that the charitable organizations provided. They also stated that the petition was already in process and they wanted to submit a new auxiliary petition. Their lawyer had already drafted the petition and, in the style of lawyers, he began his argument. "In the case with charitable actions accused Margaret Slachta, representative of the National Assembly, I submit respectfully the following petition."[104] They got so far and recognized that with such reasoning they could not gain anything; therefore, they stopped further action. This case came finally to conclusion on 31 August when the verification committee reported they had examined the petition against the representative - not revealing the name of those who submitted the petition - but made no recommendation. Even after repeatedly bringing up the request, no answer was given. For this reason the accusation was rejected and Margaret Slachta was declared a verified representative.[105]

Her first talk in the Parliament was given 23 April 1920 when the assembly dealt with the em-

---

[103] Nemzeti Ujség, 1920. III. 30. P.1.
[104] Érdekes Ujsaá, 1920, IV. 10. Vol. 24. P.16.
[105] Diary of the National Assembly, 1920, III. 31. P. 16.

powerment of the assembly to use the old budget until the new could be completed. In this talk she summarized and enlarged the content of her program announced during her campaign and suggested solutions with a proposal to remedy the problems. Great interest preceded the first woman representative's first talk with a packed gallery and a full house. This expectation was fulfilled because beyond the novelty that a first woman representative gave the talk, her new insights and many specific social themes filled her talks and justified the actuality and the value of women's passive right to vote. Margaret Slachta spoke with a clear, strong voice, very calmly, once in a while looking at her notes and with few gestures. Everywhere she was well audible - that which many of her male colleagues could not do. What she said so directly was perhaps surprising from a woman's lips; but those were true and very painful realities of life. We could be grateful for what she brought to the floor of the National Assembly. Her leading thought was the importance of protecting Hungarian mothers and future generations in view of the country. From this talk came a proposal that she submitted with general approval.[106] The periodical Nép Szava wrote of the talk: "The first woman representative spoke for first time on Friday in the Parliament. Her talk was filled with truths she learned from the socialist women. The male colleagues accepted her sympathetic proposal glee-

---

[106] Nemzeti Ujság, 1920, IV. 24.

fully, with jokes and with a sense of superiority.[107]
The outline of her talk is the following:

> Honored National Assembly! I accept the proposed law of indemnity trusting that the government will find a solution for tax-reform that will assure remedying the shortage of money that is reported in the budget. However we cannot solve this problem only with tax-reform, but only if together with tax-reform actions will be taken that empower the nation to become truly able to pay taxes. I desire to treat those portions of feminine programs that are indirectly but closely connected to this issue. When I recommend to this assembly the protection of women's vigor of life, I desire to treat this issue on behalf of women. We, Christian women do not deal with this issue, like the radicals based on class struggle, simply from women's interests, but in view of a general interest. *(Yes!)* We consider the energy of women as the source of the nation's strength. This issue was not recognized so far in view of the general interest, but held as a secondary question. If the economic interests of men suffer, the women suffer as well; but if a woman's economic ener-

---

[107] Nép Szava, 1920,I. 24.Cover page. Of the behavior of some politician the Diary of the Parliament of the same day wrote this way: "The speaker following Margaret Slachta began: 'in the Hungarian Parliament no one had the honor to speak after a woman representative... therefore, he must try not to supersede that noble influence the first woman representative offered, but must follow as a gray sparrow on that well prepared path of action that she placed before the honored assembly.'"

gy is abused, and she sends the children with reduced energy into life, it will not be possible to be remedied, to equalize. We seek strong male hands, but we shall be able to assure for the nation strong male arms, if the nation has strong, healthy mothers. *(Vivid affirmation.)*

The second aspect with which I desire to deal is this: I consider women's energies as a national asset. We shall suffer the loss of that tremendous energy that is necessary to uphold the nation's vitality if we don't assure the interest of that energy. In our present condition, the capital city comprises $1/8^{th}$ of the nation. The villages whose vocation would be to make up for the lost energies, on account of the great difference are unable to supply it. The women of the middle class stand before a great crisis. We cannot solve the economic condition of the middle class by forever making their income higher without limit. It is not possible only to demand, when we know we have no resources. Therefore, I say that the most important task of the government is to take hold of all means by which it will be able save us from this terrible disaster. Perhaps it may seem very small and insignificant - the means I think of - but I do not see right now any other solution than to introduce home-industry the way we have done in villages, based on export with raw material imported from abroad. If I look at the situation of women working in industry, we discover a terrible result. I shall try to read the statistical data of the children of women working in a tobacco factory. According to these data, 36.17% of children of working- women die before the age

4; those above 4 years 6.8%; of pre-mature birth 1.9 % and by spontaneous abortion 8.15%. Among the surviving children 20.28% are sickly; that means 72.59% get lost for the nation; 27.41 % of healthy children remain for the nation. This is a terrible reality present not only in tobacco factories but also, more or less, in all industrial factories. We may not look away from these facts; therefore I see it urgently important especially in unhealthy industries that employ women to introduce half-day terms. I find it necessary to provide more effective protection of mothers than offered so far, particularly by funds to provide help in case of illness, and for working girls and women in industry two weeks of annual paid vacation. *(Agreement.)* I find it unavoidably important to initiate industrial supervision in factories.

I must deal with the issue of wet-nurses. It should be made obligatory that the child of the wet nurse be taken to that house (where she breast feeds a child for pay) and to establish by law a foster sister-brother relationship. We must urgently demand that no one have the possibility - even if the economic situation allows it - to buy a mother's milk at a price of giving her own child into the arms of death. *(Agreements and applause.)* Questions of common morality are also connected to economic problems. Jenő Karafáth, Representative, quoted some from the data of Dr. Lajos Nékám, dermatologist (1868-1957) that in 1910 at the clinic, patients with sexual infections numbered 5773; this number by 1919 was fourfold, i.e. 22900. I take courage to add from the shocking statistical data of Dr. Nekám regarding youthful male sexual infections. According to these records, before the war, in boys of fifteen, infection was found in 1 %; now it is 8%; among 17 year olds it was 11% and now it is 26%; those of 18 years was 27% and now it is 68%. *(Shuffling in seats, one voice: 'Unbelievable, how did we get so far!')*

Honored Assembly! We plan to talk about budget but these numbers I think will leave without decision 4-5-10 milliards of deficit for the nation. Now when we speak of a Christian course, these symptoms must not be erased out of sympathy by regulations from the outside. We must be completely clear that we are faced with a total moral collapse *(Agreements!)* and uprooting it is possible only by an interior moral consolidation. *(Yes! Yes!)* We, as Christian feminine organizations of the national union party, are convinced that to solve this problem women alone are not capable. In this respect a true moral renewal can be expected only if it becomes a male movement, and we women give help to realize it.

I turn now - again in view of national economy - to school reform. *(Hear! Hear!)* My demand might seem American, but nations at the brink of survival or death must consider unusual viewpoints. I hold it necessary that, in grade, middle, and higher education, reforms be realized in the following way. The first focus should be the nation's vitality, its vigor; second, the economic stabilization and only in third place theoretical knowledge and classical formation.

We need, for the realization of this reform, not theoretical scientists but practical educational professionals, national economists, and doctors *(Yes!)* who can discover whether the small, developing 6-7 year old child is able to bear the daily 3-4-5 hour long study without fresh air. Consider in this respect how much our youth are able to bear. I found it important to deal with the reform regarding the type of education (*agreement and applause)* that we create four types of schools: household, industrial, commercial and agricultural types; such schools exist abroad. It is surprising how little our schools seem to know about life.   To only dream of great reforms makes no difference if there are not persons to embrace them and realize them. *(It is so! From the left.)*

Honorec Assembly! Our very first task must be to awaken in the entire nation the energy to act. *(True! Yes! Applause from the left.)* Where this is noticeable, those initiatives must be effectively supported. The feminine independent political organization as in the Christian Feminine National Union Party has begun rebuilding the nation cannot boast of a long political past. We, Christian women are facing, as strangers, the admirable party fluctuation that we witness now.   We are occupied only with what could practically contribute to the work of rebuilding. *(Affirmation)* Our primary principle in this is that we do not want to be helped by the state; rather, we want to do everything- even though in a small measure - that can contribute to lifting up the nation.   Today those who demand should not be the first, rather those who primarily offer.

In order to realize our political program in the first district - that sent us here - we began immediately to initiate such welfare programs that otherwise would have been asked from the state or the city. We hope that the Ministry of Treasury will not deny a minimal contribution necessary for beginning and continuing those programs *(Agreements, applauses, exclamations: That is harder! Laughter)* especially if within a short time we can report of positive results.

Honored National Assembly! The entire Christian Women's Corps stands united and disciplined behind the national assembly. *(Appreciation)* It does not want to play a glorious role, but wants to bring sacrifices to the altar of the nation. We understand these times; we know the sacrifices it demands. We recognize the tasks it asks from us. We demand a part and fight for a part, for participation in the work of rebuilding our nation. The spirit that leads us is the same spirit that inspired the heroic Hungarian women - though manifested in modern circumstances - who were not afraid of cannon fire, yet remained true women. The Christian Hungarian woman does not seek for herself political jobs for the sake of politics. *(Affirmation from the right.)* But we are not afraid of political work for the sake of the hallowed work of rebuilding the nation. We shall prove that we will continue to remain feminine at all times *(Applause at the right.)* but we are ready and capable to make all sacrifices that in the present circumstances our nation requires of us. We ask however, that our efforts will meet not only with understanding but also with effective support.

From what I presented before I submit before the honored Assembly the following proposals for decision: *(Hear! Hear!)*

The House shall direct the government:
1. To urgently modify the law, in view of the interest of future generations, to introduce and make obligatory a half-day working time for women workers in industries where conditions are harmful to health. *(agreement expressed)*

2. To place a sufficient number of female supervisors in industrial settings. *(agreements)*

3. To secure the protection and better care of mothers with help in case of illness until family health insurance can be installed; *(affirmation)*

4. To secure for each industrial worker a paid annual two-week vacation. *(affirmation)*

Furthermore I propose that the House direct the government to:
1. Enact a law to stop the system of wet-nursing or make obligatory that a wet nurse's child is raised together with the employer's child.

2. Examine and revise, according to the Christian morality, all the laws and regulations regarding public morality. *(affirmation)*

3. Order the planning and preparation of education reform - that has been urgent for a long

time - by the following guidelines: first the protection of the children' health; second: serving
economic interests (work or job preparation);
and lastly, theoretical knowledge and classical
formation. *(General applause. Several representatives greet the speaker.)*

During her work in the Parliament in 1945 -
1948, a bill came under discussion that distorted
one of the first term interventions of Sister Margaret. Punishment of "whipping by stick was repeated by representatives of the left. The truth is not
found in propaganda writings or demagogue
speeches. It is simply verified in the <u>Diary of the
Parliament.</u>

After the end of World War I, the country was
in a hopeless, destroyed condition. The National
Assembly officially agreed to the Trianon treaty on
4 June 1920; the areas annexed to other countries
were under foreign governments for two years.
Hungary was full of refugees. Following the rule of
the Council of Republic was the Romanian occupation. The country was robbed of resources, of
food supply, and found itself on the brink of death.
Some, to make a profit from the misery of everybody else, used this situation. Food supply was
manipulated in unbelievably big measure and the
price of the adulterated foodstuffs kept rising. Yet
another practice, called "chaining," became common. It meant, that while bread was sold at the
price the government determined it was sold only
on condition that another thing, with a very high

price, was also purchased. The government struggled to solve this abuse that affected mostly the poor class, children and families. The press, naturally spoke much of this problem and demanded "stick, whipping, hanging" for the abusers The Social Democrat <u>Working Woman</u> wrote: "If it is impossible otherwise, let it be stick, let it be whipping, let it be hanging as punishment for those who make prices higher. Let no exceptions be made; carry it out on everyone." It is important to remember these expressions, because, for such expressions, attacks were made on Margaret Slachta.

The National Assembly submitted to the Ministry of Justice on 20 April 1920 the legislative bill on *abuse of raising prices* according to the rules of the Assembly two months in advance in order that the representatives have time to study the issue and prepare for their intervention. The discussion of the plan was scheduled to begin on 15 June. At the beginning of the session the Minister of Justice announced that he submits the plan and the House will discuss it four months later under the title "On Criminal Law for More Effective Protection of Assets, Morality and Identity." The debate began in April. Among the first to speak, Tivadar Homonnay, strongly condemned those who lift prices, and he found the planned incarceration insufficient, and suggested *whipping* as the main punishment. The Minister of Justice protested that a recently submitted proposal to be debated later does suggest this form of punishment, but does not include it in this bill. Later on, however several representatives repeatedly speak for this punishment of profiteers. Margaret Slachta got her turn to speak on 18 June, and said: "Speaking of the whipping, we must be afraid that the most crooked profiteers will find a loophole even if a health certificate is needed to postpone the whipping." She points to the fact that the proposal *refers only to men.* If only men are intended, we shall arrive at a surprising result: profiteering will be done not by men but by women, namely the wife or relative of the profiteers; therefore it is necessary that the *law include women.* That is all she said regarding the whipping punishment for profiteering, whether it was of food or anything else. She explained her standpoint to her party members in the <u>Hungarian Woman</u> (10 July 1920): "I find it necessary that we exchange opinions. The first question: is it right for a human being to be whipped? The response simple is: *no.* The second question is: Do the profiteers, who abuse the needy situation of others only to enrich themselves, act as human beings? Those who are not held back from *making their purse fat at the price of the blood of their neighbors?* The answer again is: *no.* Do the profiteers know they are acting wrong? *They know.* But their passions are stronger than living by moral values. Since their morality has sunk below human level, they cannot be influenced with human and humane methods. If however, they experience the results of their bad actions in a form of suffering, they will remember it." She continued, "The leftist press protests in the name of Christianity against whipping. We can add - and this is addressed to the legislation to be debated in the future - we do have that much strength, having recognized the terrible decline of moral sense, we dare to take the whip into our hands to correct it."

In 1945 in the paper <u>Democracy</u>, we read that Margaret Slachta attacks started. "Those who with her and her protection experienced the tragedies of the past year could not even dream that Margaret Slachta can be attacked." However the editor of the newspaper visited Sister Margaret and asked whether it is true that she voted for whipping punishment of women. She responded affirmatively, "Today it is loudly announced without any emotion: *death to those who sell on black markets.* No one gets scandalized by it. In my opinion punishing by whipping is less serious than doing it by death. Yet many get scandalized for it In 1920 poverty was much greater than today. On the streets more than one person died of hunger and infants froze to death. In the Parliament the representatives discussed desperately how to solve the problem. It was for this reason whipping punishment was prescribed for profiteers - today black marketers." The editor asked her, "Would you vote yes today as well?" "No. I know today, how much those who administer the punishment can abuse such punishments. I already know that punishment cannot eliminate profiteering, only inner formation." In the end the National Assembly voted for punishing profiteers by whipping but without including women. The <u>NÉP SZAVA</u> wrote: "The determined profiteer's naturally will continue to cheat. They are clever enough to send their wives, daughter, girlfriend or women employed for this specific work to transact profiteering under their own name." This is exactly what Sister Margaret foresaw.

The actual whipping law, Criminal Law for the More Effective Protection of Assets, Morality and Identity, was submitted to the National Assembly on 25 August 1920. However Sister Margaret, according to the data of the <u>Diary of the Parliament</u>, had earlier asked for six weeks vacation, which the House approved. In the <u>Diary of the Parliament</u> her name does not appear on 22 July in the list of speakers or among those making interventions. In a miraculous manner one of her diaries from those days survived. Accordingly she first made a retreat in Pannonhalma; from there she traveled to Austria, then planned to travel to Switzerland. Her goal was to gain sponsors. Before her election she made some promises to the electors, as did every representative. She went to neighboring countries in August 1920 to be able to fulfill her promise regarding children. She sought out MICHRIST, the international organization that would help her to fulfill her promises. Naturally they counted on contributions from Hungary as well. In the paper, <u>MAGYAR NŐ</u>, (1921, VII. p. 8) Sister Margaret enumerated what she asked from those at home: "Assure for each child of the district their future well being." She explained that the 1st district made huge steps toward reform when it elected a woman representative. They could not create a more beautiful memorial for this reform than to help the needy children "...*by becoming sister for the parents and second mothers for the children.* Neither the lost war nor the economic collapse nor the stolen land of the nation is so great a loss as not having great personalities. *To give persons, great human beings to the country, to provide new and intense life-streams into the body of the nation from the beating hearts of the nation, this is the greatest feminine program. In this work will the Christian Women Corps create a memorial for the 1st District.*" Beyond resources from the nation there was need of help from beyond the borders, and for this Sister Margaret spent August - September of 1920 in Austria. She told in her diary that she traveled to many places outside of Vienna, and visited primarily Hungarians, but she made known to local organizations the movement of MILCHRIST, and gathered benefactors for the children with unequalled success. She returned home on 4 October.

During this time at home two new laws were created: the Numerus Clausus (1920. Par. XXV.), and the More Effective Protection of Assets, Morality and Identity by Criminal Justice, which popularly was named punishment by whipping (1920. Par. XXVI.). This law affected those who offended by pornography, killing, offenses against public health, robbery, stealing, blackmail, keeping stolen goods, cheating, arson, usury and profiteering.

The length of punishment could extend to only one year. [...]

A conscious and organized warfare of slander began against the law and, connected with it, on Margaret Slachta. The primary agent of slander was the paper <u>WOMAN WORKER</u>, beginning in 1920 and continued on many occasions to spread distorted slanders about her, "Sister Margaret speaks in the debate on punishment by whipping and at the Numerus Clausus with all her talents and outstanding oratorical gifts." Slanders were changed according to the whims of the writers; such accusations were also heard that Margaret Slachta wanted to make workers become illegal. Here is the text of a brochure from 1926: "Women, Comrades! Workingwomen! Proletars! The counter-revolution came with great fanfare and promises. Of these, only the law of whipping and the general misery of the people were realized." Did Sister Margaret know of these slanders: Definitely yes, because she wrote in <u>VOICE OF THE SPIRIT</u> on 1 February, 1943, "I was in America in 1928, and read with great interest the Hungarian leftist papers that wrote about representatives of Christian orientation. In this manner I could read about myself very instructive information, for example, that I tortured political prisoners in the jail of Margit Boulevard. First I thought to start a libel suit against them, but we were in the process of foundation and time was precious. I did not follow through with this idea." In a letter 6 May 1926, a sister working in California informed of her work among Hungarians there, "There are many good persons among them but most are organized into some leftist party or union. God and religion are banished everywhere." The sister participated in a rehearsal of Hungarian children and before leaving a gentleman, not previously known to her, came to her, with a loud voice said, "But I know who you are. We know Slachta and her companions, and the whipping punishment that she introduced against the communists for Horthy's desire and his gang." Before everybody she responded "Perhaps it would better to get information rather than mix up facts." Margaret Slachta wrote on 30 October 1926 to a co-worker: "Many thanks for the newspaper clips. I am not happy that somebody be imprisoned because of me. Maybe only my sensitivity got dull toward the slanders propagated by newspapers, reading those articles that the pornographic Hungarian papers in America write of me. They were truly terrible."[108] This was the reason that during the past 40 years whipping punishment was always attached to the name of Margaret Slachta in the Parliament and in the press. Sister Margaret bore these slanders heroically, but in the session of 12 March 1946 she gave information on her function during her term of 1920 - 1922 in the Parliament with the title "Attacks on My Person." She concluded with the following: "I respond to those who can say only 'stick!' Seemingly I must have functioned without blame if only one criticism is told, even though this does not have

---

[108] SZTTI, 1157/ 38.

basis in reality."[109]

Since information on her service in the Parliament during 1921 - 22 was given in an outline form, where it is necessary it will be filled in. "Those who speak repeatedly of the "stick", and not in a positive way, even though I wanted only to protect poor families, they turn that against me. I can be accused only for not desiring a stricter law - namely, death. They never gave a thought to all the things that I succeeded in achieving on behalf of the poor working families, on behalf of whom all my activities were dedicated. In this way, I mention the introduction the system of school nurses, and later, also that of doctors for schools." Actually only a service of social care after school was intended, but eventually a total child-protection service grew. On 30 September 1921 Margaret Slachta called forth the decree 83.519/1921 VII, suggested by the mayor of Budapest, for *raising taxation of horse races and profits from 11/2% to 2%* for charitable purposes in order to increase the funds for charity. Her proposal was accepted and that half percent supported several charitable and social institutions. The fund functioned until 1945. She also succeeded in having *tax on the superfluous rooms of luxurious homes* and used the money on behalf of people living in wagons for building small homes. From 1918 on people fled in droves from the territories annexed to other nations. Not having homes, they lived in wagons at the train

---

[109] Diary of the National Assembly, 1946. III. 12. P. 744.

stations in unimaginable misery. She expressed herself on 9 June 1921 that the law should not give opportunity to rich people to excuse their selfishness with the Christian view of right to private property. On 30 December 1921 the taxation of luxurious homes was approved for the named purpose.

The local government board overseeing the schools originally included only men. After the intervention of Sister Margaret, women received this right. In the area of national child-protection, where the death rate was as high as in 1946 she succeeded in having two women installed as government commissioners. The commissioners were installed at a ministerial level. In land reform at Nagyatád she won the right of equal ownership for women and men. This partial land reform, created in 1920, originally served only men. Sister Margaret succeeded in modifying it so that not only war-widows but also women in general could apply for land. In those sections of prisons where male guards oversaw women she achieved change providing female guards. For the workers in industry she introduced annual two weeks paid vacation. She urged a half-day work time for workers in industries that were harmful to health; feminine supervisors for women workers; better protection for mothers in the area of health care; regulation of visiting bars; reducing the percentage of alcohol in brandy; and forbidding employment of women in bars. At the time of dismissing 12,000 office workers, she urged establishment of a department to offer work training to secure jobs for the unemployed. "This is meant to secure simple training that the laid off might be able to earn their bread in another job. I urged for those in detention - who at that time were mainly communists - better provision and chance for work." Sister Margaret gave that talk on 25 January 1922 in which she described the condition of those in detention and said the following.

My intervention on behalf of those in detention is seemingly in contradiction with what I expressed in the case of profiteers' punishment with stick, and that I supported. The state has an obligation to protect the weak. Those who know the world of those who depend on pawn tickets, of frail children shedding bitter tears, who live in moldy homes, that is, the world of the miserable and helpless, realize what a terrible sin profiteering is. In my opinion those who are afraid to rise to protect defenseless people are cowards and false humanists. [...] For those who are ready to fill their purse at the price of human blood, no punishment is big enough. At the same time the law of 1920 par. IV ordering punishment by stick against the profiteers prescribes the presence of a doctor; this expresses the principle of the protection of health and safety of the body. Together with the right to punish, the right of protecting the human body is secured by this law. The state has the right to punish those who suck the blood of fellow citizens, but to physically waste away the punished with a nourishment that is completely insufficient to maintain life, and with unemployment (lack of work possibility in prisons), hurting their spirits, not even the state has the right.[110] For the workers I promoted living wages and I initiated a movement for women's voting rights that were, at that time, limited.

We have some insights into Margaret Slachta's style of work in an event preserved in the Nép Szava: "An armed gang abducted a wholesaler at 3 AM from his home in Buda. The family notified Margaret Slachta immediately who turned to the Ministry of Defense and in five days the man was released. Two more events speak of the function of the Office of Housing: 'In handling the case of poor people the office is energetic and decisive. I know of two cases from my district where the husband's wake was held, and on the next day the widow had to move from the home. Presently there is a woman in my district who supports herself and her four children by doing laundry on Mészáros Street. She received an order to move from the home on Jozsef Street.' "[111]

We can get a better picture of her work and principles from an article, "How Does a Woman Representative Work?"

A day in the office of the party...
In front of one high yellow building on Attila Street a group of people shuffle impatiently.

---

[110] In the Diary of the Parliament, 1920-21, a note is added with the signature of Margaret Slachta: ""and now in 1946?"
[111] Diary of the Parliament, 1921. VI. 9. P. 27.

They wait for Margaret Slachta, District Representative, who holds her weekly day of reception in the office of the party when everybody, happy and unhappy, can come to see her with their problems. The office of the party is a simple, poor room. From the wall, the Crucified Jesus looks consolingly on the sad and broken people. One by one the petitioners sit down before the table of the representative. Margaret Slachta listens with the patience of an angel to the long lists of complaints. She accepts each case. She does not ask for whom they voted; she accepts the case of those who belong to another district. One can see she wants with her heart and soul to solve every problem. Amazed by her, I asked Margaret Slachta her opinion of the responsibility of a representative.

'I am not surprised that you ask me that question,' she said, 'since in the present circumstances one must struggle to do one's work responsibly. Not only the electors, but in the country everybody who has a problem expects help from the representatives. It seems consciousness has diminished in everybody that the representatives must spend most energy on creating the laws that serve the common good, to develop useful regulations for ending the problems affecting the population.

'I, myself, suffer from the knowledge of how much time I take away from the common concerns while I try to solve the problems of individuals. People do not think of the high price and much shorter the representative's time to dedicate to the common good. Of course one can understand their grabbing for help. And I find myself obliged in my area to do what the state is unable. To harmonize my two obligations in my distrct I use the Social Mission Society for the care of the people. The Social Mission Society does this by involving its coworkers. I divided my district into eleven regions for meeting people's needs. Each of these regions receives a caretaker, who tends to her region's issues that extend not only to economic needs but also to spiritual and moral concerns. Beyond these I deal with problems with the help other organizations and the specific ministries. How other representatives solve this problem, I do not know. They do not have the advantage of working with fifty co-workers. I came to realize they are men but from me, a woman, the several thousand year tradition expects more, particularly in times of misery when nearly every petition coming to me starts: I came to you because you are a woman and have a heart.'

What were your achievements during your time as a representative?

She points to the wall where a manuscript is framed. 'When I received my mandate, I made a promise to my electors. My first promise was that for those retirees who turn to me I would secure, by societal manner, monthly help to complement their income. My second promise I guaranteed educational help for each child if the parents or guardians ask for it. Beyond this I provided 4,000,000 Korona (Hungarian money) through donations from abroad and home and distributed it among the poor of my district. In the Parliament my greatest achievement was raising the taxes of horse races with 1.5 % for the poor of Budapest, and that meant five million Korona yearly. At my request the Minister of Education ordered the establishment of school nurses and a system to offer social care after school hours. Moreover, at my request the Minister of Education ordered that school boards include women. The Minister of Justice gave permission that females be employed for supervising women in prisons.

'Of my future work plans, I can say that I have in mind to have a female be appointed government commissioner in child-protection. I cannot understand why this specific work is entrusted to busy men, when even a free person has a hard time to realize resolving all the problems completely.'[112]

It was mentioned that at the time punishment with stick was debated in the Parliament, Margaret Slachta was abroad. She asked and received a vacation in August 1920. In her diary that survived, one can read the following penciled inscription, "4 October 1920 Monday. We returned to Vienna. A telegram expected us to return home...to save women's right to vote."[113]

More can be learned from the report of the Hungarian Woman since it tells the text of the telegram. On 15 October the open letter of Margaret

---

[112] Nemzeti Ujság 1922. I. 3. P.6.
[113] SZTTI 12141920, October

Selecta was published:

Christian Hungarian Women! Parliament wants to eliminate both the passive and the active right for women that were temporarily regulated. It wants to finalize the law regarding the right to vote. This legislation interests us in the closest manner because it wants to eliminate both the active and the passive vote of women at the local and district elections. Since we gained political equality we have not had the possibility of debating our rights and exercising responsibilities as citizens. We want to grab the occasion of the Catholic Assembly when so many of our sisters from rural areas are present in Pest. We also ask our Protestant sisters who identify themselves with Christian politics to come in great numbers and participate in the demonstrative feminine assembly on 27 October, when we want to express our opinion on the issue of voting rights. It would be unworthy of us to remain silent bystanders while our rights are diminished and we do nothing to prevent this. The right of women to vote is not an issue of party politics; it is a question of human justice. All the united feminine organizations of the nation, the charitable, faith related, the social, the economical and the cultural are to hold local meetings on this issue to draft a memorandum to the National Assembly. They are to be signed by the leader of the groups and brought along to our assembly on 27 October. Having received them, I shall submit them on the following day to the National Assembly. Please visit your representative, ask their position on this issue and share clearly that our fidelity and persistence is not focused on the person but on the vision that they represent. If we must chose our choice should definitely be the vision, the truth and justice. Now the continuation of the issue - that is at present only at the beginning stage - what we proclaimed as a password in Christian Hungary. Hungarian Christian women line up and demand we keep our arms! If you tear them from us, perhaps a decision has been made beforehand to end Christianity and the common good to favor its enemies. If there still are some who do not understand us well we want to tell, without the passion of party politics, objectively, with conviction and united, what we think, what we feel and what we want regarding voting rights.[114]

Margaret Slachta

In the same Nemzeti Ujság appeared a report of a demonstration in favor of women's right to vote.

This afternoon the street of Pest became alive. This aliveness, a demonstration was new, new as the question, as a spirit that moved and kept rolling a great number of people on the wide lines of streets. The Christian Women of Budapest marched to the modern political front, to the streets to demand rights for women to vote, that were given to them during the counter-revolutionary time, but the present day party politics wants to take partially away. The wom-

---

[114] Nemzeti Ujság 1920, October15. P. 4

en march in silence and in a dignified manner from the Opera house to the Vigado. They carried their desires and their arguments with dignity and consciously to their assembly. Their assembly was like their demonstration: peaceful and dignified. They did not demand, but stood a test, gathered into a mass with one feeling and one idea; not like those who were forced to the margins, but like those who within some fortress set themselves up to protect their rights. Among the helpers of the Women Corps, past politics and new politics was present. The arriving demonstrators quickly filled the large hall of Vigadó. At the podium, Ottokár Prohászka and Count Albert Apponyi, representatives of the National Assembly together with the juridical representatives of the city, took place amid inspiring ovation of the participants. Margaret Slachta stood up to talk, 'We do not place our struggle for women's right to vote on the platform of party politics, we make it the issue of culture and Christianity. The Minister of Internal Affairs asked me the other day: *What would you say if those women would gather who are enemies of women's right to vote?* I responded it is not possible to build up a nation on negatives. Whoever cries *no* now is dead and, with an army of dead, one cannot rebuild.' The participants clapped for long minutes and the various societal and political organizations, one by one, proclaimed joining the struggle for the untouchableness of political rights. The intervention of Mari Rafis, a simple peasant girl of Mezőkövesd, received great acclaim. She stated that the participation of women in governing the nation is indispensable.

Count Albert Apponyi stood up to speak amid high affirmation and applauses. Following his talk with loud applauses all the representatives of rural organizations placed their memoranda on the table of the presider in favor of unimpaired right for women to vote.[115]

The question of taking away parts of women's right to vote came again under discussion in 1921. The Minister of Internal Affairs submitted a new bill that would take away the principle of secret vote. It would give the right to vote for men of age 24, who have lived at the same address for ten years, is a Hungarian citizen and has four years of grade-school education. On the other hand, women would have a right to vote if 30 years old, citizens for ten years, had four years of grade school education, had two children with eight years of high school education and a husband with a similar education. They were allowed to cast secret vote only in Budapest and in surrounding areas and under some municipal authority. Everywhere else open voting had to be held.[116] Sister Margaret gave two impressive talks in favor of women's right to vote. The first on 28 December 1921 with the title "Representatives' Right to Budget." Citizen awareness was rarely as keen as at this time when this right affected their purse, their household, in favor of the nation.

---

[115] Nemzeti Ujság, 1920. October 28. P.2
[116] Antal Balla, 1937. P 510.

Our nation is in a chaotic economic situation. We who are responsible must recognize this because this situation did not happen by itself; the National Assembly created it. There is between the practice of the right to budget and the nations' monetary situation the strongest and undeniable connection. I ask how can and will a simple citizen assure the protection of economic interest if not by the practice of indirect use of the right to budget, that is through right to vote. Here I arrive at my first argument: The first demand of the Christian social programs is to extend to women the general right to vote because the monetary chaos justifies it. If the representatives who got to the Parliament through a general secret vote will not be able to achieve better, that situation will cause a different evaluation. The citizens will not accuse anybody because they themselves decided their fate. All will eat what they have cooked. However, if I insist on preparing the food, even though I know it will burn, and force those to eat who were not allowed near the oven, then this act can rightfully be condemned. This refers very forcefully to women's right to vote. Men have strong cultural and economic connections; by their nature they can much better pressure and more consistently demand the realization of their will and interests. Women in every respect are in a more unfavorable situation. The handling of the nation's economic affairs regarding high prices affects women just as much as men; she pays taxes like men. Having less practice and a more sensitive conscience, she is affected more than men. Whatever I said regarding women's right to vote, I found important to say from her viewpoint and justice. But the same demand regarding the passive vote I want to prove from the point of the nation's economic benefit. I must state that the handling of the nation's economic affairs is very difficult since creating a balance has not been accomplished. However, that which so far seemed impossible, and since in the majority of the world nations this is the case, I see a truth expressed that in this world all strength is one-sided. If it isolates itself it will fail on account of its own weakness. The fact that men generally are more gifted intellectually than women - I say this in general since in this regard there are too many exceptions - undoubtedly the greater giftedness is also in need of complementation. From its limitations it will not rise if it compares self with the weaker and despises it, excludes from work and looks at self with contentment. Depending on its own giftedness will assure recognition for self and claim rights in isolation. Or, recognizing one's finiteness and dependence on others, will search for that complementing giftedness that is present - perhaps in a smaller manner then one's own, as it has a different kind of strength. He will seek that complement that is missing in self. In this question I must draw a parallel between the gifts of men and women. Their gifts are very different. It is characteristic that men still think that women's femininity is expressed and must be expressed solely in works in household, child-care and emotional areas. Naturally the women's femininity is expressed in the above, but what men did not see so far - and at a loss for the common good - that women's specific thinking is expressed in every area. Women think in everything with a different shading and characteristic. She handles commerce differently if she works in it; she enters differently into a workshop if she is a carpenter and handles economic issues another way if th s is entrusted to her. The opposite is also true. A man will approach the most feminine work with his male characteristics.

Based on this, I find it important to include women in the work of the nation's financial affairs. This need is not based on fashion or vain desire for recognition, but on the fact that women see things differently than men. Women will recognize things men do not; will see things that men overlook. Allow me to draw attention to some social differences. Men most certainly are better able to acquire, but less able to save. They are better in finding sources of money, to use advantages from it, but less able to accumulate. Thriftiness is a feminine virtue. Good management is generally a feminine trait and this has a very important role. There is a common saying that a farmer with a wagon drawn by six oxen cannot bring into a home as much as a woman can take out in one corner of her apron. Men, however, vindicated both roles until now in the nation's household, and it cannot be said they did an excellent job as housekeepers. They took out from the house more than carried in with six oxen, even though they did not have an apron. Women take into account even small things, they are detailed. If this is the case, I ask on this basis the inclusion of women in the nation's household! Men in their grand style spend in a grand style. The results stand before our eyes in a grand style. Perhaps nowhere else is attention to small things, on details, on saving in small things also as in handling money. On small squandering I bring an example that might seem insignificant. In Hungary at present by the general voting right there are approximately 31/4 million voters. Each vote is placed in an envelope, even though the margin of the voting paper could be made sticky so to close it. At the present price of paper in this manner 1-2,000,000 Corona could be saved. For this reason saving in small - a feminine characteristic - may not be despised and excluded. We may not forget that the entire universe is made up of small grains of sand and a great gate turns on small hinges. There is one more thing in which the way of thinking differs very much between the sexes. Men in their way of thinking are more theoretical. They see numbers, addition, subtraction, perhaps deficit or the loss of balance, but do not see beyond. Women see beyond numbers, see the people who are affected by these data. When the Minister of Treasury said this year the deficit will be 16 milliard, that is the nation will incur 16 milliard more of debt, I saw 8,000,000 persons or 2,000,000 families who will have to carry this burden. That will mean 8,000 more Corona above the present terrible burdens. I saw the many tears, the innumerable half nights of agonizing that women will spend since they have to share in this. They will have to embrace more work to meet the rising costs. I saw the pale faces of children who will not receive what is necessary for their survival; I saw fathers with careworn faces because they were not able to provide for their loved ones and, as usually happens, they will try to forget their troubles in the bar or at the table of cards and throw their families into a greater misery. We women see through these numbers, the persons for whom this will mean new suffering. The significance of this is to know that who turns to money does not only throw money away but causes suffering to other human beings, attacks happiness, perhaps kills them. Such awareness can hold one back from acting irresponsibly, while numbers do not have that power or incentive.

Whether we will make life better if we involve women in financial matters, we cannot prove with facts, we can only opine. However, the fact that men did not succeed in solving this problem is proven by the beggarly poverty and misery of the nation. I call therefore every just and objective man who loves our country to turn away from a path that leads into bankruptcy and start walking on a path of justice, love of country and objectivity that will hopefully lead to a greater happiness in our country and for our people. Women's passive and active right to vote can be justified primarily by the manner of handling of our monetary affairs and our present economic condition.[117]

In 1922 on January 28, Sister Margaret asked for time to speak before the daily agenda. She protested in the name of 170 social and cul-

---

[117] This talk appeared in a separate printing, Budapest. Stephaneum.

tural organizations against diminishing women's right to vote.[118] She spoke a second time in favor of women's right to vote on 14 February 1922. This speech was submitted in writing in an abridged form.

> For centuries, men were the lawyers and those creating laws. The basis of these two functions must be justice and legality. Men, however, wrote two codexes for law and justice: one for themselves and the other for women. Christian justice and law eliminate two kinds of codex; one principle is valid for everybody.

After some foreign country examples, she read a leaflet from 1790; the name of the author is not given.

> The Hungarian mothers' humble petitions submitted to the 'Great Men' gathered in the National Assembly, and Hungarian Fathers. The petition of 1790 was only that women would be allowed to participate in their sessions. They reason with the idea: 'the National Assembly is that place where the seeds of freedom may fall from your lips into our hearts and from there will flow into your sons and find happy growth.' The woman representative continued. Modern man will realize that his importance will grow if he raises the importance of others around him! We have to create a new world; we must be led by Christian justice and by equality in law. What has passed belongs to the past, and we must

---

[118] Diary of the National Assembly, 1922, I. 28. P. 69. Uj Nemzedék, 1922, I. 29.

walk toward the future; everybody needs to be involved equally in the struggle for it. The reason we ask for political equality is only the most elementary demand of justice; we are the same citizens and individuals of our country as men. We work like them, we carry common burdens, and we pay taxes! We are overburdened with bankruptcy, we share the sufferings caused by war! Therefore we must have the same influence, and that is our due.

Following this she gave a detailed list how modern developments, e.g. the technical civilization directed by men cast an unbearable burden on women, who had to step out of their homes and into the arena of struggle for survival, carrying a greater burden than men. Therefore, women ask the same rights as they carry burdens. It is not only women who carry a yoke two or three times heavier placed upon them by developments directed by men, but the exploited child-workers as well. Greedy capital also appeared and that, too, is in the hands of men. "...In the hands of men is creating laws, the capital; not one has the courage to raise a voice. Women are also missing who would shout out loud and ask what will happen to the woman, what will happen to children?" She mentions that when she submitted her proposal for family-wage the finance minister shoved it aside saying: "this speaks of some system of family-wage, I do not accept this proposal." "I stated always that men have a fraction of talents, women have also a fraction of talents. If creating laws would be only in women's hands they would, out of altruism, distribute all the capital at a loss for all. In the same way, if law creation is in the hands of man alone, human beings get destroyed for the sake of capital and competition in the market. That justifies the presence of women and collaboration. Men can think of women only as cooks and nursing children, and that was the case. That is the reason we have in public life so few men with high principles; public life is missing real men because, at home as children, they missed spiritual and intellectual mothering."

Sister Margaret found unbearable that women were either locked in horizon-less housework and saw it unnecessary to develop their intellect or thrown into the marketplace never considering that they had responsibilities at home, thus needing to be placed in a different manner into breadwinning situations. "This is disadvantageous for women, but not primarily for their sake, but for children, the future generation, for men and the nation." She raised her voice that women be given back to the family and at the same time "be given free development of their talents and for exceptionally gifted personalities. She mentioned Florence Nightingale, Harriet Beecher Stowe, Saint Catherine of Siena and Madame Curie. [...] She said emphatically that legislation is unjust when it prescribes two kinds of measures for its citizens and a National Assembly may not do this when most of its members can thank their election to women voters.[119]

Following Margaret Slachta, Count Albert Apponyi spoke. "The honored speaker and representative who spoke before me obliges my gratitude not only in the sense that it obliges all of us by her truly outstanding talk through which she enriched the Diary of the National Assembly, but especially because she shortened my talk. After all that she said in view of women's right to vote, I need not address this issue in greater detail because to speak more beautifully, more exhaustibly and with deeper motivation as she is not possible."[120]

The National Assembly held its last session on 16 February 1922. During this session Margaret Slachta spoke for the last time. This could be called her swansong. She summarized what we can consider her political credo:

Honored National Assembly!
I propose that when we gather tomorrow, as we generally do, let us gather for thanksgiving worship. At this time we have a special reason to do so. Never has a National Assembly gathered with so much expectation by the citizens as the present one. This great expectation was focused on the strength of Christian truths and their saving reality. The overwhelming misery of poverty, the super-human tasks and

---

[119] Diary of the National Assembly, 1922. II. 14. p. 15.
[120] Diary of the National Assembly, 1922, II. 14. P. 20

171

our limitations did not make it possible to fully respond to this expectation. On account of these and psychological functions, the uninformed masses became weak in their trust of principles and vision. The greatest evil however would be, if because of the circumstances, the Christian vision would become only a password and faith, that has been held in it, be weakened. Therefore I feel as a double obligation, we, who believe in this vision and who have not been led here by economic interest, make our profession in this vision. We must demonstrate to our nation that we continue to believe in it; that in our souls the cry to God came not from fear of Bolshevism. Nor did our prayer to God come only from a festive excitement. It came from our unshakeable conviction that in work, in sweat, amid disappointments and lack of success, we continue to believe without hesitation that our nation can be led on the path of Christian faith to happiness.[121]

The mass of thanksgiving was held on the following day in the Basilica.

It is natural that preparations for the elections to be held in June would begin immediately. However on 3 March the press announced the news that "Margaret Slachta may not run for the next election, because as a Sister in the Social Mission Society she needs permission." To receive permission she would need to change direction and, because of this, "her interior conviction is

---

[121] Diary of the National Assembly, 1922, II. 16. P. 16-59

missing" and she cannot do so.[122]

Five days later the Christian Women Corps held its great assembly. During the assembly Margaret Slachta gave a report on the results of her political function, she referred to distorted news published in some papers about her. She, as a member of the Social Mission Society, owes obedience to her superiors and they want her to withdraw from political life. At the same time she announced her resignation from the presidency of the Christian Women Corps. She left with good memories, knowing that she made a sacrifice, but this sacrifice was not bitter. Those present object to her announcement and decide to send a deputation to Edith Farkas to change her standpoint.[123] However the Women Corps did not succeed. They turned to the Conference of Bishops, asking to intervene with Mother Superior, to permit Sister Margaret to work in politics. Of this, the diary of the Bishop's Conference of 22 March 22 1922 wrote: "Even though the members of the bishops conference have great regard for Margaret Slachta's political function, it does not desire to enter into the internal affairs of the Social Mission Society."[124]

---

[122] Nemzeti Ujság 1922, III. 3. P. 3
[123] Nemzeti Ujsag, 1922, III. 18., STTI 1182/83., Uj Nemzedék,1922. III. 9. P.4
[124] The Chronicle of the Bishops' Conferences... 1919 - 1944 Budapest. 1984. p. 99., Csernock Cat. 59. 692. 1922.

From the standpoint of Edith Farkas we shall hear in the next chapter.

From Social Mission Society
to
Society of the
Sisters of Social Service

The previous chapter focused on Margaret Slachta's activities during her first cycle in the Parliament. For this reason information was not given of the happenings within the Social Mission Society. This chapter will begin with those events.

Until 1919 In the Hungarian female society, Social Mission Society, was the only unifying force of a Christian vision. With its organization it reached the entire historical Hungary. From 1919 on, new organizations were started, such as the Hungarian Women's National Association, (MANSZ) led by Cecil Tray.[125] The Hungarian National Protective Force (MOVE[126]) for which Miklós Horthy asked Edith Farkas to accept the presidency of the 'feminine' segment. In actuality she did not work in it. However, it is known from a contemporary letter of the Social Mission Society, "our situation has changed completely during the past half year; we were used to holding first place, but

---

[125] It was founded in December 1918 and existed until 1944. It was the country's official feminine organization with a newspaper title: Magyar Asszony.
[126] Founded in 1818 with a program of protecting races

now, at best, we are fourth. Ébredők[127], MANSZ, and MOVE work very hard. To this we have "our great internal difficulties."[128] About these "great internal difficulties" we can make only some guesses, but from the available documents some can be discovered. As we could see the life of Margaret Slachta and that of her sisters and their obedience were authentic. They could proceed because both Edith Farkas and Bishop Prohászka agreed to their work in the feminist movement. Bishop Prohaszka said in October 1920: "Lack of faith, immorality, cynicism and a destructive spirit is so great a danger; that makes women's ongoing organization in politics necessary. Everybody has to understand that the half of our world deserves some of what happens right now. Women are not rebelling; they are anointed for a new vocation, to be forces in the struggle for the well-being of people and of humanity."[129] Edith Farkas expressed her thoughts regarding women's societal responsibilities since 1915 in nearly twenty articles known, not only in the <u>Christian Woman</u> and the <u>Hungarian Woman</u> but also in the daily paper, <u>Nemzeti Ujság</u>. Such is one of her articles.

The Fighting Women Corps

I look at our nation with a sad heart.   Since

---

[127] The Awakening Hungarian's Organization was a totally anti-Semitic societal organization.
[128] Letter of Sister Petra Rónai to her spiritual director Gyula Zimányi August 10, 1920 SZTTI. 1182/76
[129] <u>Nemzeti Ujság</u>, 1920. X. 12. P.5.

communism, my eyes rest with hope and peace upon that huge social force we call the Christian Women Corps.   Members of this Corps are women who live spiritual lives, who see not only the faults of the left, but their own. With their radical thinking and unbending will, they are more suitable than men to stop the terrible curse: the discord. Some kind of an ancient, mother energy rises in our soul with anger over the never ending dissension and to prevent our heroes having died in vain, we are decided - heart and soul - to collaborate in the consolidation of our nation and to bring it to completion. We have principles; we know what we want: to follow Christ and his earthly successor in spiritual matters, to follow the legal head of the state in secular matters. We want work, order, discipline; we want peace. Not because of our beautiful eyes, but because of the gifts hidden in us, it would be a loss to exclude women from legislation and from any other rights of citizens. Silently and w th an organized discipline we shall pour forth those streams from which healing can be hoped.   Perhaps for months or years, maybe never, will results of our work come to light; we are satisfied with the blessings of hidden works. We only think, that in such societal spiritual poverty in which we exist, it would be good to add our treasures. The crumbling shores will be held up by millions of roots.[130]

This article appeared at the time of the

---

[130] Nemzeti Ujság 1920, X. 24. P. 4. SZTTI 693

great protest on behalf of women's right to vote. It is not possible to bear a clearer witness for an ideal. A different reason for the 'great internal difficulties' must be sought. Edith Farkas was in contact with the chief leader, Horthy and his family, on the evening of the National Army's entrance into the country. The organizations of the Social Mission Society decorated the path of the march and their representatives were among those who greeted the chief leader. From that time on the deepest friendship developed between Edith Farkas and Mrs. Horthy. They spoke with each other in a very informal way and a friendly relationship developed with him as a governor. "The Mother Superior gradually started to oppose the Christian Socialist's direction because the governor's immediate surroundings opposed it. Among the Christian Socialists the idea was spread that she influenced the governor against Christian Socialism.[131] The source of the controversy arose from another political situation when King Charles IV tried twice during a year to return (March and October1921), but the country was divided between the legitimists and those who wanted free elections for the king. The latter did not hide; they wanted Horthy for king. Mother Superior supported Horthy, while the sisters supported Charles IV. The difference of opinion was made even more difficult by the Society's financial situation throughout the nation and several of the sisters thought they must go abroad

---

[131] Rónai Petra: "The History of our Society." Testvér, 1931. IV. P. 5. The Secret Diary of P. Zadravecz. Kossuth. P. 264

to collect finances to support their activities. The third difficulty arose because Edith Farkas again chose a spiritual director, this time P. Ferenc Biró, S.J., who in 1921 founded the Society of People's Daughters of the Sacred Heart.[132] This new spirituality began within the society. The sisters who worked in fields outside did not experience much of this; but for those in internal fields and in the novitiate, the Jesuit spirituality became dominant. It is interesting that a Jesuit P. Béla Bangha had convinced Edith Farkas that the Society enter the public sphere, and when this initiative succeeded so well through Sister Margaret, another Jesuit, P. Ferenc Biró, initiated leaving it. We quote again another contemporary letter, "at the end of this month Sisters Etelka and Klotild, etc. came to Szikszó for a retreat conducted by P. Biro!! Naturally, I shall not participate, as we have to care for the house as the sisters often return from Pest. I again rejoice and thank God, I am here. I could not last longer; I came away in the last hour. My greatest pain is women's right to vote and that I may not work for it. Sister Margaret puts all her energy into it. What follows afterward, all the pain, does not depend on her - therefore I am specially glad to be here, because I do not know how I could bear to be prohibited from doing it."[133]

From the previous chapter we know that in

---

[132] Maria Puskely: Religius.1990, p. 137.
[133] Sister Petra Rónai's letter to her spiritual director, 1922. II 3. SZTTI 1182/80

February 1922 the National Assembly concluded its work. At the same time preparations began for new elections. Sister Margaret did not receive permission from her superior to accept nomination. More exactly, Edith Farkas bound permission with one condition: if she joins the movement of "free election for king." Sister Margaret is woman of principles, she did not change her conviction regarding the legitimacy of the king by succession; she rather withdrew from politics.

On 2 April 1922 an article appeared in Nemzeti Ujság with the title, "The Opinion of the Politicians on the Activities of the First Woman Representative." Like others, this one stated "Her work in the Parliament brings glory not only to women, but to Christian politics. To exclude her from activities in the Parliament is a half way lost fight for the Christian camp. Those who make her step aside, regardless the reason, do more harm to the nations' Christian social thought than a thousand enraged enemies." [134] The sisters hardly knew anything of all this. When in March 1922 preparations began for the next election - we read in a contemporary account - the Mother Superior

---

[134] This was written by Károly Huszár. Others wrote also: Ágoston dr. Bénárd, István Haller, István Rakovszky, Pál Tomcsányi, Béla Tury, an unnamed member of the Christian Women Corps, and even Gyula Gömbös. His statement contains an interesting criticism: Margaret Slachta stood her place, "she has only one fault: in political issues she is overly idealistic, dogmatic, and somewhat subjective..." Her life and political efforts are repeated anachronisms."

forbade the sisters to read newspapers; more than that, she ordered them not to vote for a Christian Socialist candidate but for a candidate of the government's party.[135] Sister Margaret stated emphatically sometime later that the separation did not happen on account of the political differences: "When the Social Mission Society excluded from its ministry political activities, it was only pain for me, and I did not have difficulty with it; I knew, if I took vows to the Social Mission Society, the goal of the superior and her intention is not my issue.[136] She has the right to dispose of me; she has the right to call me back from it, regardless how painful it is for me." On account of the difficult economic situation, and the happenings at the end of her political function when "she got into the middle of unpleasant interest," Sister Margaret asked to be allowed to go to America to make collections for the Social Mission Society. During summer of 1922 she received permission to go. At the same time a letter from the Bishop of Cleveland, OH arrived in which he asked Edith Farkas to visit him in München for a discussion about an American foundation The superior traveled with Sister Margaret to Munich because she meant to send her for leading the American mission. Following this, Sister Margaret traveled to London to brush up her English; she traveled purposefully there because her youngest sister, Alice, worked at the Hungarian

---

[135] Sister Petra Ronai's writing in the <u>Testvér</u>, 1931/5, p.6.
[136] SZTTI 1157/80 b. Sister Margaret's teaching at the end of 1926.

embassy in London.

Edith Farkas made an agreement with Ferenc Biró, S.J., without asking the sisters, to unite the Social Mission Society with the recently founded Daughters of People of the Sacred Heart. The first sign of this was perhaps that the <u>Christian Woman's</u> name was changed to <u>Hungarian Woman</u>. The latter, in its issue of June 1922, on its cover page announced that P. Biró would lead a three-day triduum in the Society's chapel. On the last day of the triduum, the Governor's wife was also present and P. Biró gave a long and touching homily. At the end of his talk the Blessed Sacrament was exposed and Edith Farkas offered the Social Mission Society to the Sacred Heart. Up until that time the sisters addressed each other in a familial way, but from then on they had to do it in a reverential expression. During the summer of 1922, Edith Farkas called Sister Elizabeth Bokor (one of the founding members) and Sister Paula Ronai, and told them she "will unite the Society with the Daughters of People and their name shall be Sacred Heart of Jesus People's Social Mission."[137] Sister Paula asked, "Mother Superior did you discuss this with the older sisters?" She responded, "Do you think I will make my decision dependent on your opinion?" Then both of them went to Esztergom and made report of this to the

---

[137] In Hungarian" Jézus Szive Sociális Népmisszió. (Translator's note. The English title is my translation.)

office of the Cardinal.[138] This was immediately reported to the Cardinal and he sent the reply he will not allow the fusion of the two.[139] Edith Farkas also wrote her decision to Sister Margaret, who was in London at that time. Sister Margaret sent several responses to Edith Farkas and in these letters one can see the anguish of Sister Margaret and her efforts to find solutions in prayer and reflection. One letter:

London, 1 September 1922.
My dear Mother Superior!
Your telegram, the insured letter and your note sent in the letter to Sister Hildegard arrived. The American visa is already in my passport. I could leave any day for America. However, I must say and with great pain that I am in an insurmountable interior difficulty about leaving because the retreat planned for the end of August is postponed until the middle or the end of September, and together with it the resolution of the internal difficulties. I would have to leave without knowing what the final resolution will be. In this uncertainty I cannot leave. Dear Mother Superior, when you called me back from the work outside, I had time to grasp the situation within the Society. I recognized how grave the situation was and that it requires a quick resolution that will bring satisfaction to all in the community. If such a resolution is not found, the

---

[138] Prelat Antal Leopold,, John Cardinal Chernoch's assistant.
[139] SZTTI 1182/87, + the author's conversation in 1981 in Buffalo with Sister Elizabeth Bokor.

present reality cannot be maintained. I pray to the Sacred Heart of Jesus (!) that the new solution of the Society's situation will bring rebirth and the solution of the problems. But what will happen if it is not found? I must write with pain, but my reality is, that I, who from the very first day, have lived through and have seen how the situation got where it is now. I, in the far away America, might not be able to serve you, Mother Superior, in the midst of unresolved situations at home. I might not find the conviction to do it. I ask your forgiveness that I did not write this immediately after receiving your telegram, but I agonized much over it - debating, reflecting, thinking, and fretting over the issue. Today at last, it is first Friday and I have a day of recollection, I came to the conclusion that leaving with uncertainty about my fidelity would not be honorable. My petition after all this is that, for the sake of my spiritual peace and on behalf of the issue, Dear Mother Superior, I may be allowed to return home. Be kind to postpone the trip to America for some time later, that I may wait at home for the final resolution of the issue, and that I may come to clarity within myself and then travel to America. My soul needs a complete security, because good possibilities and assurances about the future no longer give me peace, only the concluded facts. I deeply desire that only this time you, my Dear Mother Superior, would understand me. I am afraid that from my lines, even at this time, nothing but rebellion or something similar would be perceived. I kiss your hand and am waiting for your response.

Sister Margaret

Two days later Sister Margaret wrote to Sister Elizabeth Bokor.

After much trepidation, and reflection I offered to God this issue, and came to a final decision, of which I notified Mother Superior and Sister Superior in a letter and in a telegram. I asked that my ticket on the boat be returned and perhaps that someone else be sent to America, and for my recall after the solution of the situation. Of what I will be doing, I found it simpler, not to write and I do not write it to you either; I believe it is better. I asked for my recall for after the new arrangements so that I do not cause disquiet in our dear Mother Superior with my presence and not hold her in fear that I will attract the sisters to myself. I find it necessary to write the following, and I ask you to tell those to whom it belongs: If among the options of solution the Mother Superior chooses to unite the Society with the congregation of the People's Daughters, the way I judge the situation and guess future developments, and knowing myself, I shall not enter. I believe it unnecessary to ask for anything but that sisterly love require that we give to each other, without influencing for or against anybody, except to pray, that we pray to succeed to fulfill the will of God. However I ask exactly out of sisterly love that of the discussions for the solution everybody have information and bring in an orderly fashion, a lawful decision depending on two conditions:
1. No one may enter into the new community all at once definitively, only after one year of candidacy and one year of novitiate. Only

after that may anybody make a final decision to join.

2. For those who do not enter, a just economic arrangement be made. Justice demands this, since it is not they who leave, but the Society (the one they entered) has left, actually was changed. Giving one's best energies to the Society for the past 10 -15 years a possible job is not a sufficient compensation.

I sent these points to the dear Mother Superior that they could be read at the meeting. I ask to be notified when you received my letter. I embrace all our sisters with love and commend all to the Sacred Heart of Jesus.

Your Sister, Margaret
London, 3 September 1922

On the next day she wrote again to Edith Farkas.

London, 4 September 1922
My dear Mother Superior!
I received the letter of your great, decisive and, as you write, your final decision. With it, dear Mother Superior, you decided regarding your own person for a final sacrifice. I shall pray from the depth of my heart that you succeed in a total measure to make this sacrifice and to find that happiness the Lord Jesus promised to those who give up everything for him. If such a sacrifice is not made for his sake with total purity, we cannot persevere in it, because during the process of realization one recognizes how

much 'everything' contains in itself.

As for myself, I do not judge it to be God's will for me to enter into the new institute. If at some time I could be of personal assistance to you in something, you could always count on Cordelia.[140] The fact that I am not home at this time, I find to be providential, not because I would disturb our sisters, but because I shall not cause to you, my Mother Superior, worry with the thought of my presence. After final arrangements have been made, I ask for permission to return home, since the new situation will require more things to settle. I kiss your hand and ask God's blessings on your decision and on our beloved Society, my dear Mother Superior.

Your daughter,
Margaret

Two days later she wrote to the community.
London
6 September 1922.

From the quiet distance here I see the situation in the following manner: The fusion (meaning two branches of Social Mission) is providential. In this manner the differentiation is possible without scandal before the world. That is:
1. The possibility of separation without scandal.

2. Personal burden will be avoidable. Two bloodstreams will paralyze all activity if Mother Superior joins the People's Daughters with

---

[140] Cordelia was King Lear's banished daughter

those who find vocation to it.

3. Will completely assure unity, [...] hopefully for us, but for all others involved. All have need for the school of the good God; that He will give.

4. The fusion, even though at a high price will be a school for the men also.

I would find it a great loss (!) if this solution would not meet the favor of either P. Biró or our Father Bishop, or even the Prince Primate. May everything proceed. Let the conviction stand: the Superior decides alone, that is, she has decided. The members will have to choose. I will not enter the People's Daughters. However, I find it an obligation of conscience to serve those who are there, to give to all members objective information. I summarize:
The Mission ideal lives in my soul, I want to serve it! Please, I ask, show my letter to Superior Kamilla[141] after having read it. I do not want to be secretive until the possibility is limited! I ask everybody very much, as much as you are able, not make yourself excited. There is nothing on this earth that is not held in the hands of our loving God.
With faithful love,
Sister Margaret [142]

Though the Prince Primate did not allow the fusion, in October 1922 P. Biró S.J still held the retreat for the sisters. After the retreat Mother Su-

---

[141] The Vicar of Edith Farkas.
[142] SZTTI 332-334

perior called the community together and told the sisters that she decided against the fusion, and will realize her plan in a different way.[143] On 14 October she traveled to Székesfehervár for two days. Returning from there she placed the picture of Saint Ignatius on the wall of the chapel and took the statue of Saint Benedict into the sacristy and placed it on the top of the cabinet. With this she expressed her decision for the Ignatian spirituality, and obliged the sisters to follow it.[144]

The Social Mission Society however was so close to the heart to the Prince Primate that he appointed Prelate Leopold as an official Visitator and sent him to the Society. He reported the results of the visitation with Mother Superior. It is characteristic that he addressed Edith Farkas with title of a Lady.

Esztergom, December 4, 1922.
Honorable Lady!
The meeting of the National Organization is approaching. I take the courage to write my standpoint of the issue that will come under discussion.

The Christian Woman: This paper is the official paper of the National Organization. If the organization wants and is able to support it from its own resources, do not oppose it. The Society is not obliged to assist the paper, but in your

---

[143] Sister Petra Rónai: Testvér, 1931/5. P. 6.
[144] SZTTI 1132/87

189

status as superior by no means, and under the title of president, you may not take a position against the paper. You may, at the most, state that the Society is not in the position to support it. Regarding editing, it will depend on Your Honor to allow or not an internal sister to edit it. However it is not prudent to forbid inner members to write in it - the order's censure extends only to those articles that inner sisters write. A cruel censure will not bring good results because it will cause unnecessary bitterness; leaving out political information from the status will deprive the National Organization, of a powerful means and will disillusion many members. On the issue, Ernst,[145] I see, is of the same opinion, as I am. The goal of the Social Mission Society is much broader than other feminine organizations. It wants to organize women in such areas and inform them in which other women religious cannot. This area is exactly that which is called politics in a wider sense. Your Honor wants, very rightly, to exclude what is called party-politics in so far as this is not connected to Christianity and the church. However, politics is to some degree in the interest of Christianity and the church in as much as we demand the realization of Christian and Catholic principles in politics. If we exclude in this the collaboration of the Social Mission Society, we did not do a creative work, but a destructive one. With such restriction the So-

---

[145] Sándor Ernst, papal prelate and later a minister

cial Mission Society cannot reach its goal and in this way it has lost the basis of its existence. I have emphasized this before, Your Honor, repeatedly. I know Your Honor thinks differently now. But I warn you; I stand or will fail with my conviction. If Your Honor clings to the exclusion of politics in the National Organization also and includes the exclusion demand into the constitution of the Society, then I have resigned from my visitatorship. I have received from His Eminence the task to preserve unity. I have not received authority for the separation. I would not even accept such a tragic role. If I am unable to maintain the Society's unity, I leave the Society to its fate.

Your Honor will be bitterly disappointed, taking it to a breaking point. It will not be one or two sisters leaving the institute but 80%, and it will become evident that Your Honor did not hold the Society in your hand. Please do not put yourself into this, rather bring personal sacrifice to save your own Society, and allow the views of the sisters who grew up beside you, come to realization and who, in my opinion, have good will. If you cannot make this sacrifice, there will be a break not only now, but of the sisters who now go with Your Honor and will in the future break away. In my activity as a Visitator, I was led to protect the authority of the superior before the sisters, but with the superior I tried to have accepted that correct principle, that she must govern together with the sisters, and to pay fair attention to their views and desires; not to force on them things you see will meet with the sister's dislike or disapproval. Personalities cannot be completely suppressed even in the strictest communities. Everyone in governing must be clear about this. Whoever wants to force her will upon others should not govern. Objectivity is needed. The Society should never experience caprice, but the application of principles. It is not important what this or that person is saying, but only that which is of benefit for the Society. It is unnecessary to force some devotional practices, but it is important to assure true Catholic spirituality.

Truthfulness and humility are needed for governing. All other goals must be set aside when the matter is the survival of the Society. Your Honor has also a political viewpoint. It is exactly this viewpoint that leads you to forbid the sisters from justified involvement in politics. The sisters with their Christian and Catholic propaganda, with organizing Christian women can only be of benefit to present politicians. In acute and actual political questions that are not in the vital interest of the church sisters may not engage. However, inaction in politics will drive women to the opposing side and with it, Your Honor will have harmed those politicians whom at this point you desire to help. If you explain this to them, they will understand (!). Ernst's opinion is the same. I shall show this writing to His Eminence. If something in it is not to his liking, I shall leave it out and will not send it to you.

I believe I am not mistaken in judging Your Honor's disposition because I have observed it for a long time. I owe you truthfulness. Admit humbly your disposition, and try humbly to judge your own opinion and to value humbly that of others. Presume the best of your sisters, trust them and allow them to work. Rejoice over their success, inspire them and support them materially to achieve new successes. Then they will love you and will willingly obey you.

I recommend into your love especially poor Sister Margaret. Each highly gifted person has some faults. But Margaret is humble, she will recognize her mistakes if she is reminded with love. Please do not handle her as incorrigible and dangerous. Margaret is good, but sometimes she exaggerates. Trust the sisters leaving for America. Do not make more difficult their situation with unnecessary orders. They will have to adjust to the situation there frequently, which cannot be known here. Let us proceed on the way of unity! As soon as I notice efforts for separation, I will have finished my unsuccessful work.

With high respect,
Yours, Dr. Antal Leopold (signed.)

I have read and I agree:
John Cardinal Csernoch, Archbishop (signed.)[146]

Between the two Societies union did not happen. Mother Superior was seeking a new

---

[146] Csernoch Cat. No. 46. 3608,.1922, XI. 11. and No. 3948/1922. XII. 5. SZTTI 350.

method to realize her will. She sought and gave a new constitution to the Social Mission Society. When the new constitution arrived, the sisters turned to the Prince Primate. He gave the order by canon law that writing a new constitution may be made only with the collaboration of the sisters. If someone has such a strong personality as Mother Superior, who is used to arranging things independently, it is understandable that, for her, it would be foreign to take into consideration the sisters opinion.

Since Edith Farkas wanted so strongly this constitution, and saw that the Prince Primate did not allow it, she resolved the problem by transferring the Motherhouse to Csobánka into the diocese of Székesfehérvár, and in this way got it under the authority of Bishop Prohászka. The Prince Primate accepted the information on the transfer, and, with it, his order regarding the constitution was abrogated.[147] Of the new constitution Sister Margaret informed the sisters who left for America in January 1923.

> Dear Sisters Paula and Gertrude!
> At Easter our Mother Superior distributed a new constitution. It has two parts, the so called constitution, that includes everything, the part of government, spiritual obligations, and a part that contains only spiritual things in an outline form, called 'Summarium.' [...] The whole thing is unusual. It seems to be a copy of a medieval

---

[147] SZTTI 1157/80a. p.3.

constitution containing every small detail, for example:
'Point: 32. In the books used, no signs may be written.
37. Touching others is forbidden even it is out of joke.
69. The head must be held strait, slightly bent forward without bending it right or left.
72. Hands must be held modestly, peacefully.'

Important areas:
'In the future, politics, fighting for women's rights, aggressive women's movement, a feminist style must be missing from the heart of each Social Mission Sister.'
Vows will be taken to 'Your Divine Majesty and the Reverend Mother, Edith Farkas, Founding Superior and her legitimate successor. Industry and commerce may be practiced only with pontifical permission.

The founding Superior is not elected; other general superiors are elected for life, etc., etc.

Of course this is only a plan, but I don't believe church authority would essentially change anything. At Pentecost there will be no first vows, nor renewals. I shall write at a later time who will not enter on this new basis. I shall write when it will be more concrete. At this point these things may change; human beings can be unstable.

Here I shall compare the two:
The old: Society of laywomen with private vows.
The new: Religious congregation with simple vows.
The old: In the spirit of Saint Benedict. The new: in the spirit of Saint Ignatius.
The old: Modern, all embracing contemporary program. The new: with a program of charity.
The old: Effort to assure economic basis to be self - supporting. The new: Excludes industry and commerce, etc.
The old: Holy Spirit. The new: Sacred Heart cult.
The difference is quite much.
God bless both of you. Please, double your prayers.

With love,
Budapest, April 13, 1923
Sister Margaret[148]

Again Sister Margaret wrote:

On 17 April 1923 we received the letter from Bishop Proházka, in which he obliges us to accept the new constitution. Those who do not accept it have lost their vocation, and are to ask dispensation from vows. At this, all of us without having talked with each other responded, we did not lose our vocation; contrary, it is stronger than any time before. But we have deep concerns that the 400-year-old constitution coming from Saint Ignatius is not helpful for us. If we have to follow that we will not be able to keep it.

---

[148] SZTTI 1156/7

None of us wanted to leave the Social Mission Society. After our response, we received the letter from Bishop Prohászka in which he writes: 'those who for any kind of reason stated do not want to live by the constitution of the Social Mission Society, should consider themselves as having left the Society.' We did not understand why we were sent away only because we expressed our concerns about the inability to live under the authority of that constitution. (?) There was no legal basis for this. However, we accepted it because it required a process of development whose bridging seemed impossible, and for the reason that it will be more beneficial for the community if we leave![149]

In this way the Society of the Sisters of Social Service was founded on 12 May 1923. It was completely "un-planned" so much so because the founding sisters at the time of founding were in three different countries. Those in Hungary lived in three different places, in Budapest, in Szikszó, and in Taliándörögd, three sisters in America, four in Temesvár. In 1948 at the time of silver jubilee Sister Margaret said the following of the foundation

I return to 1923. We are the conscious carrier of traditions. Our birth is in 1923, yet we know that our vocation did not start then, but in 1908 in the Social Mission Society. We have no reason, my dear sisters, to spread a veil over that year when the Society, out of God's grace, was born. At that time we acted with our best con-

---

[149] SZTTI 1157/80.

viction and intention, and accepted what happened to us. When we return now to our Society's cradle, our grateful respect is lifted to both our Mother Superior and Bishop Prohaszka who have entered into eternity. They may have been led by human considerations - but with 25 years it is perhaps not an audacious belief – but gave us a response that the decision and action was the will of our good God of Providence. As long as our Society lives that long our gratitude will have to live for those to whom Providence gave the grace for the Hungarian social field pioneers of a modern organization with vowed members. We need to cultivate a grateful love for Mother Superior, who for fifteen years gave us a home, and through whom we received our vocation. When God will allow us to meet in eternity, then, having left our earthly relationships, we shall look back with amazement at things that we see now but halfway developed.[150]

Reading this one may think that during a quarter century difficulties may fade away and we "shall remember only beautiful things." It is therefore important to quote more from the attitudes of 1923 when Sister Margaret taught the sisters who were sent away:

Our spiritual attitude toward the original group of the Social Mission Society:

1. Mother Superior began the pioneering. Such kind of foundation was unknown in Hungary. Her connections made the founding and sus-

---

[150] The <u>Testvér</u> 1948/8. P.3

taining of it. We may say truly, she began everything out of nothing. In the members there are gifts, like organizing, etc. that are missing from her, but they could not have been developed unless she gave the environment to it.

2. She trained a group. From the beginnings at Elnok Street, Margaret, Etelka and Elizabeth remain today. The Mother Superior rang a bell in the desert; she had no one except the above to train the new group. The experiences - the more bitter they are, the more precious they become - they are priceless. There was a cost for these experiences and for 14 years the Social Mission Society paid it.

3. She nourished and made ripe public opinion. The People's Daughters found a prepared soil. We must think of the old stem of the Social Mission Society, as one being the work of Divine Providence. It would be false and frivolous not to hold them with the feeling of love, gratitude and respect. We should have the same concern for the Social Mission Society as we have for things we protect and would cause sadness to lose. This is my first home, the educator of our leading sisters - my mother - I love and pray for her.[151]

The Founding Minutes of the Society of the Sisters of Social Service expressly states:
We decided that in case of separation we shall

---

[151] SZTTI 1227/5

always honor Edith Farkas as our foundress. (Separation: It was the suggestion of sisters that the Social Mission have two branches those who follow the original constitution, and those who follow the new. For both Edith Farkas be the superior. With this they would have liked to avoid the scandal of splitting apart.) She did not accept the idea of separation and the legal bond between us was destroyed. While we cannot consider the Mother Superior our foundress, I propose, since we embraced her ideas, she gave us possibility for life, we shall therefore always remember her with gratitude and love and will include her definitively in daily prayers. All agreed with joy.[152]

This was done in daily community prayers until the death of Edith Farkas in 1942.[153]

In 1927 Sister Margaret recalled the happenings of 1923. "This was not an ordinary fight, some admirable inner nobility was expressed. Mistakes, yes, did happen; it would not be true if I failed to say that very regrettable things happened to us. But we are here on earth; we are fallible human beings. Only those who never sinned throw a stone on Social Mission. It is very true that to be with saints in heaven is joy and happiness, but being together on earth is something totally different. We know from Scripture that between

---

[152] Sister Margaret Slachta's proposal in the Founding Minutes, The Testvér, 1932, February, p.45.
[153] The community prayers of the Sisters of Social Service, Szentes, 1931. P. 37.

two nearly perfect persons, Saint Joseph and the Blessed Virgin Mary, painful misunderstanding happened. Yes, this is where we are. These were sad events that we have to forget. We started out with the clothes on our backs in the house of the Erzsébet Királyné Street with four pots of jam. These were the times that became the source of inexhaustible happiness."[154]

How did the relationship continue between Edith Farkas and Margaret Slachta? The little we know is that Sister Margaret held the Mother Superior always in grateful love. In 1941, hoping that time has mitigated the painful memories, she personally sought a meeting with Edith Farkas. The occasion was offered by the Chapter held by the Sisters of Social Service that had as one of the agenda points the relationship between the two organizations. The Society of the Sisters of Social Service did the first step within the Chapter making the "proposal to hold jointly a festive meeting with the Social Mission Society under the auspices of the Holy Spirit Association. Moreover, with the leadership of the two societies it proposed to make a joint pilgrimage to the grave of Bishop Prohászka. Lastly, the Chapter planned to greet 'Mother Superior' and intended to publicize in the press.[155]

---

[154] SZTTI 1157-80

[155] SZTTI 540/27 Prohászka Ottokár according to the writings took the side of Edith Farkas. Stadler Frieda (1888-1969) pedagogue, organizer of women movements, author, editor, leader of the Catholic Girls National organization (KLOSZ) said to the author that she is willing to swear that

The appropriate section of the Chapter Minutes were sent to Edith Farkas with the following letter:

Highly Revered Mother Superior
We are attaching a part of our Chapter Minutes in which we discussed establishing a good relationship with the Social Mission Society. We ask your Highness deign to accept it on your part. All of us are filled with joy over the thought that a loving relationship will exist between the two Societies. We desire this within ourselves, but the difficult times and the uncertain future urge us to eliminate everything that could stand in the way of peaceful collaboration. If our Highly Revered Mother Superior accepts our thoughts, that will be so much a greater joy, since we stood from the beginning by the conviction, that while differences in principles designed different paths, that should not influence loving relationships.

We shall never forget what we expressed in the founding minutes on 12 May 1923, that our origins are rooted in the Social Mission Society. Mother Superior awakened vocations of the founding members; and the social programs of our Society originated there. For these we decided that we would pray daily for Mother Superior and the Social Mission Sisters. Our en-

---

she quotes exactly: Somebody asked Bishop Prohászka, that he, who always stood at the side of the weaker, how he did not do it in this case? Bishop Prohászka responded: I stood in this case also with the weaker."

tire community has done this for the past 19 years.

We ask that you deign to receive our Society's respectful delegation.

With high respect and unchanging gratitude,
Budapest, 8 July 1941
Members of our Chapter[156]

Each chapter member signed the letter, drafted by Margaret Slachta. Among them seven were founding members of the Social Mission Society. Edith Farkas did not receive the delegation. Sister Margaret continued to try until she succeeded to be received personally, and could visit several times in 1941. "Last year, the Mother Superior was willing to establish relationship with me, for which I often have asked her without success. My conviction is, even if people walk on different paths, personal relationships need not necessarily cease. During the last year I could visit her several times, and for this I am very grateful to God. It would have been a great loss for my soul if she would leave into eternal life without having met.[157] About this, Sister Margaret reflected with gratitude in a letter in 1955.

At the news of Edith Farkas' death Sister Margaret hurried to her wake. She could, however, not participate in her funeral. She had to travel

---

[156] SZTTI 540/66
[157] The Testver, 1942/4. Cover page.

to Bratislava in the case of the Slovakian Jews,[158] but the Sisters of Social Service participated as a body in the burial ritual.[159]

It is evident that in the soul of Margaret Slachta and that of her sisters, reverence was alive regardless that they had, for reasons of principle, followed different paths.

---

[158] Ilona Mona: <u>Margaret Slachta for the Slovakian Jews</u>...p. 391-400

[159] <u>Testvér</u>, 1942/4. p. 4

A Superior Created by Whip

On 12 May 1923, the Society of the Sisters of Social Service was founded in Budapest at Queen Elizabeth Street 17 in the chapel of the Social Mission Society's Mercedes home. That home was not inhabited and Edith Farkas wanted to sell the house. However, because the newly founded group needed a home, she allowed them to use it at the most for three years, but if Edith Farkas could sell it sooner, then for a shorter time. At the moment the sisters had a roof above their heads. The Mercedes home had provided for a jam workshop since 1921. This work was begun by the sisters to have some financial basis. Of the early difficulties, a small paper, the <u>Grey Veil</u>, wrote jokingly: "Application! The editors of the <u>Grey Veil</u> seek two proposals for two-story high chairs so that at a table, where there are 17 places, 34 persons can take meals." And: "I sat down comfortably on the arm of the sofa, until the glass of which six of us drank, arrived." The community was faced with two great tasks: to acquire a home and to elect a superior for the Society. The manifestations of Margaret Slachta bear witness, she did not guess that the confidence of the sisters would be focused on her. "In a most determined way, I did not want to be superior. I had two motives for this. I wanted very much to do developmental work on behalf of the Society; therefore I found it more beneficial if the administrative work would not take my time.

Secondly, I did know, it is impossible to meet with opposition for years and not experience wear and tear; and on account of which one cannot use one's gifts the best way for the cause. I desired to use all that God gave to me for the benefit of our Society's life with the fewest obstacles."[160] A letter that she wrote to Sister Augusta in Temesvár on 5 June 1923 is a shining testimony to the truth of her motives. "We shall hold elections for the general superior, and we pray daily for this intention. I remind you that among the points you all accepted, one prescribes that a superior may occupy herself only with the internal affairs of the Society. I ask you, write us, what do you think of Sister Maria? Our nominee, practically unanimously, is Sister Maria; in her person all of us are at peace. She is a person of principles, intelligent, spiritual, and self-sacrificed."[161] "As for myself, from the beginning I did not want to be a superior, not from the motive of humility, since this in my opinion is not a question of humility, but out of practical reasons. Regarding being a superior I have somehow always a feeling as if I want to run away from it. The sisters' affection and trust placed repeatedly a burden on it." [162]

Of this there is a good example in 1928 in the assembly that substituted for a Chapter. Sister

---

[160] SZTTI 1217/59, p.3.
[161] Sister Mary Schwartz: in Szolgálat, 1982, ps.401-406, Pneuma, Hamilton, 1992,p. 2-4
[162] SZTTI 1218/58

Margaret, as the presider of the assembly, said: "The Society is based on a theocratic foundation, but is totally democratic and expressed by the accountability of its leaders and by elections. Let us practice that virtue which is demanded of us as members of a Society called conscientiousness. I must live by the sense of responsibility and humility with my rights."[163] When elections were on the agenda, Sister Margaret told the following, "In connection with elections, I shall tell you what I would have liked to tell you for five years, but you did not allow it. My soul desires to serve our Society with all my energies, but not in the place where I am now. It is clear to me, that everything depends on God's grace; also my energies are insufficient. Regardless how excellent your collaboration is, the sense of responsibility, the concerns and that part of governing that cannot be taken away are very hard on me. I long for a year when I could live for formation work, and - freed from the preoccupations of governance - I could spend time regaining my physical strength. (On 15 November 1927 she had a gall-bladder operation, removing 87 gall-stones.) For this reason I recommend not to nominate me. I ask, let us witness to the fact that the office is viewed as responsibility and not as an honor. Afterward let us pray and discuss this issue with total peacefulness."[164] Following this, Sister Margaret recommended, instead of

---

[163] SZTTI 1153/ 2, p. 1
[164] SZTTI 1153/2, p. 7.

herself, Sister Paula Ronai[165] and she explained in great detail why she considered Sister Paula as superior. Sister Paula responded that it is her conviction that the time has not arrived for Sister Margaret to leave her post. Another sister said: "A mother risks frequently her life to bring to birth her child. The Society of the Sisters of Social Service is a great child, I nearly could say, that for giving it birth, a mother may not hesitate to give her life, regardless how cruel this may sound, time is not here that she may lay down this work." Sister Margaret sought now a different argument: her physical condition is not the most important, but the fact: "I had no novitiate. In the Social Mission Society we became all at once sisters, and there I worked nearly always outside. Now I, for the past five years, walked again by my own will. I want to ask for myself the opportunity and the possibility to live under the condition of obedience, because in the past I did not develop in myself the spirit of obedience."[166] However, that year was not given to her; she was re-elected.

It is natural that a behavior within the community brings about negative responses; in many a lack of modesty developed. They began inter-

---

[165] Maria Paula Rónai 1886 - 1968, High School teacher, entered into Social Mission Society in 1912. She left for an American assignment in 1923. She entered from there to the Society of the Sisters of Social Service. Later she was the vicar of the General superior and the Central novitiate's director.
[166] SZTTI 1153/2 p.9.

rupting the speaker, and despite their immaturity they took on a critical position. This gave impetus to developing a faulty concept of authority in those who were not mature enough to realize what they were doing.[167]

In 1930 it seemed that Sister Margaret could return to public service. The Christian Socialist party nominated her to be a member of the Capital City Commission and elected her for Angyalföld. She could realize her desire to hand over her service within the community to someone else. Nobody among the capable sisters was willing to take over this responsibility. Unfortunately a sister, who was not fit for it, accepted the service. Sister Margaret began again her public ministry with joy, and it seemed that at the elections of 1931 she could run for public office under the Christian Women Corps. However, she was hindered by an electoral swindle. The parties who wanted to run had to collect a defined number of signatures. The Christian Women Corps had to collect 2800 signatures; instead they collected 3800. The commission of elections examined the signatures and if not approved the candidate could not run. In the south section of Budapest only four parties were allowed to run. [...] [168] The Christian Women Corps, together with ten other parties could not run. There was a great bitterness within

---

[167] SZTTI 1217/59 p.4.
[168] I did not enumerate the parties that were deprived of running. (Translator's Note)

the small parties, wrote the <u>NEMZETI UJSÁG</u> in its 25 June 1931 issue. Sister Margaret in that same paper called the action a shabby trick. She thanked those who collected the signatures and those who gave their signature for their trust.

In the meantime serious problems arose within the community. The inability of the new superior became so evident that Sister Margaret recognized there was no other choice but she re-embrace the burden. In 1932 the sisters re-elected Sister Margaret, and the superior who had to step down, left the community with eleven sisters in 1934. In 1935 they founded the Society of Parish Sisters of Daughters of Saint Peter.

These happenings impacted Sister Margaret very deeply; she came to realize in 1935, twelve years after the founding, that she must stay at her post. During the Chapter, Sister Margaret communicated this to the sisters. "Looking back on many years I see myself in this work that God allowed me to do. It is a great suffering for my soul to see myself in such a great task with my, I could say playful personality that does not reflect much on self, and after a happy childhood, grown during a happy youth and not becoming mature for life and for handling such weighty situations. When I said in my report that the sad happenings of the recent past had a maturing effect on us, I said it primarily about myself, my dear sisters. To-day I stand before you as a different person from how I functioned before. I thank God that I do not recall all my actions all the time; if I would I could not bear it. But because they are continuously before me, I realize how much loss I have caused to our Society with incorrect courses of actions. I give special thanks to those sisters who consciously bore my special mannerisms that I cannot change, and despite them, supported me in doing the work. In my soul an ongoing gratitude is present for all those sacrifices and the selflessness I see in the sisters who work with me without wavering. We are each other's crosses, but if we are able to bear each other's burdens we can become each other's blessings. For being a superior and carrying out its responsibilities, I am a different person today and hope that, with your help, I will make fewer mistakes in the future."[169]

Governing was always difficult for Sister Margaret. We shall quote another of her thoughts: "The sisters always hold me as founding superior. In fact right from the beginning, I have said that this does not correspond to reality. From the Social Mission Society we were sent away; we were expelled, including most of Society's outstanding members. It would be naïve to think, that I founded the Society of the Sisters of Social Service. If God would not have chosen those sisters, who were like pillars, in no way could our Society have grown to what it is. In that development, I am only a part. We included in the founding minutes that we brought with us the ideas of the mother superi-

---

[169] SZTTI 499/15a p. 9-10.

or and we remained faithful to her original vision. On our part, we only created a structure for realizing that vision."[170]

Upon founding in 1923 the first priority was to find a means of support for the members. After the Trianon peace edict, possibilities in Hungary did not exist. Opportunities abroad had to be found. Before anything else, however, they needed to obtain ecclesial approbation, and for that, a Constitution had to be written. During the summer of 1923 Sister Margaret discussed it with sisters and wrote a draft in Tömös, Transylvania. The draft constitution was sent to Rome to Cardinal Justinian Serédy, a canon lawyer, for evaluation. Sister Margaret then arranged for sisters to travel to America to collect money for a motherhouse to be built. The younger sisters were sent to France and placed in convents to work, where they got food and lodging and could send their earnings back home. Sister Margaret herself went to America on 4 November 1924, stayed until 12 December 1926, arriving back in Budapest on 22 December into the acquired Motherhouse. Her letter, written on the ship is very characteristic. First she wrote from London that she sailed on the ship Aquitania and comments "on the boat one does not sense in the beginning of being on the ocean, because the ship is so huge, one can walk back and forth on it and not realize that under it an immeasurable amount of water." She continues to de-

---

[170] SZTTI 1155/25

scribe the ship, expresses her sadness over those working in its bottom. "During the second night, as I did not feel well, I remained on the deck. There was a strong wind. The terribly large body of the ship ran against the wind. From the two contrary forces colliding with great speed a terribly loud hurricane began. Such was never heard on dry ground. Into its concert the sound of water screeched up. As much as one can find delight in such a discomfort, I rejoiced in the creative genius of men for building the ship. How sad women are not able to open up and develop their own gifts. Ultimately what is an Aquitania in comparison to a soul or to life processes, and to spiritual life-giving? We have that; but we are not aware of it. The majority of human beings, I believe, do not become aware either. In reality everything is carried by the soul, but it cannot be seen; just as the majority of travelers do not think of the conductors though it is with the fruit of their energy that the train proceeds." Even from this short part of her letter Sister Margaret's two basic ideas can be seen: her profound respect for the women's movement and the value of soul.

She spent nearly two years in America and Canada. From Los Angeles to Canada she traveled the continent giving talks in English, German and French. The news of her talks reached the press. From New York the news reached all the American states that the Hungarian National Assembly's first woman representative, Margaret Slachta, (written Schlachta) arrived in the new world into the mission of the Sisters of Social Service. The <u>New York Times</u> and all the greater American newspapers wrote long articles about Margaret Slachta. From Richmond, the metropolis of the state of Virginia, she received an official invitation.

Sister Margaret arrived in Richmond on 1 May. No famous Hungarian person had ever made such a visit. She gave her talk with the title: "Dismembered Hungary", in the Catholic Women's Club. The beautiful hall was packed full by the news of her talk. After the talk, according to American customs, the participants raised questions. She had to talk for hours of the Hungarian conditions, of communism, of the Sisters of Social Service, of their mission, of everything, of which very little was known in America. On the following day Margaret Slachta gave a talk in the Richmond Women's Club. This club was Virginia's first for women, of which much has been told in the history of America... Sister Margaret gained the good will of the audience. Her talk was frequently interrupted with their stormy applause. On the following evening Sister Margaret gave a talk to the Young Women Association. Those present did not want to leave the hall and Sister Margaret had to stay there for a long time to respond to their different questions. The following day in the morning Sister Margaret gave a talk for the University of Richmond's women students. When the male students got wind of it, they together with their professors wanted to hear her. It meant that instead of the half hour talk she would give there, she spent a whole day at the Westhampton College. She had lunch with the students, and afterward spoke of Hungary's history, geographic and economic situation, and of the unjust treaty of Trianon. The University of Richmond was a Methodist University and no Catholic person had given a talk there before. In a short time a great enthusiasm arose for her and she had to return. In the meantime, Sister Margaret traveled to Washington D.C. to participate in an international women's conference. A few days later she returned to Richmond and gave a public talk about Hungary. For this occasion they obtained the city's theatre without a fee. Her talk was communicated in paper, on posters for several days, and the patrons of her talk were the governor of the State of Virginia and his wife, the mayor of Richmond, the Catholic bishop and several Protestant ministers. Given the culture there, it had a great significance that a foreigner could bring together the leading men of all religious faiths.

One cannot imagine a more enthusiastic celebration even at home than the one Margaret Slachta brought about there on 15 March. At least in Virginia people gained a different picture of how Hungary became the First World War's victim. The role of Sister Margaret's talks had great significance, because she made known to the Virginians the thousand year old Hungary.[171] Sister Margaret not only made known Hungary, she also came to know Canada and the United States. Even though everywhere there were many difficulties, she decided that sisters remain in both countries serving primarily Hungarians émigrés. The bishop of Los Angeles sent, at his own expense, the first two novices in 1928 to the Hungarian novitiate. The Society had gone to America and Canada because they had to go abroad to make the founding fiscally possible. The Society took root in both countries with much work and many sacrifices. Sister Margaret's experience in America was published in 1928 with the title, <u>Elkapott Sugarak,</u> (Captured Sunbeams.) and she wrote in the foreword: "These are the collected joyful experiences I gained during my stay in America; not as all America, only some trends on the face of America. We cannot take home dollars, they avoided us, but we take home the spirit, whose breezes gently stroke our faces. A young, lovely, fresh, confident, helpful spirit that can rejoice." She brought not only the spirit, but also an idea of what was possible that she tried to realize at home. On the tenth page of the book we find a confession. Seeing in America Christmas trees for the public, she recalled an experience: "I wanted to raise at that time in the 1st district (as Representative in Parliament) such a tree for the homeless so they would have at Christmas like other people enjoy in their homes.

---

[171] <u>Magyarság,</u> 1925. VII. P. 9 was the title of the artice.
SZTTI 657

216

But I was deterred from my plan because it was not 'customary.' And I had not enough strength to do it anyhow. I did not know that this is done already somewhere. Now therefore I also take a gift for myself from the Everybody's Christmas Tree: the conviction that if anybody wants to realize something, she should only consider whether it is good or not?"

Sister Margaret returned home for Christmas in 1926 and at Christmastime of 1927 candles were lit on Everybody's Christmas Trees in fifteen places of Budapest. Since the Society could not own institutions, the ownership of the committee of the Everybody's Christmas Tree came from the organization of the School Sisters, but Sisters of Social Service worked on the committee. According to Sister Margaret our Society works namelessly even in public service. On the success of the first Everybody's Christmas Tree we quote a contemporary letter. "We had to overcome unbelievable difficulties because the Ministry of Interior did not want to give permission; they feared the loss of silence of the streets, etc. But Sister Paula, with her unbelievably tenacious energy, gained the permission and made it happen. They called and asked workers and they collected ten tons of candy and chocolate. Everybody received and so much remained that the sick with incurable illness in the hospital, the institute of the blind, the disabled children all received some. Under the Christmas tree they had choir, music. The ladies were so enthusiastic that they wanted to begin the preparation for the next year. At Octagon square (Budapest) all afternoon the hymn was projected: 'Glory to God in the heavens and on earth peace to people of good will.' They said it was like half of heaven."[172]

The movement about the Everybody's Christmas Tree lived on until 1947. On 24 December 1944 one single tree secured on a truck went around in the city that was totally surrounded by the Soviet army. According a contemporary account, "Sister Margaret came with us on the truck that stopped at each busy point of the city. Through a loud speaker Christmas hymns were sung until Christmas Eve. Instead of the customary gifts Sister Margaret distributed Christmas candles, which at that time were a great asset. A Hungarian soldier was the driver and at the end he asked that the tree be given to the army that they too could celebrate Christmas - who knows, perhaps for the last time. When it turned dark they forgot that the city was under blackout rules. With the candlelit tree they hurried through the street and across bridges. Above their heads the death-dealing planes gave their deep sounds, but no words were said, everybody was ready to face the consequences."[173]

A contemporary wrote about Sister Margaret's return: "at the train station a great crowd

[172] SZTTI 1184/5 p.2.
[173] SZTTI1168, p.41.

gathered. The flowers she was greeted with were taken home in laundry baskets. Sister Margaret herself became very surprised at this picture at the East train station: 'an angry man said even a king is not received in this way.' In Hungary nobody was welcomed back with so much love and trust. That people expected so much from her frightened Sister Margaret."[174]

Sister Margaret and some sisters gave a report about the work abroad (America, France) to the Hungarian public in the "old parliament." The palace on Sandor Street was the place where politicians met until 1902 (today it is the Italian Institute). This building had such a big hall - a capacity of several thousand persons. Magyarság wrote about this event, "After two years and two months of absence, Sister Margaret Slachta arrived back in Budapest with a group of enthusiastic Sisters of Social Service, who during their absence offered to Hungarians in America invaluable service of charitable mission. For the non-Hungarian speaking people they realized an even more valuable work by giving information about our nation. The Sisters of Social Service and their leader held a meeting in the old parliament building giving information on their work abroad. The meeting was announced for Sunday at 5 P.M., but by 4 o'clock, there was not even standing room in the huge hall where more than five thousand ladies were jam-packed. Those who arrived later had to stand in

---

[174] SZTTI 1184/4

the corridors. Those who came at 5 o'clock could no longer enter the building. Hardly ever before had so valuable, intelligent and attentive women staged an event as this."

The Society of the Sisters of Social Service, when their first steps were completed, was obliged, for lack of resources, to reduce its activities. As so many times before, they had no choice but to turn for help to America - to beg there, but also to remain in America to give. The sisters thought that in rich America they needed only to ask and receive. However, when they arrived they saw they are richer; they have to give to the poor and abandoned Hungarians. They discovered the emigrated Hungarians in spirit were very poor. The sisters visited thousands of Hungarian families. Children who no longer spoke Hungarian were taught to read and write and to pray. They told them of the dismembered Hungary and awakened in them love for their "old home country." In less than two years the Sisters of Social Service created homes for themselves in Buffalo, NY, Los Angeles, CA, and Stockholm, Canada and proclaimed the truth of the Hungarian reality to them. A part of the group remained, and from these homes, they continued their mission.

After this, Margaret Slachta began to share about the work done in Hungary. A beautiful motherhouse of the Sisters of Social Service was built in Budapest. During her talk she gave thanks to generous co-workers. At the end of her talk she outlined work plans for the future.[175]

These works were connected with the process of founding. Steps had to be taken to attain a novitiate; and it was necessary to have a constitution approved by ecclesial authorities. For these two issues Sister Margaret took steps while in America. In April 1925 the paper, Nemzeti Ujság, published Sister Margaret's article: "Let us Save For Our Country Hungarians Who Went Abroad." In the lengthy article (a full page) she explained that other nations' children abroad keep together but not the Hungarians. They have no organizations, no parishes, schools; they will be lost for Hungary. She also delineated how this could be helped in an official and non-official way. Then she wrote the characteristic lines, "Divine Providence lifted us with a strong arm at home from our previous works - from our former environment. Now we bless that providential arm, because if He had not obliged us, we would not be scattered over the world. We would not have seen our nation's slow decay beyond our borders; we would not have become conscious that part of our mission could be to prevent it. Out of God's goodness the Society of the Sisters of Social Service has passed the phase of life or death; she can open her small gates of a novitiate for inquirers."[176] After Sister Margaret made this call, somebody asked her, "How dare you seek novices when you do not

---

[175] Magyarság, 1928.II. 8.
[176] Cardinal Chernoch Cat 1817/1925. 5.15

221

even have a house?" She responded, "I do not seek persons to live in the house, but workers for the Church." It is sufficient to say, that the novitiate opened with 32 novices.

Sister Margaret sent the constitution from Canada to Cardinal Chernoch for approval. In the accompanying letter she gave the reasons why the constitution contained some points that might seem unusual in the eyes of clerics. They are necessary, because "we feel we must enter into the world where, amid life's struggles, thousands and thousands of souls get lost and are cast to the representatives of materialism and atheists. They are in the forefront of development and gain their victims with ease. One of the very definite points of the constitution is that the Society may not own institutions under its name and may not lead movements and organizations. The second emphasized point is that the Society will support itself through work of its members; it may not accept subventions from authorities; they may accept donations only if they do not oblige the community to some specific actions in return. However, the Society wants to be engaged in movements and political works; for this, they have to seek finances. To provide for these activities the Society organized the Testvér Szövetség (a Sister-Association) that functions as an economic association created by laypersons with the aim of giving support to the Society." This Sister-Association ran a jam workshop, a knitting workshop, and later a home-industry association, a bookstore and a press.

Some Sisters worked in the jam production, the knitting workshops and in the bookstore. Later, sisters led the home-Industry association. To initiate and keep this going and to overcome human difficulties was an unbelievable burden.

Sister Margaret found that developing novitiate instruction was one of her most important tasks. She herself wanted to attend the first group of 32 novices, to introduce them into the spirituality of the Sisters of Social Service. Part of this work was to guide individuals in their spiritual difficulties; she did not find it to be her special gift. We share two of her admissions.

She wrote the first from America in 1924 to Sister Paula, with whom she became friends in 1905 in Kalocsa, and who entered later into the Social Mission Society. In January 1923, Edith Farkas sent Sister Paula to the U.S., where she joined the Sisters of Social Service. Sister Margaret wrote: "I hope you will sense that past events changed me, and what you missed very much in me, even if not in an adequate measure, you now will find in me. I learned to give work out from my hands and at times I am glad if I do not have to work; I am able to rest, enjoy others; that means even to recreate, etc. I will never have a vocation to individuals; it will always be sensed that my world is working for causes. But my attitude is now different toward individuals than before. There are many things I regret - like always hurrying - when I did not see the individual, and kept running, running."[177]

The second self-disclosure is from a letter of 1933. "My spiritual life is very simple; I have problems infrequently. Therefore it is hard for me to understand how some can find problems in so many things; why do some little things become immense pain for some; why do some things become big complications; and why do some have to spend so much time solving their problems and require so much time for spiritual care?"[178]

She explained her principles about leading a novitiate in 1933 in Goldenstein, near Salzburg, Austria at the Conference of Modern Catholic Women Organization. A paper with the title, "A Schönere Zukunft" (A More Beautiful Future), stated:

A very impressive example: Sister Margaret Slachta's insights regarding spiritual life.

1. In the development of a soul one thing is essential, love for God and good will toward human beings; everything is only a means on behalf of the sanctification of the soul. Striving to love God is essentially different from striving to become perfect. A soul that strives only to love God will be self-forgetting and generous. Those who want to achieve perfection will unnoticeably grow in selfishness.

2. The sisters are formed in a positive spirit. Everything that God sends or allows, joy or suf-

---

[177] SZTTI 1154/54
[178] SZTTI 1217/59, p.5.

fering has the spiritual purpose of growth. Sacrifice is not a goal for sanctifying; it is only a
means.

3. From this follows forming for spiritual freedom and joy.

4. Forming for total selflessness. Sisters must
exclude from their individual and from the Society everything that would serve its self-interest
or glory, and serve only the good of the church.
Nearly everybody works under the name of other organizations in movements and societies.
They are truly workers of Catholic causes. In
our vision striving to maintain good health and
giving consideration for young members plays
an important role.[179]

It is superfluous to emphasize that Sister Margaret
painted her own spirituality.

She considered it was her responsibility to
promote vocations. Beside other works, she published a book in 1928 with the title: From the Desert to the Center of Life. Her opening words: "The
idea that a soul may give herself to God with a
bridal love is as old as the Church itself. For a
person who dedicates herself to God in such a
love relationship, it is secondary what type of work
she will do and within what structure she will live."
The book covered the development of religious life
beginning with the hermits to contemporary times.
Following she described the spirituality and vision,

---

[179] Schönere Zukunft, 1931. II. p. 431-433. A translation is in:
Testver, 1931/4. P.8 Imagine

the structure and ministries, and the history of the first five years.

The year of 1928 was concluded with another trip to America, from November to April 1929. The result of this trip was that the bishop of Los Angeles embraced the travel cost to Hungary for the formation of the first two American novices. This was a very great happening. At the arrival of the two young women born in America, Sister Margaret said the following to the community:

> All of us here, except perhaps the youngest, can witness how God built us up step by step out of nothing, since these few years are nothing. A second continuation happens outside the borders of Hungary. This least expected growth, continuous building, happens in America. At the time when God scattered us '... as a flower scatters around its ripe seeds,' it seems our Society spreads in a similar manner. Today, when our two Californian novices will arrive, receive them in your souls as you witness the building up of our Society overseas in America, the first nation of the world. The jewel of America is California. This nation was won by a persistent energy for work that made it fertile and happy. Now think of it, this America that disdains the world, received a small Society, whose roots are in Europe, and from a most despised nation. From there it asks Sisters of Social Service to serve Spanish and English speaking people. Imagine this situation: these two novices come a terribly great distance; they do not speak our language and are not familiar

with our customs, and have been accustomed to the American comfort. Theirs is a different world. They will return to a nation where Sisters of Social Service are wanted very much, and where they will not serve Hungarians but Americans. From this a branch with a different language will develop. God faces us with the task: to nurture on our stem a foreign branch that, in its own time, will dig new roots or will remain with us. It depends on us if they will remain with us. We are faced with two options; one is that we will be better professionals than the Americans. The second is this: that those who will occasionally come will find such a fire, such warmth, such a spirit and life, and sisters of whom they sense can nourish them. The Bishop sent them here saying: 'I wish they bring such a spirit with themselves that I came to know from the first sisters coming from home.' One that he emphasized was that God gave us as a grace for the start, that despite being scattered, living in impossible situations, the whole group kept together. He came to know our sisters as servants and that they could hold their place and remain faithful to their vocation. For this reason, let us accept with holy reverence, not because of their person, but because of what God desires from us and God builds in us. And let us thank Him for giving us always some compelling task that demands more from us. Not that we may look better, but to become better! Let us thank God that each year we are given a new possibility, to recognize how His divine hands build our walls higher.[180]

---

[180] SZTTI 336. Sister Margaret did not read the typewritten

At the end of the novitiate the two American novices took their vows, and took leave from the sisters in Hungarian. [...][181]

The trip to America was necessary by Sister Margaret, partly for community reasons and partly for business of the home industry. As mentioned before, the Society wanted to support itself by work; the sister association directed by laity but for the benefit for the social ministry and of the Society provided a means. In the markets of America the authentic Hungarian embroidery, embroidered clothes, blouses, etc. easily sold; these were pre-pared by the home-industry. This manner of fund-raising ended during the 1929 economic crash. The young, six-year old Society grew slowly for lack of resources, and the ministry output could not meet expectations. During the retreat of 1929 Sis-ter Margaret spoke about this situation: "Do not think of what people say. They cannot realize what it means to start out of nothing during these difficult conditions. For growth, time is necessary. To lay down the foundation, to go on, to develop, to do everything all at once, we have to sing in six melo-dies. Since everything needs to happen all at once, development is slower."[182] Sister Margaret was mistaken. The Society had to sing not in six voices,

---

form of her talk.

[181] I left out the "good-by" words of the two American sisters, I could not translate the broken Hungarian into equivalent English. (Translator's note)

[182] SZTTI 899, p.40

228

but in many more. They got some taste of it. It began developing simultaneously on two continents. In Europe in Hungary, in Transylvania annexed to Romania, and from there they went soon to Bucharest, to work with Transylvanian servant girls. In 1927 the community received invitation to Kassa (Kosice), and started living there as minorities in the newly created Czechoslovakia. Work was underway in all three countries of Europe, each under differing social, national and political conditions. On the American continent, Canada and the United States differed from each other. These services are all under the direction of Hungarian sisters. At that time the Society had to struggle for approval with canon lawyers for the simple, but novel constitution that they considered modern. (Approval was not gained until 1935.)

In the meantime Sister Margaret also lived her civic vocation. In December 1929 she was elected in the capital city under the Christian Economic and Social party to represent Angyalföld, a very poor section of the city. Sister Margaret continued to do city politics for two years, but did not renew it. At the chapter of 1935 she gave a report of this work. She organized courses for manual works without fee with 124 participants and three groups of the Working Girls organizations were established in the territory. She started a program of milk-without-fee for children and succeeded in placing twenty abandoned aged persons in homes of charity. Several adult education courses were established and many in-kind donations were distributed.[183] The 1932 budget discussion of the capital city should be mentioned. At the 20 November session Margaret Slachta spoke of various problems in social-politics. Her professional presentation was received with great success. Szerena Stern, a social democrat, also gave a very professional intervention and caused as deep an impression as the previous speaker. Sister Margaret went to the social democrat representative and congratulated her very warmly.[184] Recall that Margaret Slachta was engaged with workingwomen in the National Catholic Women Protective Org. Her first public activity was her talk on behalf of protecting workingwomen. Neither the Catholic Women Protective Org. nor the Social Mission Society saw it necessary to work on workingwomen's issues. Sarolta Koranyi initiated an organization of Catholic workingwomen in 1911. However this well-developed organization was destroyed during the communist government in 1919. On account of the illness of Sarolta Koranyi in 1920, she was not able to start organizing them again. In 1931, the Sisters of Social Service embraced this work. Sister Margaret entrusted this work to Sister Paula Rónai, who with two young sisters, Natalie Palágyi and Hedwig Jolsvay began organizing the working girls and workingwomen.[185] For Christmas in

---

[184] SZTTI499/50

[184] SZTTI 481. Fővárosi Közlöny. XLII, issue 69. No 1931. XII. 22. 1422, 1424.

[185] Of this movement wrote Hedwig Jolsvay and Ilona Mona with the title Christian Working Women and Working Girls:

1931 the first issue of <u>Workingwomen</u> was published and it became the paper of the movement. In it Sister Margaret wrote: "Working Girls, do you want to have an organized sisterly circle, education, spiritual and intellectual development, feminine ongoing education and professional development, better knowledge of your rights and responsibilities, economic and legal protection, good health and noble recreation? Come into the Catholic Working Girls Organization! Trust in God, in yourself, in your good friends, and in your better future! Work for happier working girls!"[186]

Her second great accomplishment was creating the Holy Spirit Association in 1934. Its aim was defined in the following way: "We want to create a religious-ethical movement to lift persons from the paganism of materialism, so that the nation may be re-born from the Holy Spirit."[187] This aim was promoted by organizing groups, with spiritual programs and particularly with the paper <u>Voice of the Spirit</u>, whose chief editor would be the Spirit. The paper promoted deepened reverence and worship of the Spirit and building a church in honor of the Holy Spirit. It emphasized prayerful help to the souls in purgatory according to the teaching of the communion of saints. However, from the first issue one finds references to both the

---

DN and DL. <u>In the Unfinished Reform Era</u>, Rome 1990. pp. 106 -110.
[186] "The Working Girl," Occasional Information.1/1. 1931 Christmas, cover page.
[187] <u>Testvér</u>, 194000/1-2. P.2

eastern and western collectivism. "...God destroys the army of Satan with its own arms! Not only will this inner accounting meet Bolshevism, all nationalist crazes will face this hidden Waterloo inner destruction." The October 1939 issue was censured several times; a half page was deleted from Sister Margaret's article on "The True Well-being of a Nation." From February 1942 the <u>Voice of the Spirit</u> became the mouthpiece of the Christian Women Corps, in order that "political life will embrace Christ's joy-giving truths." The paper served this role until March 1944 when it was the first of the papers suppressed by Nazi government.

It was mentioned that building a church in honor of the Holy Spirit was a goal of the Holy Spirit Association. "The cult to the Holy Spirit is purely spiritual. Therefore it is necessary to build a material body for it. This will strengthen and inspire human desire for the Holy Spirit." The Society wanted to build such a church of the Holy Spirit that somehow would express the being of the Holy Spirit: "...it should be monumental, because the Spirit is immeasurably great; it should be rich in color, because the Spirit is lavishly rich. In each of the church's detail it must be made with the right material, because the Spirit is true; it must be warm, spreading joy, because the Spirit is sweet and consoling..."[188] Sister Margaret wanted the church to be built on a mountain so that it would be

---

[188] The style of the writing suggests that Sister Margaret wrote it.

visible from a great distance. With naiveté, characteristic of Sister Margaret, she went to Prime Minister Gyula Gömbös to ask about Gellért Mountain, more exactly the Citadella. After listening to Sister Margaret, Gömbös took off from his jacket the medal of his party and asked Margaret: would you pin it on you? Sister Margaret, as a response, lifted her Holy Spirit medal and said: "I already chose an emblem."[189] The prime minister denied the request because the mountain might become important in the event of a war.

The Society of the Sisters of Social Service received approval of their constitution in 1935 from Prince Primate Justinian Cardinal Serédi. Sister Margaret would have liked that the constitution contain spirituality material - something that later Vatican II decreed. The cardinal/church lawyer insisted on a dry legal wording in the constitution. Therefore, Sister Margaret wrote the constitution in two forms: one for the church authorities, the other for use by the sisters. [...] [190] Sister Margaret requested church approval of the spiritual part. Cardinal Serédi responded to her: "The part of the constitution written for the use of the sisters cannot be considered as official. Only that part is official that is not in contradiction with the constitution ap-

---

[189] SZTTI 1219/10 No date was written. It must have happened between 1933 - 36, because Gömbös died in October 1936.
[190] I left out the sample of the two kinds of constitution, because the present has two parts, one the spirituality and vision of our Society, and part II its law. Translator's note.

proved by me." Thus, the trailblazer idea of Sister Margaret had to wait thirty some years, when Vatican II ordered the same. By that time even the sisters had forgotten that this was Sister Margaret's pioneering idea.

The year 1935 was rich in community events. The possibility of a foundation in England seemed plausible. A British inquirer thought that through her contacts she could found the community in Scotland with the help of a Hungarian sister who could speak fluent English. The initiator wanted quick success, therefore she admitted everybody who wanted to join without testing. At the beginning of 1935, Sister Margaret traveled there and saw that the founding could not survive; therefore she closed it down. She dismissed the British sister and came home with the Hungarian sister. In Hungary it was only said that founding happened too early; it was not possible to uphold it.[191] Years later she wrote in a letter to the sisters who were sent to make a foundation in China: "...I find that founding with 10 or 12 persons is too many in the novitiate. Who knows what they think about vocation? Besides we should not accept them under the title as novices. If some have entered as novices, it is very difficult to send away those who do not have the qualities for religious life. I shall never forget the sad initiative in Scotland, where I received the

---

[191] SZTTI 1161/2. P.9. Sister Margaret's meditation, 1937. II. 10.

never forgettable slap on the face."[192]

The other important event was the five-year approval of the constitution.   From the time of founding twelve years had passed, the entire Society was filled with joy, with confidence and gratitude.   Following Pentecost, the Chapter opened in with the sisters from California attending.   The members of the chapter represented 198 vowed sisters who worked in six countries (two continents) twenty dioceses and in 33 places.   At this chapter Sister Margaret made this confession: "One person can work more on an intellectual level, the other more by intuitive feelings.   I belong to the latter. Therefore I am asking for your patience not only for my possible weaknesses, but also when intuitive insights lead me in a direction for which I cannot give reasons."[193]   On 3 September 1935 Sister Margaret left for her third trip to visit California.   She arrived home at the end of September 1936.   During the time away from home her sister, Mariska died on 7 October 1935; her mother died on 16 January 1936 and her father two weeks later on 30 January.   Sister Margaret received the information of their deaths much later because she was on the road.   In a letter of condolence she wrote of her feelings of that period:
> ...in four months I lost my mother, my father and one sister.   I felt as if my soul was broken to pieces.   But not only the passing of time healed

---

[192] SZTTI533/3, Letter of December 9, 1947,
[193] SZTTI 499/58, p.6

those deep wounds, but on one occasion - without having thought of such things, or having seen such things - in some spiritual manner I met my parents, who greeted me joyfully and with direct warmth and they radiated their joy into my sad soul. This spiritual meeting was certain and definite, that I could determine from which direction came this voiceless greeting. They did not stand beside each other, one to the right side of me the other to the left. I know the truths of our faith not only by faith, but also from experience.[194]

This great trial immersed her more deeply into the mystery of God's will. What she understood in this, she tried to help others to understand. Relating to a chapter on suffering,[195] she wrote the following:

...our human heart feels pressure every time we hear the voice of Job. I write because I would like to make conscious in connection with this chapter a capacity in our possession that for most of us is not conscious and therefore it does not fulfill in us its mission. This is the soul's intuitive gift. It is a wider horizon of the supernatural in the living. It is the depth and the height of existence, and since these reach the supernatural, we cannot enter with intellectual understanding, as they are beyond the natural

[194] SSA-B, Margaret Slachta's letter to Joseph de Heinrich, 1951. II. 10.
[195] From the book of Rev. Lippert S.J. on the book of Job, ch. "You Created Pain." Testvér, 1936/ 5. P.64, Voice of the Spirit, 1936/4, p.2.

intelligence. The soul comes to know the most sublime realities of the supernatural world with the intuitive gifts. The intuitive gifts are our soul's highest perceptive powers and the most neglected ones, so much so that most persons have no knowledge of them.

Coming to know through intuition happens differently from those we come to know through reason. What we come to know in a natural manner is information, knowledge; what we receive based on intuition is life, strength, an essential content that cannot be translated into human speech; it cannot be shared with someone else in its true content. However, a natural knowledge can be shared. The essence of being and the ideas of the Creator cannot be perceived even with intuition. But with intuition it will enter our soul as reality, as a most natural experience, that the ways of God, their extent and his thoughts and means cannot be understood. With this experience, tormenting desires to know and want everything come to rest. It becomes clear that insights into existence are like flashes; they are projections of reality coming from a different content, like the law of suffering that embraces everything. If we are unable to understand being even with intuition what role does intuition have at recognizing suffering? The soul feels that He, who holds her in his hands, is a different being from what could be thought of in the light of the world's cruel happenings; and from this the soul can know that the reality of existence, of being, is different from its symptoms. The soul feels security, the nearness of God, intimacy, certainty, and they bear witness, they convince and give security. She has a living consciousness of the being of Him who governs the world; this consciousness speaks of goodness, of mercy, of understanding, of sympathy, of compassion and love. This consciousness is living, is strong, is so certain, though it does not give concrete knowledge it gives unshakeable security - despite terrible happenings or frightening events - that they are different from what they seem to be; they are in reality in wonderful harmony with and the beautiful expressions of the will of the Creator.[196]

Sister Margaret speaks of this inner joy in many of her teachings. Let us come to know one more: "...I could not say that my life was sheltered (during the war, during the process of nomination and as a representative, and the happening in 1923) ... and yet I must say, the more time passes I am the greater amazed that in a supernatural life even here on earth how deep, how profound and how sanctified happiness can be."[197]

Her life was certainly not sheltered. In 1937 her school celebrated the 50th anniversary of the Marian Congregation. In the name of the students she gave the greetings. Giving appreciation for the work of the superiors of the School Sisters for developing the school, the following confession slipped from her mouth: "...Divine Providence ordered that the direction of our small organization

---

[196] Testvér, 1936/ 5. P.64, Voice of the Spirit, 1936/4, p.2.
[197] SZTTI 1191/17, Her meditation in 1937.V. 10

the Sisters of Social Service be in my hands. In my younger age, I imagined that a superior gives the orders and spends the greater part of the day with pious thoughts and spiritual reading. Since then I know well how much those who direct a spiritual organization have to count, struggle with financial concerns and deal many practical questions. I know now that the visible work of each organization is like a wreath whose flowers, their beauty and aroma, that is their intellectual and spiritual achievements are turned toward the world. The members and especially their superiors have the role to be the wire that holds together the flowers; that means doing the practical work and dealing with material issues[198]

The aim of the Sisters of Social Service is to give "workers who are called and are professionally prepared to the Church and secular society"[199] primarily through its members, but also through a wider circle - through those who in social work see not only breadwinning but also their life's vocation. Sister Margaret began organizing the School of Social Service and naturally applied for permission from civil and church authorities. From the church there was no objection, but the minister did not want to approve a social work school because he said he may not allow it before the state had such

---

[198] From the Newsletter of the School Sisters of Notre Dame of Kalocsa, manuscript 1937-38. XV.

[199] From the Constitution of the Society of the Sisters of Social Service, I. 2.

a school.[200] In the end permission was granted and the school opened on 3 November 1937. At the "Veni Sancte" following the opening ceremony, not only the representative of the Archbishop, but Károly Szendi, mayor of the capital city and the vice mayor with their council were present together with the representative of the Ministry of Education. Károly Szendi said among other things, "I look forward with great joy and hope to the functioning of this school." Sister Margaret gave the reason (among others) why the school will function on a Catholic basis.

> ...Each religion gives eternal viewpoints, but Catholicism states with incomparable force that persons who are inwardly strengthened, possess an unbroken spirit, and are enlivened with eternal hope and love can be true care-givers of people. From the viewpoint of those who receive services other basis cannot be imagined. They will work in fields where life tears apart with iron hands, where raw forces fight each other, and where people's tears are flowing. This requires not just monetary help, food or clothing, or heating stamps. This work expects much more. It needs sisterly love, affirming inner strength, and shared energy. Those who will be served will ask primarily for work, housing, medication, or money; but they have more profound and perhaps unconscious requests. For example, where is justice for their lives so full with thorns; why is there so much suffering, and where could a much-desired life be found

---

[200] SSA-L. The letter of Margaret Slachta, 1937. VIII.. 22

240

instead of ongoing death. For this reason the School of Social Work must stand on a Catholic base. It is our conviction that only such workers who are anointed by the Spirit, strengthened in grace, and have the experience of being children of God, warmed and put on fire by sisterly love can bring blessings and solutions into the world of those in need. [201]

This is how much the newspaper published. Sister Margaret said much more. This is what we know:

...I am glad to be a citizen of a nation that burns red and green as an island in an ocean. May God permit that the traditions of Saint Stephen will never be lost; and the flow of red lava will not go through our nation. Much more do I hope that students who study in this school - my sisters, myself, and our co-workers - all will remain, even if Divine Providence would allow the hardest, that people imbued with the spirit of Saint Stephen will not lose out. [202]

Sister Margaret said all these things in November 1937 shedding light on the future when, in Hungary, most of the people, even the most learned, dismissed the idea of Nazism and Hitlerism with a wave of one hand.

The first students of the School of Social

---

[201] Nemzeti Ujság, 1937, XI. 21. P 19.
[202] SZTTI1225/1, p. 3. Red= Bolshevism, Green = National Socialism. In Hungary the swastika followers wore green uniform

Work were assigned to the movement, Hungarians for Hungarians, started after the fist decree of Vienna in 1938. These social workers received on 6 December 1938 a small album as a gift with the title: <u>Message to the Bridge Builders</u>. In it Mrs. Horthy, the wives of the leading politicians, and those who had roles of leadership in organizations of social work areas, persons who held responsibility for the common good in Hungary wrote some guidelines. Sister Margaret wrote:

...A good ending is more important than a good beginning. Otherwise the great enthusiasm, the sweat demanding work and sacrifices will collapse into nothing; and a bad continuation, or an unfinished job will be worse than not beginning at all. The social delegate in the movement will experience from the first day that her work is difficult; more than that, the process of re-annexing is not a program full of flowers. It will be a shocking process, even when leaning onto the heart of the motherland with joy of freedom. Those will do a good job:

1. Who do not cling to fantasy-painted pictures but cling to reality and the soil of justice and are conscious that on earth everything, even the holiest idea, such as the re-annexing will happen through work with sweat, with struggle and earthly limitations. On this she will not get scandalized, rather she will know that beyond material help a spiritual influence has a greater impact and she can offer that if she works with mature, grace enlightened harmony of soul in

her daily labor.[203]

2. Who work with a pure motive. Not from vanity, not for success, not make believe, not for recognition.

3. Who forget themselves and enter totally with a maternal love into the mentality, the feelings of people in the re-annexed territory in order to introduce them, without shock, into the re-united Hungarian mentality.

4. Who do not keep in mind an accusation, a hardness, a lack of understanding, and do not hold others on account, but immerse these rebuffs into the ocean of suffering with modesty and offer them up for a happier Hungarian future.[204]

A great event in Hungary in May 1938 was the XXXIVth International Eucharistic Congress. Naturally the entire Society and Sister Margaret participated whole-heartedly in its preparation. A place was prepared in the motherhouse for the

---

[203] By the Decree of Vienna in 1938 parts of historical Hungary that were cut away after World War I. were re-annexed. (Translator's note.)

[204] SZTTI 655. Messages were written by: Mrs. Miklós Horthy; Mrs. Béla Imrédy (the wife of the Prime minister); Richard Bikraurer, the leader of the Foundation of the Filadelfia Diaconisses' of the Reformed church's Organization by the shore of Danube; Mrs Gábor Massanek, the president if the School-care Institution; Countess Rafael Zichy, the president of the president of the Catholic Women Association; Edith Farkas, the superior of the Social Mission Society; Sister Margaret Slachta; and Mrs.Géza Brontsch, the president of the movement: "Hungarians for Hungarians."

guests coming from overseas, and the sisters collaborated in every way for the success of the Congress. Sister Margaret was so deeply impacted by the congress, that she bought the altar created by Ödön Lechner for Heroes Square; it would serve as the altar later for the Holy Spirit Church to be built. This beautiful plan together with many other things became victim to the World War II and the events that followed. After the beautiful and uplifting days of the Eucharistic Congress the ideas of National Socialism were gradually introduced into Hungary. On the doorstep of the war, Margaret spoke to the Christian Women Corps, on 6 January 1939, the customary meeting beginning each year, "...All injustice and all violence is a boomerang that hits those who threw it. Let us never walk on the road of violence, never of injustice; let us keep our sober judgment and arrange all things with a Christ-like spirit. Based on my belief in Christ, I oppose injustice regardless whom it affects..."

In her talk she explained that we must be careful, because if we swallow the German poison; we shall lose our Christianity and ourselves. Hungarians must weigh with national self-respect the German happenings. In Germany work is done with very dirty means; we must firmly resist being drawn into them. "...The German anti-Semitism fights against Bolshevism. From an ethical point of view they are worthy of each other. In this case God feeds a killing beast with another killing beast. Today our task is to realize Christ's truths; let us not shout Barabas instead of Christ. In this situation our Christianity is at stake; that we may not give away."[205] This was a worthy direction for the years of 1939 -1945, when Sister Margaret was led by intuitive inspirations - doing otherwise not explainable actions in connection with the given happenings. It is certain that in the midst of the cacophony of voices of those days, she had to proclaim Christian truths with a leading voice and in actions.

---

[205] SZTTI, 147. Sister Margaret's talk on 6 January 1939.

Free From Public Opinion

The history of Europe between the two World Wars has appeared in many studies. In this chapter we will try to share the ideas of Margaret Slachta of those times. Naturally - since they were contemporary - they cannot agree with the credibility of those that were later discovered, and on which the light of historical distance shed a different meaning. Nonetheless, it describes a human being who from the first moment saw clearly the dangers and the inhumanity of the national socialist worldview and tries to do something against it.

Hitler rose to power in Germany in 1933. The basis of his system was the mythos of "blood and race" (therefore Sister Margaret calls it materialistic). From this arose the driving force of anti-Semitism that he spread all over Europe with educated agitators. The other driving force was the idea of one great empire, the Third Empire,[206] ir which all German-speaking people will be united. Both forces led toward war. Sister Margaret observed with great attention the events in Hungary but also happenings in world-politics. She recognized fully the dangers of Nazism, and she prepared primarily the sisters and secondarily the Christian Women Corps. Sisters were prepared by

---

[206] The first empire was from 800-1648, (from Charles the Great until the end of the 30 years war') the second: from 1870-1918, and the third was meant to be Hitler's own empire.

her teachings and meditations. For example, when Chamberlain and Hitler discussed the question of the Sudetan territory (1938, September), in a very Sr. Margaret-like manner, she connected to her meditation that political event:

> Hitler says, "...peace depends on Benes,[207] because he does not want to allow that the German speaking Sudetan territory should belong to Germany. The Benes regime, that created Czechoslovakia, unquestionably unjustly, feels pain and loss if Germans want to take it away. So are we, too, when God takes away some things from us, perhaps because we got it in a sinful way - when we sinned and would need to make reparation, we forget how much we offended God, and we only see that suffering awaits us... even though only justice is fulfilled on us. It is difficult for us to step out of our subjectivity, but we must do it at any price, because with persons entangled into subjectivity, nothing can be achieved; they will always have the last word.[208]

During Autumn of 1939 when the Molotov/Ribbentrop pact[209] came about Sister Margaret taught the sisters: "We have to do a great work in order to make ourselves independent of public opinion, of the viewpoints of the times, from all influences of nations that function without concepts

---

[207] Eduard Benes was the president of Czechoslovakia
[208] Teaching of Sister Margaret, September 30, 1938.
[209] August 23, 1939. On 1 September the Second World War began.

of law. Germany ceased to be a lawful nation; it based itself on brute force...it lost the war when it made a pact with the Bolsheviks. Let us practice, in ourselves, fidelity to values."[210]

Sister Margaret gave the Christian Women Corps information on the political worldview at their opening meeting on 6 January. From 1939 on, it was always focused on conscientization of Christian values and need to increase society's resistance. Because now "...we come to oppose those who think of themselves as Christians, but in their actions they denounce Christian teachings step by step."[211] The essence of the theme of Sister Margaret on this first meeting of the year was: Today Berlin is the center of the oppressive and anti-Semitic worldview that is spread all over Europe.

> It is easy to put into flames that world, where people hunger and where the ethical basis is broken up. Hitler looks toward the Ukraine, he forgets, that where one train track goes, another parallel will return. Now our country is in danger of Hitlerism. The prime minister acts like the protector of the levee, who for saving the levee opens the sluice gate...this means a so-called Jewish law is in preparation. In connection with this the Corps declares the following:
> Standing on Christian basis, we cannot agree

---

[210] Teaching of Sister Margaret on 6 October 1939.
[211] Magyar Sion, 1943. XII. 25. Margaret Slachta: The Corps now.

with the Jewish law. Contrarily, it proposes the following for the sake of not offending the Christian order of law:

1. It cannot confirm a date establishing who the law considers to be Christian.

2. It may not dismiss a Hungarian citizen of Jewish religion in order to fill the job with a foreigner (German).[212]

The Pesti News, a liberal paper, gave information on the meeting of the Christian Women Corps. The year of 1939 was rich in happenings. On 10 February Pope Pius XI died. "The whole world looks toward Rome; it expects what modification the change of person will mean to the ongoing ideological struggle," wrote Sister Margaret. On 2 March, Pius XII was elected. His actions were looked at for decades in a negative light because he kept "silent"; he did not condemn openly Nazism or Bolshevism. His predecessor, whose secretary of state he was, did so. The preparation of the two encyclicals condemning the collectivist systems (Mit *brennerden Sorge* on 14 March 1937, and the *Divini Redemptoris* on 19 March) was the responsibility of the Papal Secretariat of State. It is unnecessary to repeat what they proclaimed.[213] The new pope found it to be more important to help where he could. Of his first encyclical, *Summi Pontificatus,* and his Christmas proclamations

---

[212] SZTTI 147.

[213] This is witnessed in the Editrice Vaticana in 10 volumes from 1970 on, where documents include the activities of the Holy See from 1939 -1945.

we shall speak later in this chapter. On 1 September 1939, Hitler attacked Poland and in accord with the Molotov/Ribbentrop pact the Soviet Union did not delay to claim its rights. The fate of Poland was settled and Hitler could begin the list of his suicidal victories in Europe. The re-annexation of the northeastern territories (in March) re-established the Hungarian border with Poland, where both civilian and army unit refugees, like a flood, entered into Hungary. At the direction of Sister Margaret, the Society accepted Polish refugees and the priest who celebrated daily Mass was also a Polish refugee. From that time on the sisters fasted two days a week and the saved money given to the Polish refugees. Beyond that, Sister Margaret raised her voice on behalf of the Polish refugees in the <u>Voice of the Spirit</u>. In the 1 October 1939 issue she wrote an article entitled "Principles" which was censured and cut short. The beginning of the article speaks of what is a state's good: "If therefore a state gives an example that contracts, with a given agreement or unwritten laws, that requires sacrifice they need not keep when they collide with present-day interest; the state teaches the citizens to practice this in their private lives. This materialistic principle will bring about ethical decadence that will, in economic areas (commerce, honesty, loans) and in moral life (friendship, spousal relationship), allow momentary self-interest to become decisive." Following this, Sister Margaret wrote of the statement of Beck, the Polish prime minister; but from that point on the censure deleted the article. In the deleted part Beck said: "Peace is very good! One can give away very much for it, but not honesty! The country of the Polish people was erased from the map; still *they are the victors - they gave a martyr's witness to human morality.*"[214]

The fate of the Polish nation was followed by the Baltic-states, and Finland would have followed but the Finnish took arms and resisted. "The first legend of the Finnish freedom fight began," wrote the <u>Esti Újság</u>. "Fifty deathly tired Finn soldiers arrived after four days of fight with 180 Russian prisoners of war." The Finnish soldiers recounted that for 24 hours they fought without food or water with the outnumbering forces in two meter high snow, when "a radiant angel with immeasurably big wings was spread over the front protecting the Finns; the Soviet soldiers seeing it threw away their arms and surrendered."[215] It is natural that Sister Margaret spoke of the Finn's heroic struggle on 6 January 1941 to those who gathered together. "The Finn's spirit of heroic resistance, even in the face of death, is an example that states: it will protect to the last man its sovereignty and freedom, to which each nation has a God given right." The Finn's gave testimony that the strength of a nation does not depend on the number of its citizens, nor on their murderous weapons, but on the spirit of their sons and daughters. The Christian Women Corps was also strengthened in their consciousness of vocation:

---

[214] The draft of the article was preserved in SZTTI 1207,
[215] <u>Voice of the Spirit</u>, 1940. IV. 1. P.8.

"their program of realizing a Christian Worldview is eternal, just as a spiritual vocation of a woman is eternal in human history. We must get ready to hear the voice of the Spirit when our nation, among the line of small nations, will also fulfill its vocation."[216]

At the yearly opening meeting 1940, the proposal of the Christian Women Corps to the Prime Minister opposing the planned law depriving Jews of employment was read. Each of the participants signed it. The law depriving jobs was the second Jewish law. (1939. IV. Limited all those qualified as Jews from public and economic areas). With this, Sister Margaret stepped into action. At a time when "literary discussions developed fear in the educated and strengthened concern for what will happen to them in a Hungary after the war hardly anything was said of what had to be done here and now against Hitler's Germany."[217] [...] In 1940 the northern part of Transylvania was re-annexed to Hungary; in return for this, together with other obligations, Szálasi had to be freed from prison. "As soon as he became free, he gave his great program talk supporting the movement of building up the Carpathian-Danube-Great Nation. It was the all embracing concern of Europe". This meant nothing other than Germany. He might just as well as said: "Hungary should not exist, it

---

[216] Voice of the Spirit, 1940. II. 1. Cover page.
[217] Julius Juhász: Hungary After the War, 1938-1945. Bp. 1986. P. 144.

253

should be Germany." This is how Sister Margaret quotes him in one of her teachings. She said: "We can pin on the emblem of mourning without fear, because our nation as a home-land no longer exists. Now is the time for struggle. We must fight for souls, for the rights of law and for Christianity. We must take hold of all means to keep our children and our youth Hungarian. We must face reality; our nation is lost and exists only outwardly."[218]

The time of war arrived. The month of September 1941 was spent in joy over re-annexation, while the re-annexed Transylvanian areas were under military administration. The officers poisoned with ideas of Szálasi began shocking actions. They took from Miercurea-Ciuc on 8 December 1940 nine Jewish families to the wildest areas of the snow-covered Gyimesi Mountain at the Romanian border. They suffered for a day under the sky from hunger and cold and the totally exhausted people were returned to Miercurea-Ciuk, to be taken after a day to Kőrösmező at the foot of the Carpathian Mountains. From there they were forced across the Russian border.[219] Sister Mar-

---

[218] SZTTI 1161/43. Sister Margaret's teaching after the event of giving freedom to Száasi.
[219] Tamás Majsai: An episode from the history of Jews during World War II in northern Transylvania. The actions of Margaret Slachta on behalf of the Jews deported from Miercurea-Ciuk. In: MEDVETÁNC, 1988–4-1989-1 + the deportation of Jews from Miercurea-Ciuk and Margaret Slachta's intervention on their behalf. In: Braham R. L.: Studies on the Holocaust in Hungary, New York, 1990.

garet learned of this event from Sister Judit Veres, who was a social worker in Miercurea-Ciuk. On 9 December 1940 Sister Margaret wrote a letter to the pastor: "We received desperate news from Miercurea-Ciuk, that the military deported 30 Jewish persons without any previous notification, who suffered for weeks at the Romanian border at the wildest area of the Gyimesi Mountain and were taken afterward to Kőrösmező. Regarding their issue, I am guided only by the responsibility placed upon us by Christ's command to love our neighbor - and patriotism. It is terrible for me, that they who have been returned to the homeland should face injustice from Hungarian authorities, only because they belong to this or that race."

She asked the priest to get information on the case from both the military and the administrative authorities and to ask the offended as well. "I need completely trustworthy data, otherwise I cannot believably intervene with the specific authorities."[220] We quote another letter. The child of the writer was deported across the Russian border from Kőrösmező: "Dear Sister Margaret, I was able only today to thank you for that immeasurable sisterly love you bestowed on me. I do not have any news yet of my child; all my hope is that Sister Margaret will get to him. From anybody else I could not even imagine that much love and conscience on behalf of such a case."[221]

---

[220] SZTTI 1131/12.
[221] SZTTI 1131/2

When the atrocities were repeated in June 1942, Sister Margaret asked Countess Móric Eszterházy to intervene. In her letter to the Countess she wrote: "On the copy of the letter in the case of Miercurea-Ciuk I left out the address, that my name be not an obstacle to the possibility of a good realization of the issue, knowing the Minister of the Interior is angry with me."[222]

We do not know the reason of the minister's anger, but we guess that she must have approached him frequently about the Christian Women Corps. On 10 December the Minister of War assured Sister Margaret in a letter that in the army those assigned to various tasks[223] count as soldiers and receive the same treatment as the regular soldiers. He wrote this in response to Sister Margaret's proposal in which she asks the minister to assure the "physical and spiritual well-being of them." "It would be completely superfluous - to give religious and charity organizations opportunity on their behalf. In the same manner no unfairness happens to those drafted to work, because they too, receive the same treatment as the regular soldiers."[224] Accordingly, Sister Margaret raised her voice in 1940 on behalf of the

---

[222] The letter is about the new deportation she wrote to Sister Margaret.
[223] Those who were assigned to background tasks were Jews. (Translator's note)
[224] SZTTI 1128. Károly Bartha Minister of War's original letter.

drafted work force Jews. "The second Jewish law (1939) led to the creation of the flagrant discriminative system against the army work force and to its gradual extension. From among the few who objected to it was Margaret Slachta, the superior of the Society of the Sisters of Social Service, who tried to awaken public opinion, and tried to influence military authorities to end cruelties against the persons forced into labor."[225] She tried in other ways to help. In July 1940 we came to know from a letter she wrote to the superior of Los Angeles, Sister Frederica, that she turned to the Archbishop of Los Angeles on behalf of Antal Fleischer;[226] however she received a negative answer. But she tried another way to gain for the artist a letter of invitation that he be able travel abroad. It seems, this was also unsuccessful, or perhaps because of the ongoing war the response arrived so late that travel was no longer possible. In October, written in a letter to Sister Frederica, she wrote to pray for Dr. Imre Magyar (a famous medical doctor) who was just then drafted into military work.

Of the other "inopportune" actions of Sister Margaret we learn from the Uj Magyarság, national socialist paper of 24 June 1942. It published a condemning article about her, because she raised

---

[225] Braham, r. L.: The Hungarian Holocaust. Budapest. Gondolat... p. 358.
nat[226] Antal Fleischer 1889-1945, conductor, music pedagogue, composer

her voice against a bill that would order the confiscation of all Jewish holdings. Sister Margaret wrote a letter and sent it to all of the representatives in the Parliament asking them to make their decision based on justice and law, not according to the terror of the streets. We know of this action only through the newspaper. It was reason enough for the minister's anger. The theme of the meeting with the Corps on 6 January 1941 was the question, "Who is Hungarian?" but from a completely different viewpoint than the contemporary "Hungarian race" would hold it. The Voice of the Spirit printed in October 1940 the writings of Irene Eva Leszkay: "Hungarian Confession." She wrote, "Hungarian is one who from her ancestors is that; but also those whose name is foreign, but in spirit belong to Hungary. Hungarian are those whose ancestors sought a home, bread and work here. Their name became Hungarian and that of their friends. Those too, are Hungarian who for a long time spoke their native language, because nobody forced them otherwise; together with bread and roof they received human freedom, and that made them Hungarian. Hungarian are those whose ancestors came to this land when, after the Turkish occupation, the land became depopulated and it needed to be re-populated. And Hungarian are those who did not have bread to sustain them and were forced to emigrate abroad."[227] The students

---

[227] The text of "Hungarian Confession" is found in several variations in the Voice of the Spirit. In the issue of 1940/12

of the School of Social Service on the 6 January meeting presented this text. Sister Margaret encouraged the members of the Corps to persevere and to work against those movements that aimed to undermine our faith and national identity.

By 1941 nearly all the nations around Hungary were under Nazi authority. The persecuted, whoever could, fled to Hungary where they were in comparative security. However, in 1941 the National Control Commission Center of foreigners began actions against persons illegally present in the country and the deportation of Jews with Hungarian citizenship began. Among those who raised their voice against this, Margaret Slachta had an outstanding role "with a clarity of foresight, and intransigence not possessed by many theologians and church people, and with a greatness of the few, she stood up with a passionate desire to work for the persecuted Jews." Among Church people in June of 1941 she belonged with the very few who knew their task. By letters she turned, not only to the competent authorities, but also to Mrs. Horthy, with whom she had not maintained any relationship since 1923. She informed her of the terrible things she witnessed personally regarding Jews. Here we quote only from her letter after the trip to Kőrösmező. "My highly Honored Lady! For me, half of a case is always the fact that each human being is a child of God; the other half is what

---

the text was shortened for schools. That text is found in corrected form in the issue of 1941/3.

will happen to us if our country veers away from the principles of rights, sinks ever deeper into de-moralization?"[228]   Sister Margaret verbalized in these sentences her two main principles for her opposition to that terrible contemporary worldview: true Christian faith and the love of country based on that faith.   Her manifold interventions and the objective report did their job.   On 15 August 1941 the Minister of the Interior ordered the immediate end to the deportation of Jews.   Ámos Pasztoy (National Control Commission Center) had initiated the deportation; he was executed after 1945. Sister Margaret learned of his execution only after she was an émigré.   When she learned of it, she wrote to Edith Weiss:[229] "For me, each order to execute is shocking.   I went to him after the first deportation of Korosmezo, since he ordered the deportation and told him about the turn of wheels, I felt it was useless to reason with him with higher principles.   His reply was such that gave basis for his condemnation."[230] The activities of Sister Margaret on behalf of the Jews had consequences. The Hungarian Royal Gendarme's Investigation Center ordered confidential, inconspicuous observation of her on 21 October 1941.[231]

---

[228] Tamás Majsai- Ilona Mona: Notes to the history of the deportation of Jews of Kőrösmező. In the yearbook of the Ráday Collection IV-V. Budapest. 1986. 195-237. P.217.

[229] Edith Weiss was hidden and saved at our motherhouse; she financed my escaping in 1952. (Translator's note.)

[230] Letter of Sister Margaret to Edith Weiss, 1951. II. 23. The original is in the SSSA

[231] MOL K 149-1941-8-1626, SZTTTI 1130/1.

1941 is significant not only on account of her public activities but from a community point of view. In 1935 the Constitution was approved for six years; after a trial period it needed now be submitted for a final approval. Sister Margaret attempted to convince the Cardinal to postpone the Chapter until after the war, since the sisters from abroad were unable to attend and their observations and interventions were necessary. But the Cardinal did not see postponement possible. The Chapter had to be held, and it was from 29 June -8 July 1941.

In March 1940 the Hungarian Bishops Conference organized a commission: "to assist morally and spiritually those Hungarian believers who are affected by the so called Jewish law." The commission had 21 members, among them three women, one of whom was Margaret Slachta. In October, the Hungarian Holy Cross Organization was founded to give to those affected by the laws spiritual, social, charitable and societal assistance. Margaret Slachta was elected as co-president.

The Christian Women Corps held its' meeting on 6 January 1942 in the Marble Room of the Hotel Gellert. Sister Margaret proclaimed the year's work plan in undisputable terms:

It is important on Christian basis that all citizens of the nation, including Jews, have assured their natural rights: right to life, right to sustenance, right to family, right to have children. The Christian Women Corps walks on the basis of Christ's truths and believes only in Him. At this point our nation is favored by a great power (German), but tomorrow we might become castaways if they feel we are no longer necessary. On our country, a worldview storms across that will leave behind smoking ruins, bleeding stumps, weeping people, and destruction. Our program for this year is to work with printed material and living words to lead the masses back to Christian faith, to the recognition of the essence of truth and to its experience. The majority of people only attend liturgy but do not know the truths of faith. They do not know how faith's values and national life are interconnected. It is a miracle that with the brown and red trends (Hitlerism-Communism) Hungary still exists.[232]

The persons present celebrated the speaker for long minutes. Not only the Catholic but also the secular and the radical press reported this event.[233]

But the German ambassador raised a charge against her with the Ministry of Internal Affairs. At the lower courts both justices condemned her. She appealed to the Kings Table (the highest judiciary forum at that time) and the council of Töreky

---

[232] SZTTI 725.
[233233] Pesti Hirlap, 1942. I. 8. P. 7. Magyar Nemzet, 1942,I. 8. P. 8. Nemzeti Ujsag, 1942. I. 8. P. 3.

acquitted her.[234]

How were "printed words and living words" re-alized? In February 1942 the <u>Voice of the Spirit</u> began working for the spiritual front and its pages were offered to the Christian Women Corps, be-cause the Corps was led by the same truth and values on a civic level that the <u>Voice of the Spirit</u> led in faith life. There is only one kind of morality; whatever is wrong in personal life is wrong also in political life. From this issue on until the suppres-sion of the <u>Voice of the Spirit</u> in 1944, it published continuously the material of the Worldview Course. The best-known theologians and professionals wrote the studies and material of the Worldview.[235] Later this material was printed as a handbook for those who would organize such courses. The first of these courses was held in the hall of Saint Ste-phen Society's publishing house. Subsequently they were conducted wherever Sisters of Social Service worked. By November the course material was available in a condensed form and was pre-sented in the rooms at the Catholic Circle by members of women's movements and later by Sis-ters of Social Service during the National Catholic Conference. (6 October) Before this date, during summer this Worldview course was taught to young women, who wrote down what impacted

---

[234] Diary of the National Assembly, 1947,II. 25.
[235] Among others: Antal Szütz, Schp, Dr. Antal Éber, Dr. Endre Hamvas, Dr.Béla Kovrig, Zoltán Nyisztor, Zsigmond Michalovics, etc.

them the most. Their responses impressed Sister Margaret very deeply: "I have a great joy; actually I do not desire anything as much as to guide my sisters toward such a world, whose vision makes me so happy." On 23 November the outline of the worldview course was presented to the leaders and participants of the course. "The material of the course seems at the beginning to be clearly religious. It will become clarified for us that the life of faith, or the lack of it, is the most decisive dimension of how our individual, societal and governmental life is formed."[236]

The year 1942 began with tragic events in neighboring Slovakia. Slovakia received independence after the Czech republic was dissolved. But after three days Slovakia placed itself under German protectorate. The sad results of this decision were felt very soon. In March 1942 the deportation of Jews began. Tiso, the president of Slovakia (a Catholic priest) responded to the greetings of the diplomatic body that Slovakia sides with the "new Europe" (meaning: National Socialism). The actions of state reflected that view. Naturally, from the historical northwestern part of Hungary (annexed to Slovakia) - whoever could, fled to Hungary. From these refugees came the first news of deportations in 1942, and they asked for protection from the Hungarian Holy Cross organization and from the Hungarian Jewish Protective office. The Apostolic Nuncio in Hungary, Angelo

---

[236] Voice of the Spirit, 1942/10. P. 103.

Rotta, wrote to Cardinal Maglione in the Vatican on 13 March 1942 that the deportation of Jews had begun in Slovakia. The Nuncio learned this news from a refugee who asked him to make intervention with the Holy Father on behalf of the Slovak Jews who would be deported to Poland.[237]

Margaret Slachta, the co-president of the Holy Cross Organization, was also in touch with the Hungarian Jewish Protective office. She was asked by Baroness Edith Weiss to visit Slovakia and get firsthand information of the situation and do as much as she could. The response of Margaret Slachta is dated of 22 March 22 1942: "... If there is hope to do a service for the issue, I shall go with all my heart and soul."[238]

She traveled sometime during 25-27 March 1942. Because Edith Farkas died on 24 March, Margaret Slachta paid her respects at her wake but could not participate in the burial on the 27th because of her trip to Slovakia. Since Margaret Slachta was born in Kassa (Kosice) she had strong relationships with relatives and friends in the historic northeastern part of the country. In harmony with her mission she turned to the office of the emigration leader, Dr. Isidor Koso. We know this from a teaching to the sisters: "In Bratislava I tried to soften the heart of the rigid leader of the emigration office toward the case of the Jewish

---

[237] Le Saint Siege, 1941-42, p.457.
[238] SZTTI 381/2.

children, whom the Turks would have been willing to accept; otherwise they would certainly meet death. But he was unmoved." [239] From this quote it becomes clear that Margaret Slachta went with a ready plan to Bratislava, arranged diplomatically, that the non-aligned Turkey would accept underage children if they received permission to leave Slovakia. The relevant Slovak officer denied the request, witnessing his characterization of Margaret Slachta: "she is spiritually dry, heartless, with false reasoning and is a fanatic."

This short stay of Margaret Slachta strengthened her conviction of which she spoke on 6 January: "this public mentality storming over nations brings immorality and destruction." This destruction began in neighboring Slovakia, but it did not stop at its borders. Therefore, as soon as she returned, she reported her findings to all competent authorities:

Regarding the latest happenings in Slovakia in view of concrete Hungarian interests: The details of the happenings will not be enumerated because they agree with what the press communicated. If they differ it is because the reality is more sad and shocking. Whatever the official information, it is only words and do not speak the truth. The direct Hungarian interest is that Hungarian nationals who are sent to concentration camps receive protection not only in Bratislava, but also in other camps. An even more

---

[239] SZTTI 1196/19. P.4 latest

important implication is the present human trafficking. It is a proven fact that Croatian and Polish women in great number were sent to bars behind the front to be prey for soldiers. In some serious credible places, they are convinced that Slovak and Jewish girls will take the place of the already exhausted women. If this new source cannot provide enough replacement, the Germans will take Christian women without qualm of conscience the way they did in Poland. German women however will be spared. The Slovak nationals are the ruling group; however, there are, in that country, Hungarian nationals who are hated by both the Slovaks and the Germans. It is a given that further German demand will be filled by Hungarian women. It is the moral obligation of Hungary as a neighboring country not to overlook how helpless people are driven to death or into sexual slavery. Our endangered Christian and Hungarian sisters' possible sad future is a new motive to prevent this unparalleled moral destruction. It would be necessary to experiment with a strong action because the German audacity became stronger by the fear of the small nations. At one point it will be necessary to experiment with a strong action to see what will be the German response; so much the more because of the great loss of blood, Germans will depend on nations' willingness to help. If the Germans never experience moral resistance, they possibly will take women from our nation.[240]

Both the church and the national forums re-

---

[240] SZTTI 381/7b

frained from dealing with "other nation's internal affairs." We must accept "that we may not believe tender feelings and spiritual zeal are able to achieve great results." The sisters naturally kept silent about this trip, but some things gradually came to the knowledge of those who needed protection. One refugee from Slovakia remembers this: "The Sisters of Social Service hid me until the time of liberation in various of their houses without anything in return...they did not accept from anybody else either. I have of Margaret Slachta most idealistic memories. She is very simple, refined, courteous and very willing to help, she dealt with each person as if she would be her sister or a good acquaintance."[241] Sisters were able at the time to do only so much.

During the autumn of 1942 the first air raid hit Budapest. One bomb destroyed the villa of Lajos Zilahy. The author and his wife lost all property, his wife all her jewelry, and the author's royalty rights both within the country and abroad. He lost his share of income from the Pegazus and the Hid Companies. He also offered the rights of authorship of all his future works and their property on Áfonya Street for a school to be built for gifted children in order that they could receive a higher Hungarian, and, in a true Christian sense, better education. Sister Margaret gave them a high recognition [...] and this was the beginning of the friendship between her and the Zilahy couple.

---

[241] Károly Hetényi Varga. 428

Twelve hundred persons attended the meeting of the Christian Women Corps at the beginning of 1943. The essence of the talk by Sister Margaret was that the army protects the external front: the geographic borders, economic interests, the life of its citizens, and the body of the nation. The internal front is the spiritual, the mentality. On this front the citizens are to protect the divine and human rights, the laws based on the divine, the mentality of the nations, those spiritual dimensions on which nations are built. If a nation no longer lives by those, it dies. On this front the soul of the nation would be protected. On the war-front one might trample and overcome a nation. Killing it is possible only on the internal front. Brothers, husbands, sons and fathers protect the national body; women rise up on the internal front to protect the soul of the nation. She asked:

Who betrays the internal front?
Everybody who offends against moral laws!
Those
- who side with violence and deny principles of rights.
- who cowardly keep silent when they should speak up on behalf of true and forgotten issues.
- who protect self, folding her arms in her lap, when she should protect the persecuted.
- who abuse power, demean others, torture them and make life bitter.
- who nurture hate in the heart and   empty

love from it.
- who do to others what they would not want to be done to themselves.

And if all of these are done by a nation, it has lost the entire war on the internal front, because it has left the Christian basis that upholds a nation and with it has killed its own soul. It has committed suicide.

Ending her talk Sister Margaret said: "...now when the masses' better self is silent, when violence creates orgies, nations betray God and rush into suicide. I shout into the night: 'Whoever feels she wants to protect, with Christ, the internal front, join us.'"[242] This meeting was held on 6 January; but already, in the January issue of the <u>Voice of the Spirit</u>, the New Year's Letter was published. This letter informed those Christians who wanted to document they are not Jews; they are the Aryans. Sister Margaret frequently emphasized that during those times they had to understand some who claim themselves Christian, but in reality are pagan materialists. During that time a well-educated lady came to ask admission into the Society. During the conversation with her she said: "Why does the Bishops conference give out such prayers in which we pray for everybody? The Jews and communist are not our siblings, since we are Christian!" Sister Margaret said to her: "There would be logic in this reasoning if you say since we are new pagans." She tried to make this under-

---

[242] SZTTI 1943/2, p. 18-19.

standable in her New Year's Letter.

New Year's Letter [243]

In regard to:
- those drafted into military service and those at home,
- the statement of the Minister of Defense,
- Christ's admonition: the measure you mete out will be the measure you get,
- crooked lines of Providence and the graced life's logic of laws,
- the fact that persons will reap a happier New Year from what was sown personally by them.

My dear sisters,
I write to you who face the New Year with tears in your eyes, deeply concerned, and have no minute without thinking of your drafted father, husband or son. O how you would do everything to assure those at the front protection by Providence from cold, rain, wind and swamps, enemy bullets and torture! If you let go of wanting their protection in the *form* as you see it to be best, and surrender to God *its manner,* you will assure for them the divine protection. 'How?' you ask. In many ways! However, I shall write first *how you can prevent* it from happening. This, too, has many forms. I shall mention only one. You will deprive your own loved ones of God's protection if you are indifferent to the worry, the concerns and the tears

---

[243] From the "Voice of the Spirit" (Lélek Szava) Vol. X. No. 1, January 1, 1943.

of another mother, wife, or child. You will deprive your loved ones of protection if you desire
only your own understanding, care, and help.
You will deprive them of protection if you view
with coldness, ill will, or malice the pain of others. What is even worse, if you desire for others the evil or suffering that you want to prevent
by your prayers only for your self or your loved
ones!

Do you want a double measure of divine Providence for your own in the midst of dangers?
Welcome into your heart the fate of others, especially those who are hard for you to love.
Welcome one of your enemies - one who
cheated or hurt you. Receive these into your
heart to the degree that when you pray for your
own, you send a true prayer for them to God
who is a God of all.

Open your heart to a person drafted into the
work camps,[244] shunned and excluded by pre-
vailing social attitudes from a neighborly acceptance in society. *Have the courage to cast
out* indifference from your heart during these
deathly serious times; expel loveless-ness and
hatred. *Dare to recognize* at the center of your
heart that the *other* mother and her son are your
sister and brother. Open your heart to her pain
and give a helping hand to carry her cross.

---

[244] Translator's note: During the Nazi time men of Jewish
background were not drafted into the armed forces. They
were assigned into work camps to do supportive services
during the war.

Dare to proclaim that the only Christian path for a public official is the one followed by the Minister of Defense who states without hesitation, that service in work camps is a service for the nation and not a measure of punishment. Their physical well-being and their honor is protected by law just as much as of those in the armed forces. *Dare to confess*, this is your viewpoint and conviction! *And dare to act!* Dare to ask, insist, demand from your relative who happens to be a commander in the work camp to be such a superior as you desire for your son to have in the armed forces or as a prisoner of the enemy. Proclaim to him the eternally valid words of Christ: 'The measure with which you act will be meted to you.' [245] God will act likewise - punish or protect, reject or be merciful - just as you are compassionate or cruel.

Daughters, wives, mothers do you understand that there exists a mystical bond between family members? Common blessing or curse is the fate of those who belong together? You protect your own in the face of God's justice when you are sisterly and merciful to others! You cannot go personally to the front to shield your loved ones from harm with your body. The Angel of God will take to them your sacrifices, your compassion and justice. Whatever you did for the son of another mother will be the protective shield of your own son from bodily and spiritual harm.

Divine Providence might not bring back from the

---

[245] Mt. 7: 2

front your own even if you act with love and mercy. However, you do not know of how much heart-wrenching suffering, torture, or despair they will be spared by the Lord! If our all-loving Heavenly Father deems best - and it is difficult even to say - not to bring back your loved one, God will place him into the palm of His hands in peace, and silently lift him into eternity for and on account of you, because you welcomed into your heart a loved one of another. Your love for another has protected and prevented your own from unnecessary suffering, hardships, bitterness and humiliations. You loved with a Christ-like love. Your love's blessings hover over your loved ones. Your mind might not perceive at first the connection of what you do for others to what happens to your own. Your heart and your faith however can follow Divine logic that writes straight with crooked lines. Your love, like an electric current touches the source of all graces. From there it streams back as a protective blessing from Divine hands onto your own who are fighting at the front.

If we think in terms not only of individuals but entire nations, whose forces protect or attack, hate or love the opposing forces, nations too, will reap for its army and its national body what it has sown. It may save or lose their entire armed forces. It may save or destroy itself as a nation.

Once more, a happy New Year to you my dear sisters! Happy New Year to you, who now understand the key to your happiness during the coming year! The key to a happy New Year rests in your own hands.

January 1 1943
Sister Margaret

According to the known documents the country's public opinion was very favorable regarding the New Year's letter. However it enraged László Endre, Vice Bailiff of County Pest, who at the county's public meeting on 7 February 1943 officially condemned it: "I received information with the deepest shock that Margaret Slachta began such a movement that protects those in labor camps. At a time when the inhabitants of the county know they are Jews, they fire up a peaceful nation against each other, against Hungarian laws meant to defend the body and soul of our nation from those (Jews) who damage. The county and its inhabitants strongly condemn this initiative."

Sister Margaret did not delay in defending her truth. In the paper, <u>Nemzeti Ujsag</u>, her open letter was addressed to the members of the Pest County municipal authority.

The information given to the members of the Pest County public meeting regarding my New Year's letter contains statements that do not measure up to objectivity and are completely contrary to truth. They suggest the report was given without having read the letter. Therefore it is reasonable for me to inform the members of the municipal authorities and the public whom several papers might have misled. Given the content of my New Year's letter, it becomes clear that it was written on behalf of the soldiers who fight in the war. The essence of the letter is the following: Everybody is concerned for their relatives who are on the front. They cannot send them human help, but we know from our Christian faith that we can send Divine help if we pray for them. However, prayer from a hating heart, from one who is indifferent to other's suffering, or who rejoices over their pain cannot receive hearing. For this reason we must empty our hearts from all loveless-ness toward anybody. Especially we may not allow ourselves to despise or hate those drafted into forced labor; rather we must want just treatment for them, that is, we are to include them in our Christian charity. If we act in this manner God will listen to our prayers and will help our sons and husbands who fight on the front. This is the content of my New Year's letter. My statement would not be complete, if I do not add the following: I summarized my New Year's article in such a very short way that, from it, some could understand that I suggest to include our drafted work force into our love in such a manner that this love be manifested only by feeling, and would not contain that loving needs to be given in actions flowing from the truth of our faith. In order not to misunderstand my meaning, I state the following: I stand on Christian values without compromise. Therefore I profess that love obliges us to respect - without any exclusion - the God-given natural rights of all human beings; and that they may not be taken away from anybody. Such rights are: right to life, right to sustenance; physical well-being, freedom of conscience, and the right to private property gained in an honorable way. Moreover: Chris-

276

tian morality does not know collective retalia-
tion. That is exclusively God's right, which has
the goodness to serve justice to those who in-
nocently are burdened in a collective suffering.
Human beings cannot to do this. Human beings are allowed to punish only individual sins,
and even that only through the judicial system.
On the scale of justice, specific racial rights do
not exist; morality is the only issue there. I apply all these to those who are drafted into the
national workforce. And I shall close my statement with the following: God's judgment will
spare only those persons (those nations) who
primarily admit their own sins and repent for
them – and those who, together with repent-
ance, weep with those who weep; who share in
the sadness of the sad; who have compassion
for those who suffer. That is, on their soul the
Christian sign shines forth: love. On the other
hand, all believers of the religion of hate are the
enemy of their own selves, of society and of
their nation.[246]

The New Year and the Open letter's impact
was very great. The <u>Voice of the Spirit</u> continued
to be censured. [...] The influence of the <u>Voice of
the Spirit</u> is characterized by the fact that on 19
March 1944 it was among the first among those
that were suppressed.

When she was abroad in 1951, Sister Margaret received a letter from liberal politician Béla
Fábián with the following text: "Perhaps you still

---

[246] <u>Nemzeti Ujság,</u> 1943. II. 13. <u>Magyar Jövő</u> 1943, II. 24.

remember when I last visited you in Pest at the Thököly Street with Hugo Csergő. We wanted to tell you how highly we esteem the work that the <u>Voice of the Spirit</u> is doing." [247]

News came from Slovakia again. The Minister of the Interior announced on 8 February 1943 that they would empty out Jews from Slovakia deporting the 20,000 that were still there. On 19 February the newspapers announced the worldwide news that, while the United States is at war with Italy, the Italian authorities gave permission to Spellman, Archbishop of New York, to visit the American army and spend days in the Vatican. Archbishop Spellman worked earlier in the Papal State and was counted as a friend of Pope Pius XII. Hearing this news, Sister Petra Rónai reminded Sister Margaret that the Archbishop knows her and our Society. When Sister Petra returned from America in 1931, the Archbishop traveled on the same boat, and celebrated liturgy for the travelers. After a Mass he went over to Sister Petra, greeted her and told her that he knows the American Sisters of Social Service, and their superior Sister Margaret.[248] Thus arose the opportunity to travel to Rome and, with the help of the Archbishop, ask an interview with the Pope on behalf of the Slovakian Jews. Sister Margaret went immediately to ask for a passport, but the Minister of the Interior rejected

---

248 Béla Fábián was a liberal politician/lawyer he was freed in 1945 from Kőrösmző and immigrated to the USA in 1948.
[248] SZTTI 1212, <u>Memories of Sister Petra Rónai</u>. P. 60.

her request. The friends of Sister Margaret knew of her plan, and Lajos Zilahy was surprised seeing her on the street. He asked: "Are you here when you should be in Rome?" Having understood Sister Margaret's situation, Zilahy asked for a cultural visa from another minister. On the plane that flew once a week, there was one more seat available. On it, Sister Margaret arrived in Rome the evening before the departure of the Archbishop (March 3rd.) She went immediately to see Archbishop Spellman, but he was not yet at his lodging. Sister Margaret waited. He got home at 9 PM. He received Sister Margaret and, after listening to her, he called the Vatican immediately and arranged a hearing with the Pope. Archbishop Spellman said that he was prepared to do everything to help the unfortunate human beings. Of the ten volumes containing the saving activities of Jews by the Holy See, the 1943 volume speaks in detail of the intervention of Sister Margaret (p. 22-24); the meeting with the Holy Father took place on 11 March.[249] "It was totally unexpected that she could get a turn as there were fifty persons before her on the list." As a result of the meeting Pius XII ordered the seven Slovak bishops to go as a body to protest against the deportation with the President and each of the ministers. Moreover the Pope ordered that in each church a pastoral letter of protest, signed by each bishop, be read at Mass. As a result of this, the

---

[249] See: Sister Margaret's thank you letter to Pope Pius XI for the interview, In <u>Sister Margaret Slachta's Christian Public Life</u>, p. 142.

deportation did not take place.[250]

While in Rome Sister Margaret wrote the "World-View Creed,"[251] a summary of those supernatural truths that lived in her soul. The basis of this creed is the Encyclical of Pius XII, *Summi Pontificatus*. The Voice of the Spirit published the encyclical, and a quote follows: "Laws on natural rights rest on God. ... The human family is basically unified; God is Father of all. This supernatural truth creates the unity and the strong mutual bond among them. The Church of Christ serves the supernatural unity and greets joyfully the particular and partial energies of nations only when they are not against the responsibilities flowing from the common human unity and its common vocation."[252]

In 1943 Sister Margaret began the Movie-Front. Her aim was to offer good and positive ideas to society with the help of films. Each month she would rent a large theater, present a constructive film and highlight its moral messages. For example: "The Iron-Crown" is the symbol of justice; therefore evil tries to destroy it but is unable to do so. The players express that human beings, with their actions, write their own judgment. Sin contains its punishment in the way a seed contains the

---

[250] SZTTI 382. Ilona Mona: Margaret Slachta for the Slovak Jews. (1942-43)

[251] See: Sister Margaret Slachta's Christian Public Life: Worldview Creed, p. 148.

[252] From the Encyclical: Summi Pontificatus.

280

plant. The buried iron crown comes to the surface; justice is served and those who fought each other are reconciled. The march of world history is portrayed with the eye of people looking to Rome, where the power of the iron crown, truth without arms, but with spiritual strength, calls into fighting lines the nations to unite under the reign of Redeeming Truth. Margaret Slachta made efforts that those in power viewed the film. The Christian Women Corps covered the price of the movie. On 8 February 1943 the invited military, those of the military academy and the police, twice filled the Hungarian Cultural House. Sister Margaret offered the worldview highlight and her talk was interrupted several times with loud applause. Each time she explained that those in the work force are equal soldiers with those fighting on the front. She emphasized that they are obliged to deal generously and courteously toward the enemy soldiers who were overcome.[253]

In a conversation Sister Margaret told that she realized how movies affect human beings psychologically; it recreates and focuses persons on the topic without tiring them. They will notice only what is shown and how it affects their feelings but they do not engage with the meanings. They do not select out the good from it and experience the evil without criticism. She started the movie-front to enlighten people by highlighting the

---

[253] Voice of the Spirit, 1943/3, p. 34-37. The film earned the great Venice price in 1941.

worldview dimension and awaken them to making conscious their Christian role and not be defenseless to destructive impressions. Film, Theater, Literature wrote: "Margaret Slachta is one of the most interesting and significant women of our day. What is the secret of her exceptional influence? The attractive gentleness, understanding smile and patient goodness that enfolds her entire being; we come to recognize that it is possible to fight for something with love." From the following exerpt of the article it becomes clear that a play has to be artistic, because then it can mediate the truly good. It is important that artists stand on high moral level, because an artistic creation is a projection of the artist's interior being. Responding to a question she says of the feminine vocation: "The woman is the life-giver and nurturer of human beings on the earth. She is that not only in a physical but also a spiritual dimension - not only in the family situation but also in the life of the nation. Both keeping a nation in existence or its destruction is in her hands. How sad that women are so poorly aware of their magnificent nation-upholding vocation."[254]

The year 1943 was a year of jubilee. The Society was twenty years old. At the district assembly after the Pentecost festive thanksgiving the Society looked back on the past years. The sisters give a report of their ministries and decided on the activities for the coming year. Sister Margaret gave a talk to the sisters and the associates who

---

[254] Film, Theater, Literature, 1943 IV. 16.

were present. In this talk she gave thanks to God for the fruits of the past 20 years: growth in numbers, large fields of work, economic growth, but most especially for the inexpressibly great gift of the Holy Spirit, protecting the sisters through the uncompromising true Christian spirit during the time when the spiritual plague - meaning Hitler's ideology - burned up everything. In 1942 a sister, converted from Judaism, was elected to be the district superior, and Sister Margaret rejoiced for this profoundly. After this she continued with encouraging words: "We must now persevere only for a few months to protect ourselves with a hard fight from the attacks of the netherworld's spirits. There will no longer be a war, but it may happen that when we return to peaceful conditions the sky will become dark again, but the darkness will be for a short while. This will be payment for everything in which our nation has sinned. *(She meant the laws against Jews, the fate of the forced laborers, etc.)* It may happen that turmoil will follow, and nerve-wracking times will break upon us; it may happen that we lose our house. The decisive, the important, the only essential element is the untouched, graced spirituality by which, in the midst of war and inner collapse and during conditions of war or peace, we serve eternal values in the individuals, in society and in the nation."[255]

This talk may have influenced Sister Sara Salkaházi, who during the fall of that year begged

---

[255] Testvér, 1943/7. P.2

permission to offer herself as a victim of the Society, "...if persecution of the church, the Society and the sisters happens." In Sister Sara's prayer of offering we also find the ideas of the New Year's letter: "...if you personally cannot go to the front, take upon yourself the blow meant for members of your family." God's angel went there; Sister Sara took upon herself the blow meant for the Society.[256]

The paper of Lajos Zilachy, Hid, celebrated the jubilee of the Society with the title: "In Service of the European Spirit." The three- page article was illustrated with many pictures. It described extensively the activities of the Society and its history in a short manner, and concluded: "The Society of the Sisters of Social Service is the only ecclesial organization whose idea was born in our country; its center is here; its foundress and the leadership are Hungarian. Beyond several European countries it is present in Canada and California. The Society enkindles on two continents torches of light - it fights without compromise against lies, hate, paganism and false Christianity. She selflessly prepares a home for the coming peaceful era for which each honest person longs with a pure heart. The Society observes public life with courageous criticism, raises her voice against

---

[256] Sister Sara Salkaházi (1899-1944) was shot into the Danube on 27 December 1944 with her co-worker Vilma Bernovits and four protected Jewish persons.

untrue and destructive platitudes."[257]

The Christian Women Corps also celebrated its 25th jubilee. At a meeting on 28 November Sister Margaret delivered a review, "The Christian Women's Corps Now." (see text on page 409). The news reported:

> The Christian Women Corps celebrated its 25th jubilee. As part of the Hungarian public life that takes seriously Christian politics and Christian public behavior in the true and natural meaning in the midst of so much misunderstanding, distortion, this jubilee is a good occasion to think with reverence of the merits of Margaret Slachta. How much different would have been the fate of the Christian politics, if it would have followed the positive ideas and plans of Margaret Slachta. For her, Christianity meant Christ-like love, Christ-like behavior. She suffers with those who suffer, she does not make a difference between the suffering and those in trial; she suffers with them and in the midst of all difficulties she finds solutions to help them. She holds Christianity by the true meaning of its words and has faith according to the guidance of a practical Christianity that extends to everyone. She is the genius of love, of pure Christianity, of goodness. In our public life she is alone; therefore she is a shining example around whom do not prepare with words a beautiful wreath but to whom gratitude streams with such warmth that moves the heart of eve-

---

[257] The Hid, 1943, X. 15. P. 22-24

rybody in the midst of this stormy era.[258]

The true stormy era began in 1944. At the meeting of the Christian Women Corps on 6 January the Christmas Proclamation of Pope Pius XII was presented by 25 public personalities with the leadership of Sister Margaret. Archbishops' Vicar Dr. Endre Hamvas offered the closing words. The essence of that proclamation was the following:

> Whoever desires that the star of peace arise and stay above society, make the effort to return to human persons the dignity that God bestowed from the beginning. They should reject every form of materialism that nations use as means for domination and absolutism. They are to give to work the place that God assigned to it from the beginning; awaken in human beings a consciousness of rights that are based on God's reign and protected from all human absolutism; promote the development of a governance based on rational discipline, noble humanness and Christian worldview's sense of responsibility. [259]

Sister Margaret emphasized in her presentation that human beings may not dictate morality; they must obey God's laws. To study these laws would be the Women Corps most important task

---

[258] The Present Era, "The paper of the Hungarian Conscience" 1944. I. 1. P. 3.
[259] The radio proclamation of Pope Pius XII at Christmas, 1942.

for the year.[260] However this could not happen. On 19 March the army of Hitler occupied the county. From 5 April it became obligatory to wear of humiliating sign (the yellow star); the air raids began in Budapest and in the greater cities, deportations into the concentration camps began and those seeking refuge appeared at the motherhouse. Sister Margaret emptied out the motherhouse. Only those sisters remained whose presence was essential. Naturally, she remained there. The sisters went to sleep in Zugliget, at the villa of Mrs. Steffanits. The motherhouse, the two villas on the Báthori László Street, the school of Social work's boarding space and several other places where sisters worked were filled with those who asked refuge. Everyone was received in the name of God. On one occasion someone asked about payment. Sister Margaret sent him away saying that with money he could find lodging anywhere else; here everybody is received in God's name. Knowing some were in need, Sister Margaret visited and offered help. Naturally to do all this she had to win her sisters concurrence: "The vocation of our Society is to represent an uncompromised Christianity and we are obliged to make all sacrifices on behalf of the persecuted." [261] The sisters understood this and agreed; they surrendered their identity papers to those who, in possession of good papers, could feel secure (they were documents witnessing non-Jewish identity).

---

[260] Voice of the Spirit, 1944, I. 15. P. 11-14
[261] Handwritten memories of Sister Petra Ronai. P. 108

The situation in Budapest worsened after the Arrow Cross came to power 15 October 1944. Sister Margaret placed the motherhouse under the protection of the Vatican and Sweden, because Sweden took under protection Hungarian prisoners of war and all prisoners of war in Europe. For this reason the Arrow Cross recognized, for the time being, Sweden's protection. The conditions after the German occupation are well documented in what was preserved in the National Archives. Deportations began. The Hungarian Red Cross and the Hungarian and Protestant Women's National Associations asked the Prime Minister to be allowed to give first aid and refreshments to those who were to be deported. The petition was signed by the widow of Istvan Horthy, the volunteer chief nurse of the counties of "Pest-Pilis-Solt-Kiskun, and the first army division. The petition was dated 20 June 1944. The Secretary of State submitted it on 14 July to the Prime Minister, after the last train deporting people had left.[262]

It is impossible to give information on the entire activities of the Sisters of Social Service but we shall relate the happenings at the motherhouse, because Sister Margaret was there. The sisters kept the decisions made during the retreat of 1944. Sister Margaret asked them, "...are we ready to perhaps lose everything as a conse-

---

[262] Hungarian National Archive K64-1944-43. Of the last deporting train: "The history of 1944". Edited by: Ferenc Glatz. Historia Yearbook, 1984.... P.82.

quence of persevering in our convictions?"[263] She taught the sisters on 29 June 1944, "...to these drowning people, let us be merciful. Think about what if things would happen to us that which awaits them."

Archived documents tell of one threatening event.

On a foggy and frightening October night, the sound of heavy boots and harsh words interrupted the silence of Thököly Street convent. The Arrow Cross gang from across the street broke in on Margaret Slachta accusing her and her sisters that the wife of a well- known Jewish writer is hiding there with false papers. The men were shouting, but the sisters tried to convince them, quietly but firmly, to leave. The men did not leave, but with guns in their hands they searched the entire house, entering even in the sisters' rooms. They were looking for one hiding person and found 140. The various kinds of papers, documents, letters of protection, passports became useless in a few minutes. The Arrow Cross took all of them to the big dining room and started questioning them. In the meantime they insulted Margaret Slachta with rude and course attributes; they even hit her with a stick. She did not react to this; she was not concerned for herself.

During those times she truly lived for saving the persecuted.

---

[263] The meditation of Sister Paula Ronai, 1946, X. 13.

During the German occupation she placed the persecuted in fifteen cities and villages. She helped everyone who turned to her; nobody needed intervention from higher ups to dry up the tears of the suffering. She collected false papers; the sisters sent their baptismal certificates to every part of the nation, and made them available to the persecuted. Those who were hunted were sent to good places - some to Pest, some to Buda, others to rural places. She hid a thousand persons. Some she helped to flee from the ghetto, even from the deportation wagon. From the thousand, all but twelve were saved. Those who were hidden came from different social strata. Some were hidden because of their race, some others who because of their political convictions. At the motherhouse some well-known persons were also hidden like Emilia Markus and her husband and Oszkár Pradányi, after being freed from the Arrow-Cross house. Others included Eugene Heltai and his family; Antal Fleischer, conductor; Tibor Wilt, sculptor. At the pinnacle of the motherhouse the flags of Sweden and the Vatican flew, because Margaret Slachta worked shoulder to shoulder with the Swedish ambassador and the Apostolic Nuncio's office.[264]

During the spring 1945, publishing was allowed:

> Margaret Slachta tells how she has saved a thousand persecuted persons. It is a great

---

[264] Democracia, 1945,X. 21. P.5

blessing that there are persons who with self-sacrificing courage, heroic soul opposed the evil spirit of persecuting human beings, and took under protection those pursued to death. 'We only did our obligation; we lived our vocation, since this is why we are on earth.' Her transfigured face, lit up by a childlike shining eyes and a conviction from her soul. Thus she tells with simple words the history of saving persons: 'We were allowed to save many human beings in great danger. There was a time when 650 persons were hidden in our motherhouse, but the work of saving happened in our institutions and in rural locations as well. This organized hiding of more than thousand persecuted from the pursuers' was possible only because all the sisters and coworkers united their efforts with us in fulfilling our obligations. Those protected were mainly poor, nameless persons, who were totally defenseless in the face of persecution. We did not choose between persons. Those who asked for protection, or whom we could bring out from the ghetto, we protected. We - truthfully stating - did not want to be primarily of help to the outstanding personalities of public life, but for the simple people only because they were human beings and were persecuted. They were worried and crowded together in our rooms like herring; a number of them passed days and nights leaning against the wall of the chapel. We gave them our rooms, our beds, our entire house; the sisters found lodging somewhere else. We enhanced the security of those we protected because each sister gave her birth certificate to women, and we tried to get false papers for the men. They all studied day and night the data of these papers, that they would know the life-saving information if awakened during night. There were frequently police raids, and search of the house.

In the house across the street the Arrow Cross party had its headquarters. They came, searching for Jews. At one time forty of them entered our home. They were a loud gang. I stood up confronting them. They degraded me with obscene words, pushed me aside, hit me. I was able to keep my peace. With a quiet voice I said to their leader, 'Do you think in this manner you can build a better world?' My peace had its effect on them. They did not hurt me again, but they gathered forty persons from among the hidden, those who seemed suspicious to them or did not remember their new data. At this point we were called to account. The leader stated: 'I shall not charge the superior if she promises not to hide Jews any more.' Faithful to my vocation, and by the demand of my convictions, I responded: 'I do not promise. We came to serve God and to love people. I shall take, from now on, every opportunity to continue doing what I have done so far. [265]

Tibor Wild, sculptor, also told that when members of his family asked for refuge they received it immediately.

My father-in-law was sent to Nagyvárad (Oradea,) where he lived most of those times; my

---

[265] A Reggel, 1945. IV. 30. P. 7.

wife was sent to Miskolc - as if she would be a sister and a novice. This is how I got in touch with Sister Margaret. She told me such things as: 'Tibor, I need such and such kind of papers.' Since I did not have other activities I began working for her, so much that frequently I traveled with her. At the motherhouse on Thököly Street I was allowed to enter into the section for sisters only. She called me *Paul Who Damages*. Once she told me, 'Imagine Tibor - it's terrible - these hidden people call me a saint.' I responded, 'It's possible that you are a saint, but also very talented.' On another occasion, Sister Margaret told me a little girl came here; her father and mother were deported. The girl was just arriving home when they took her parents down the stairs. Her father made a sign with his eyes not to recognize them. This unhappy girl told me that in their home in the wardrobe the have much money and she has no penny with her. 'Tibor, their home is on the Almássy Square, you must enter it and bring the money.' But how are you able to think such things, I told her, since that home is locked down. 'Please just go and bring the money,' she responded. The following thing happened. I looked at the house. It turned out that between the home's bathroom and the neighboring home's bathroom there was an airshaft. I could not do anything else so I rang the bell of the neighboring home. It was a terrible risk. At that time they could have called the police immediately. They did not do it. They let me in, opened their bathroom window; the other bathroom window was open. Since between the two windows there was a distance of about one meter and below

them a deep airshaft, I stepped over into the other window. I took the money, and thanked very much the neighbor's help. That was it. Sister Margaret had such great moral energy, whatever she said counted to be an order. She saved not only Jews but also communists. I could tell such things. On one occasion I took a child with papers to Fot. I was well dressed and I had also a small beard, and went with the child to the Eastern train station. I bought tickets and entered with the little girl into the compartment next to the dining facility. I asked the girl to bring me a bottle of beer. My briefcase was full with papers that could be filled out. I put on glasses and lit a cigarette. It was customary that after the train left the station a gendarme came to see the identification papers. The gendarme opened the compartment door. I took off my glasses and called to him: 'What is it, my son?' He saluted and left. When I told this to Sister Margaret she said, 'You are like a rascal!'
[266]

Tibor Wilt was sent to György Aladár Street, into the Steffanits villa in Buda, where the sisters from the motherhouse went to sleep. They went there for Christmas Eve and remained there, since the Russian army reached New Saint John's Hospital by 24 December. The sculptor was the "porter." This made it possible that in those parts of Buda that were first overrun, the artists living there

---

[266] Conversation of Dr. Pálma Szoőke, SSS, with Tibor Wild, sculptor, from a magnetofone.

could meet on 26 January 1945.[267] About the "convent" of the György Aladár Street, Etelka Dömötör wrote, "...Hiding people happened in this Way: at the Szép Ilona tram station Iván Boldizsár lived, from here the home of the Zalai Street was only a few minutes distance. Walking up on Zalai Street we reached the sisters at the Steffanits villa. When there was a danger of checking identities, those who were hidden by us, could be sent to the Boldizsar's or to the sisters."[268]

From Christmas of 1944 the villa was the place of refuge for the young women of the area. They were dressed in the sisters' uniform with veils to protect them from the sex-hungry Russian soldiers. Of the situation at the motherhouse Waldemar Langlet, second in command of the Swedish mission, wrote with impressive, beautiful words:

...I worked most often with the Sisters of Social Service. They are such Deaconesses whose superior was Margaret Slachta. I never knew a woman blessed with such intelligence, courage and heart. This manifold institution played the greatest role during those difficult times in our efforts to save people in danger. The superior, Sister Margaret, was our most faithful and most apt co-worker, who in the area of social work won for herself the greatest distinction in the entire nation. One day she called me unexpected-

---

[267] Körkép, 82. Géza Ottlik: The Other Hungary. P.484.
[268]Tekla Dömötör: Shamans in Pest-Buda and its Surroundings.1987, Budapest, p.108.

ly, 'They are here. Come, help us.' Inside a smaller room we found total turmoil; in a larger room there were pressed together weeping men, women and children. Around them were the Arrow Cross soldiers with arms - pistols, hand grenades. Only Margaret Slachta was quiet. She called Msgr. Gennaro Verolino from the Apostolic Nuncio's office, and he arrived shortly. Soon Wallenberg himself got there with the order of the Ministry of Interior stating that those with a Swedish protective letter may not be touched. Sister Margaret consoled everybody, never losing her peace of mind. Later in the evening, as so frequently at that time, there was an air raid and strikes. The saved persons held thanksgiving worship in the shelter. I embraced Sister Margaret and kissed her forehead. A lady sitting close by asked in a loud voice, 'How does it feel to kiss an angel? Because just now you kissed an angel!' Arms, looking thin from losing weight, were raised up in agreement, 'Yes, yes, she is a real angel', people shouted from all sides in a place lit poorly, with only one candle. I never experienced such a touching, festive hour. One could feel oneself in the midst of the first Christians in the catacombs.[269]

Other witnesses, Dr. Imre Magyar and his wife, told

During the years before the war I, as the doctor

---

[269] Langlet, Waldemar and Nina Langlet: <u>The Swedish Saving Activities</u>. 1944. P.87.

of the Society, was frequently in the mother-house because Sister Margaret in her caring love called me immediately when a sister had even a small illness. Meeting with her was always a deep experience; her personality was radiant. Much kindness flowed from her as she turned toward anybody. That, for me, was unforgettable! I remember well her presentations. She spoke fast, but very understandably. What she said could have been immediately printed. During summer of 1944, I saw those who were hidden, to whom Sister Margaret opened the motherhouse's doors. She sent me a message to come because she can protect us. My wife was under their protection at Jankovich place.[270] On one occasion the gendarmes had come to raid. Sister Margaret happened to be there. She told the gendarmes she would give refuge to everyone who was persecuted for things of which they are not guilty. One of the gendarmes told her, 'Keep your mouth shut!' 'I shall not shut it if someone is persecuted unjustly,' answered Sister Margaret, 'because it is a sin before God.' As much as she was refined and fragile in build, so determined was she.[271]

It belongs to truth to mention here the saving action of an episode that is not written down but happened. The author of this book visited the motherhouse during fall of 1944 and heard the fol-

---

[270] Balaton-Jankovich place: here the Christian Working Women and Working Girls had their rest-resort. Here children and young mothers' were hidden during the Nazi times.
[271] Dr. Pálma Szőke, SSS conversation with Dr. Imre Magyar and his wife in 1979. Saved on magnetofon.

lowing. A few days ago the Hungarian police surrounded the house. Everybody in it was deathly
afraid of what would happen. However, it was
strange that they did not come in, and after a few
hours they left. It became known later, a police-
chief friend of Sister Margaret came to know that
the Gestapo prepared to raid the motherhouse.
However, there was an agreement between the
German and Hungarian authorities that where one
works already, the other will not interfere. For this
reason he ordered the motherhouse to be surrounded until the German Gestapo came. When
the Gestapo arrived, seeing that the Hungarians
were there, they left, and considered the case
closed.

The summer of 1944 offered one more service opportunity to the sisters. "The unspeakable
sufferings that burdened the Jews drove them in
masses to the Church. Many perhaps hoped they
would be saved - even though Christian faith did
not mean any advantage. Others found some understanding and love. Parishes alone were unable
to cope with the overwhelming amount of work.
The sisters offered their services to organize
courses of instructions necessary before baptism.
Collaborating with the Hungarian Holy Cross Association, they organized instructions for about
10,000 persons with eighty instructors offering 160
24-hour classes.[272] Sister Margaret published a
booklet at Pentecost 1944 with the title: <u>Fire of</u>

---

[272] <u>Testvér</u>, flier, 1945, September, p. 3

Pentecost. Members of the Christian Women Corps took the booklet to the head of houses marked with the yellow star. The booklet outlined how the Ten Commandments and Christian morality are to be realized, it called for special attention to the voice of conscience; reminding persons of the responsibility that God expects from us.[273]

On the worldview front Sister Margaret offered another service. The second Vienna decision cut Transylvania into two parts. Bishop Áron Márton remained in Gyulafehérvár (Alba Julia now), Romania. The part of the Transylvanian diocese that remained in Hungary was governed through a vicar, but at times the bishop went to Kolozsvár (now Cluj-Napoca) for functions (ordinations, confirmation). On 18 March 1944 he went to Cluj-Napoca and before the people filling the Saint Michael's church he condemned the persecution of Jews that happened in Hungary. He reminded the people of the great commandment to love one's neighbors and also that we all are children of one Father. The talk of Áron Márton was duplicated in the office of the Holy Spirit Association in Budapest and made available throughout the entire country.[274] Sister Margaret founded the Holy

---

[273] "Star marked houses" were those where Jews lived outside of the ghettoes. The talk of Sister Margaret at the National Assembly 1947. IV. 16. P. 10.

[274] Uj Élet, 1946. VIII. 22.Sándor Szenes, Unfinished Past, Budapest, 1986. P.236. The complete text of the talk is found in: Lászlo Virt: Áron Márton the apostle of Conscience. Budapest. p. 107. SZTTI 1162/23.

Spirit Association.

On 27 December 1944, God responded to the 1943self-offering of Sister Sara. Based on treason, the Arrow Cross dragged her away on that day with four of those who were hidden and with Vilma Bernovits, a religious educator. According to custom of those days, without any hearing, they were shot to death. Before her execution – as one of her murderers recounted – she knelt down and made a great sign of the cross.[275] Since her abduction happened in the city under siege and the execution happened during the hours when no one was allowed be on the streets, the motherhouse was not informed of her absence until the following day. Not knowing what happened, there was hope that she might be in one of the Arrow Cross prisons. Sister Margaret went with two sisters to the City Hall, even though shootings happened very frequently. One of the sisters' asked her: "Are you not afraid?" "Yes, I am afraid, but I go anyhow with you."[276]

One could enumerate many happenings of the siege and the times of the Arrow Cross, but we shall end with the lines of Sister Margaret, "I thank God with inexpressible gratitude that many members of our Society, and among them myself, could

---

[275] Károly Hetényi Varga: Those Who Were Persecuted for Justice Budapest, 1985, p.437. Ilona Mona: The Life of Sister Sara Salkahazi.
[276] SZTTI 876. Memory of Honora Pawlik, SSS

be of help to the persecuted." [277]

---

[277] SZTTI 1109

The Only Man in Parliament

The year 1945 began while Budapest was still under siege. The last Arrow Cross raid at the motherhouse occurred on 7 January. They came for Sister Margaret, asking for Slanda Margit. The porter told no such person is here. Sister Margaret just happened to come up from the cellar. "Who are you?" asked the man. "I, too, am a sister," she replied. On the 13th fighting stopped around the motherhouse and on the 18th the entire Pest side. On the Buda side fighting lasted until 13 February.

Many tasks awaited Sister Margaret. The foremost was to know what happened to the sisters who were in Buda and in the rural areas of the country and, after that, what she could do for the betterment of the country? What was to be the role of the Society in the work of re-building? She had to make connections with the community members who found themselves again in a foreign country (Transylvania and the northern parts, now Slovakia; and the sisters abroad). Perhaps there would be possibility for public service.

At the district assembly in 1945 - recalling the events of past years when the Society had to disobey human laws to obey God's laws - Sister Margaret found it most important that in spirit the entire Society be re-founded in the sense that members strive with total consciousness to rebuild on the supernatural basis. She considered :

God's very great grace that the sisters remained free from the poison of National Socialism. Now however, they would have to fight against another poison, materialism, with total consciousness and act from a supernatural foundation. "...Divine Providence wants to give work in this new world that was born in the midst of tremors, storms and horrible events but not according the spirit of God. We hope that God will allow us to have a role in re-baptizing this pagan world."[278] Every sister made a thirty-day retreat during which they reflected on supernatural principles and values.

During the middle of March the British and American Military Missions occupied a part of the motherhouse. With this, normal life could begin. Because of their presence, necessary building material, glass for windows and sufficient food was provided. Actually so much food was provided that the sisters could open a soup kitchen, which at the time of general hunger was very significant. Through their presence, correspondence could begin with the sisters in America even though the general postal service had not begun. Messages could be sent and received through the western guests. "...Our poor motherhouse became an international center; today fifteen British pilots will arrive; there are already twenty newspaper men here. Right now the Chicago Tribune's man is here, yesterday the Chicago Sun's. The New York

---

[278] SZTTI 1148

<u>Times</u> and the <u>New Chronicle</u> people have left."[279] It is quite natural that one of the American sisters' wrote: "...There is no week when one of the American radio stations would not speak of Sister Margaret's heroic resistance and of saving the persecuted." [280] The sisters had to move out again from the motherhouse. One of the classrooms of the School of Social Work was transformed into a bedroom where ten or more sisters slept.

Margaret Slachta began in March 1945 the preparation of her return to the Parliament. She submitted the petition to the National Commission of Budapest for authorization to begin organizing the Christian Women Corps. Even though she had resisted openly the German and Arrow Cross repression her petition was denied.[281] The <u>Voice of the Spirit</u> was not allowed to appear either - only some leaflets substituting for it. In 1928 Sister Margaret had expressed why and how much it is necessary to embrace public responsibility.

> ...It is a grave mistake that people of faith spend all their efforts on those who got shipwrecked in life. We must seek out the source of misery and illness. The source is those who hold in their hands power, evolution and revolution, and most of all control over bread for sustenance -

---

[279] SZTTI11∠9/9

[280] SZTTI 667/f.p. 6.

[281] Of the possibilities of creating a party see: The interrupted era of reform. From the flyers that were printed to substitute the <u>Voice of the Spirit</u>.

those who are in the position to satisfy human needs. There, unfortunately, are no people of faith who could offer life. The Church teaches that we are to work against the sources of problems. We say at this point of the development in society, 'Those who stand in the center, who hold power to legislate, to execute laws, control money, found enterprises, build capital and culture, all who hold the ability to create well-being are the greatest enemies of the church and religion.' We must fight in that forum for the millions whom they will subject to misery of both body and soul. However, we cannot oppose the sword with a stick, a cannon, or with pitchers of water. If the enemy has a press, we too need to have a press; if they have political power, it is necessary that we have political power. There are some who use their power for evil; we must use it for good, because we serve the earthly and eternal good of people.[282]

In 1945 Sister Margaret emphasized that a party that names itself Christian, and acts as a Christian, must be clear that faith embraces and affects the entire life; faith must transfuse all dimensions of life; otherwise the only true value on earth, the soul's vocation to eternal life, will suffer loss.[283]

This can be manifested in public life when God's will for moral order is always taken into consideration; that before any laws, orders or

---

[282] Sister Margaret's Teaching on 19 February 1928.
[283] Uj Elet, Prague, 1932. Vol. 11. P.412

arrangements can be made, they must be measured against the ten commandments of God, because that summarizes God's will regarding the moral order. From this follows the recognition of human rights, of which the principles of law, legal security and lawful order are created. Besides human values it must protect eternal values. It must assure the collaboration of Church and State. It must allow the specific values of each social class. It must protect the honor of women and family life, because these protect the health of the nation and future generations. The condition of harmony among the nations is the recognition of small nations' God given purpose. The degree of values must be considered in a right manner: first is God; the second is human beings who carry eternal value and only after that come material goods.[284]

...Though in political life we meet with so much falsehood and oppression, we may not draw back; rather we must participate in it so that goodwill may become victorious.[285]

After the difficult years of war and dangerous efforts to save people, everybody was hoping with great desire for peace and democracy - in a noble sense, governance by the people. They hoped to have a government created by vote that would express the will of the people. Instead, a

---

[284] The Christian Women Corps sends a message: Send women representatives into the Parliament. Leaflet, 1945 October.
[285] Voice of the Spirit, leaflet 1945. IX. 10. P. 2.

dictatorship by the Soviet Union was forced, step-by-step, upon the people. The statements of the victorious great powers, but primarily of President Roosevelt were taken seriously by the entire nation. In those statements the four spoke of freedom, or the rights of self-determination of nations; of forms of governments and freedom to choose the form of government; of free contribution to sources of resources, and finally a peaceful, free life without oppressive poverty.[286]

They tried to understand the mood of the nation by first – against usual customs – to hold elections of the municipal authorities in Budapest, and only afterward hold the national elections. Since neither the Independent Democratic People's Party nor the Christian Women Corps received permission to run, the Independent Small Landowner's Party won 22 seats. The municipal election was held on 7 October 1945. Margaret Slachta published two leaflets for this occasion.[287] The first leaflet became the center of attack, because she dared to raise her voice on behalf of the many who were detained and held in custody. The Világosság 16 September issue stated: "Is this the Voice of the Spirit? – No! This is the shocking voice of the Arrow Cross and the reactionaries!" According to their statement the leaflet attacked paragraph-by-paragraph those arrangements that democracy had brought to control resistance and un-

---

[286] The Interrupted Era of Reform, p. 281.
[287] Voice of the Spirit, IX 10, 1945;

ravel the Arrow Cross. The newspaper summarized the content of the flier. The leaflet of 7 October "The Editor's Message" responded to the paper.[288] This is the text written to the <u>Világosság</u>: "I receive with gratitude your quote from the <u>Voice of the Spirit</u>, because those who read it can see, whether they proclaim 'agitations against democracy into ears without suspicion or not.' " The elections resulted in 51% for Independent Small Landowners Party. Margaret Slachta and Natalie Palágyi were elected in the city government together with two members of the Christian Women Corps, Margaret Krén and Elizabeth Pusztaszeri.

For the National election three flyers were published. Among them was "The Christian Women Corps sends a Message: Send women representatives into the Parliament!" It enumerated in great detail the program for election and announced that the Women Corps would run under the Citizen's Democratic Party (PDP). The parties joined in an independent front that "those who decide the future of the nation want to create a common list"; but this did not happen because of the resistance of the PDP. If they would have accepted this plan, elections would not have been needed; but the parties would have made the decision among them in what proportion the mandates would be divided. However, the elections were held and so the nation's thinking and its general

---

[288] <u>Voice of the Spirit,</u> X. 7, 1945.

desire was manifested.[289] It got manifested because the Small Landowner's Party won with 57%. On 27 October another attack appeared in the newspaper, Haladás, from the pen of Béla Zsold. He recognized that "the work of its human-friendliness and heroism is mentioned by everybody with reverence but distinction is to be made between human and political gratitude. All this does not give Margaret Slachta the right to again have a role in public life." The same is emphasized by one reader of Haladas, whose letter is published on 3 November: "Regardless what merits she gained in the past for her loving behavior, the nomination to the Parliament of the good-hearted Margaret Slachta is an excellent trick. The Christian course should not have a role again." It is a sad human shortsightedness to think of the Christian course in such a way of one who participated for only two years in the work of the National Assembly; and was so human-friendly as to raise her voice on behalf of communists held, at that time, in custody; (1920-22), and whom the leading politicians prevented in 1931 from having a role in public life.

In a letter dated on 6 November, Sister Margaret wrote: "We are after the elections. On account of the very short time and the lack of preparation we gained in Pest only two man-

---

[289] The message of the Christian Women Corps, leaflet, p.3.

dates."[290] Truly there was only one month between the two elections and compared to the other parties, Sister Margaret did not have the financial resources for her campaign. Yet she was glad to be able to enter the Parliament again. But before that she went through a serious illness. Shortly after the elections, one night she became very ill and it took several hours before a doctor could be reached. On 14 November she was taken to the Fasor Hospital where Doctor Ádám performed surgery on a stomach stricture. She continued to attend to her community tasks from her bed. On 17 November she wrote a letter to Los Angeles. In it she told that through the Catholic Women Association they plan a census in the capital city. In the statistical papers she wrote, "I tried for hours to figure out with the greatest care the name of each column, not I alone but in conversations with the best statisticians. It happened that both of us forgot to insert the "natural death" column, since this is no longer common; everybody falls victim to some tragedy, or violence or war."[291] She left the hospital on 5 December 1945 but spent a long time recovering. In 1945 she was also called as a witness in a lawsuit of the Peoples' Court. This

---

[290] On the party list of the PDP Sister Margaret won and on the list of the Small Landowner's Party Sister Marianne (Anna) Veres received a mandate, but only until March 12. On that date the presiding council of the Small Landowner's Party excluded Sister Margaret together with 20 representatives from the party. Sister Marianne continued as an Independent until 1947.

[291] SZTTI 1132/29.

incident served as a cause of attack according to the whim of authorities. In the 9 July 1985 issue of the periodical, Life and Literature, Béla Lévai wrote with a title: "Summoning a Phantom." In it he added his own recollection to the report of Zsuzsa Thúry "Sad Memories of the Past." In her article she spoke of her participation in judicial processes of war criminals as the editor of the New Word. She recalled the process of the interrogation of Peter Hain and on the same subject that of Koltai-Kundicz. The latter was accused as a cruel man who "tormented hundreds of political prisoners." After a break "a small old woman asks if she may be permitted to give that man some lunch. She is none other than Margaret Slachta the representative." The author of the article wanted to characterize Margaret Slachta as a friend of the Arrow Cross and someone sympathetic to the Nazis; that Margaret Slachta "who among those religious who participated were the Sisters of Social Service outstanding in leading the spiritual battle against Nazism."[292] It is surprising how much was not written down by Bela Levai. He should also have written that Margaret was called by the counsel of defense as a witness - like the brother of Zsuzsa Thury, who testified that Mihály Borsai advised her in time to avoid the press and cameras. The lady editor can thank that she did not face the fate of the photographers who were identified as Jewish. No one would think of accusing Zsuzsa Thúry of protecting the Arrow Cross. Moreover from the testimony of

---

[292] The History of 1944. History Yearbook, 1984. P. 51-52.

Margaret Slachta it became clear that Koltay-Kundicz broke into the motherhouse at Thököly Street during the winter of 1944, where there were hidden approximately thousand Jewish persons and others who were sought by the police. She gave testimony with great courage during those trying times.[293] With the same courage and firmness she faced Koltay-Kundicz, who in the end had to leave without taking anybody captive.[294] He only asked Margaret Slachta to stop this life-saving activity. Sister Margaret responded: "Look, we gave everything to God, if now we do not help other human beings, we would gravely offend God." Surprisingly, he left and never returned. Sister Margaret went to the hearing to witness to his good deed - he did not take anybody from the motherhouse even though he could have done so. To make such a testimony also required courage, because those present at the hearing, waiting for the outcome, derided her as a witness for the defense, regardless that she fought for the rights of the persecuted since 1938, and risked the life of the entire Society for them in 1944. [...]

Margaret Slachta practiced love not only in easy understandable ways; she practiced love in ways hard to understand, and even, for some, a scandalizing Christ-like love for the enemy.

---

[293] Zsuzsa Thury: "The Sad Memories of the Past, 3 Hearings at People's Court" in Life and Literature, 1985 VI. 28.p.3.
[294] See: The Life of Margaret Slachta. Chapter VIII. p.131

On account of her stomach surgery Sister Margaret could not begin her regular work in the Parliament until 1946. Since the Small Landowners Party was in majority - we must learn about the relationship of Representative Slachta and that party. Sister Margaret's political vision in 1945 was still similar to that party but, by the time of elections in November, their ways parted. In January of 1946 her vision became quite contrary. Sister Margaret's opinion was that before and during elections it was not communicated to the citizens that this Parliament planned to change the form of the state.[295] Changing the form of the state is the business of the entire population and it must be decided by the vote of the people. This vote, she believed, should be postponed until after the peace-treaty was signed. In the discussions in Paris there would be very strong enemies and therefore all energies should be dedicated to the preparations of the treaty. However, in the debates in the Parliament, no one sided with her opinion - even those from the Small Landowners Party. The vision, worldview and political pluralism of that party guided them in their stance of political questions. A very strong opposition happened in regard of changing the state into a Republic. A part of the Small Landowner's representatives held that the decision be made by vote of the citizens

---

[295] See :Sister Margaret Slachta: Christian Public Life: "Changing the Nation's Constitutional Law." Talk given in the Parliament January 31, 1946, From the Minutes of the National Assembly, 1945 I. Vol.1945, Nov.-1946 May 9.

only after the country achieved a total independence.[296] This was not only announced by those representatives but also supported by actions. Proof of this is found in her correspondence from emigration. On 16 February 1950 she wrote to István Kray: "It is shocking that when Bálint Czupy was able to collect 160 signatures in favor of kingdom as a state form, that the party with a 51% majority remained silent (during the debate in the Parliament." *(Sister Margaret erred, the party had 57% majority.)* István Kray responded on 13 March: "...The signatures against republic as a state form were collected not by Béla Czupy, but by Lajos Hajdu Németh. They stopped short from the last consequences because the group of Ortutay rejected the initiative and the signers remained in minority. Their initiative was voted against. The representatives thought in such circumstances that it is better to remain in the party for later actions and remain in majority against the People's Front."[297] Sister Margaret knew of this decision because on 31 January in the debate of the law-proposal she said, "The vote based on party-decision makes doubtful the validity of the law because, in this case, voting was not made freely." On 1 February 1946 for the protection of the law that was created with but one opposing, a new law proposal was discussed in the Parliament, "On the Protection of the Democratic state

---

[296] The Interrupted Reform era. Rome, 199990, p. 290.
[297] SZTTI 1204/11c.

and the Republic's Criminal Law."[298] Unfortunately it happened again that nobody except Margaret Slachta raised a voice against it during the detailed discussions. Based on this, a law made it legal to file proceedings against those with convictions different from that of the system (e.g. Mindszenty, etc.) and to destroy the Small Landowners' Party. By June 1947 the party existed in name only.[299] Sister Margaret said in a trusted circle, "...I met in Sopron...with a representative of the Small Landowners party, who imbibed some alcohol and gave an expression more than usual of what was in his heart, while he held fast my hand and kindly said: 'You always cause us shame in the Parliament.' "[300]

Sister Margaret found voice with democratic representatives. On 6 December 1946, "Today I spoke with a social democratic representative and, I must say, it seems there are more and more threads developing among them with me..." The Diary of the National Assembly contains her words, "I owe my respect to Anna Kéthly, president of the House, and would leave with a feeling of loss if I were not allowed to say what I wanted to express during my intervention, that not only the respected left, but the right values her equally. To

---

[298] See: Margaret Slachta's: Christian Public Life, "Protecting the Democratic State and the Republic's Criminal Law." Talk given in the Parliament 12 March 1946. P.27.
[299] See: Margaret Slachta and the Small Landowner's Party. Weekly Newspaper, 1992 III. 13
[300] Teaching on 12 March 1947. P. 4

this I want to add only - that on one occasion - Count Albert Apponyi gave as high an appreciation regarding her function as we hold for her."[301] Even among the communist representatives there were some who were kindly toward her; one even introduced his wife to her and took leave from her saying, "Look, even among the communists some are good."

Some of the words of Mihály Károlyi are missing from the Hungarian edition of the assembly diary. It reads: "Even though Anna Kéthly resigned from her office in the Social Democratic party at the time of the fusion of the working parties, she still remained in the country. Women, as it frequently happens, act with greater courage than men." In the English edition, however, the foot note reads as follows: "The second exceptionally courageous woman was Margaret Slachta, the only one in the Parliament who in 1946 opposed the change of Constitutional law declaring the country as a Republic. During the persecution of Hitler she saved many Jews. Since she was a fervent Catholic and a conservative, she opposed the new Hungarian governance after the end of war. [...] She was elected into the new Parliament. After one session in the Parliament, I expressed my reverence for her courageous stance. Being close to her, sitting below her row of seats, I knew that, in the past, she was one of my most fierce enemies. She was very surprised but, seemingly,

---

[301] Diary of the National Assembly, 1946 Viii. 24, vol.435

she was glad for it. Because of her outspoken interventions her popularity was very, very low in
New Hungary and her situation became more and
more uncertain."[302]

We could see that Margaret Slachta's first
service in the Parliament was dedicated to social
issues. In 1945 the situation changed completely.
The state, at least in theory, embraced the social
program. Most issues were around principles.
Sister Margaret stood on the basis of Christian,
Gospel principles: "I judge everything from the
viewpoint of eternal goals and the value of souls.
Whatever destroys, impoverishes and ultimately
causes unhappiness for human beings. The tragedy of present times is that unfortunately human
beings do not think. They remain on the surface of
existence, they do not even guess that the solution
of humanity's grave problems lie in the living laws
at the depths of existence and in their faithful realization of them."[303] She expressed these principles
in a leaflet published on 10 September 1945
where she wrote of her program; and in her interventions she attempted to realize them. Therefore
from a practical point of view and humanly speaking the three years in the Parliament (November
1945 - June 1948) cannot be called successful.
Her interventions met not only with opposition, but
also with slander and mud throwing. The attacks

---

[302] Memoirs of Michael Károlyi. Faith without Illusion. First
published in London, J. Cape, 1956 p.383.
[303] Movie, Theatre, Literature, 1943.IV, 16.

directed against her distorted the view of her personality and her principles. Only her faith and her sense of mission upheld her. Margaret Slachta had a living faith that directed public service. Her consistent fidelity to principles was not understood even by some of those who felt for her. She wrote: "Even the best seed can not bring forth a plant if it does not have the proper soil into which to spread its roots and from which it could draw life. This is how we are with the most important reforms, with the most burning questions. They are only seeds; their soil is the understanding that is present in society." [304] Neither then nor since was the necessary soil created for the ideas she represented in the Parliament. She was conscious of this when she said in the community of sisters: "I would not be discouraged if I meet with no understanding. I only desire to fulfill what I feel in my soul to be my responsibility. I pray constantly that God help me to accomplish my mission! It does not bother me what happens outside if I do what my soul says. My job is to work; blessing it is God's."[305] She admitted publicly: "I am not a politician. All my political knowledge is the Ten Commandments, but I know that therein resides the secret of the possibility for human well-being and happiness. It may happen that I shall not live long enough to see the realization of these truths, but the solutions are in these: principles of law, security based on law, and

---

[304] Hungarian Woman, 1921/5.
[305] Her teaching 1947. III. 12.

law and order." [306] The security of these she found only by upholding the political system inherited from Saint Stephen. For this reason she raised her voice against the constitutional law of a republic. The issue was not kingdom as such; it was what is said these days as being European. She spoke in the name of those who wanted to retain the tradition of Saint Stephan. [307]

"Margaret Slachta was hardly able to say her intervention. Each of her sentences was interrupted with rude, tasteless words. Those who thought of themselves as democrats could not bear the only opposing voice. The way this gray-haired, fragile women stood in the fire of attacks, it could not be mistaken who represents human rights and freedom of speech," wrote the Magyar Nemzet forty years later. [308] The contemporary press, according to its political standing, either debased her or only quoted from her intervention without comment. Hungarians in America received information about this or that other intervention of Margaret Slachta a long year later on the pages of Krónika. It introduced its information with these words: "From these quotes our readers can recognize that in the year of 1946 Margaret Slachta was the most courageous, most outspoken, most Hungarian member of the National

---

[306] Sister, 1947/1. P.8. Sister Margaret's talk on January 6, 1947.
[307] Diary of the National Assembly, 1946, January 31. See also: Margaret Slachta: Christian Public Life, p.19.
[308] Magyar Nemzet, 1996, II. 1. p. 10.

Assembly."[309]

For the protection of the now established republic in Hungary, a new law was introduced on 12 March 1946. During the debate Margaret Slachta remarked, "...a law is created only when some need justifies it. It is therefore not clear to me why is it necessary to decree so many punishments of death and life-long imprisonment when they, according to statements made at the time of creating the previous law, did not exist."[310] Against the ruling party, (Small Landowners) the opposition, (Social Democrats, communists), she states that the law is not necessary, because it can lead to abuse. After the law was adopted, it was discussed in the National Assembly that all regulations may be made by the authority of the central government. She dared to state that those kinds of regulations were practically always abuses. For example: rescinding the right of counties and cities to self-government; or giving permission for less preparation of teachers, and even of doctors! From such regulations dilettantism, lack of professional preparation follows, and therefore she cannot vote in favor of these.[311]

During the debate of the nation's budget [312]

---

[309] Krónika, Amaricn -Hungarian Newspaper, 1947.V. 15.
[310] Diary of the National Assembly, 1946, III. 12. Kronika, 1947. V. 15
[311] See: Marçaret Slachta's Christian Public Life, p. 27.
[312] See: Margaret Slachta's Christian Public Life: "Budget, Private Property, Economic Development." P. 70.

she mentioned the general lack of trust; the government does not keep its word, it hides from the public what it plans to do with their small private properties; it does not stand on ethical basis toward the weak and abuses possibilities. In this talk she mentioned the January 1947 "uncovered" treason of the Small Landowners Party: everybody has a conviction, if the authority does not give a way for it to be expressed, it will start organizing in the underground. Therefore she proposed in February 1947 amendment of the law passed in 1946, that bore signs of impatience, oppression and fear, asking that it be re-worked by the National Assembly in the spirit of democracy and freedom. "... since history has existed, we see that oppression is possible for so long, but it never results in strengthening the power of those in authority." When she said this the Diary of the National Assembly reported: "Disturbance on the side of the communist party and a representative of the Small Landowners Party remarked: 'They cannot stand Margaret Slachta.' After that another of that party said: 'All together the other side has less value than she alone.' " During the debate of the Justice Portfolio of the National Budget,[313] she spoke on behalf of the independence of the judicial system. "A representative of truth and justice may not be a member of a party; otherwise it will not represent truth and justice but the interest of the party. Unseen truths, silent as they are, are without com-

---

[313] Margaret Slachta's Christian Public Life, "Justice Portfolio of the National Budget," p. 76

promise and implacable; but if they are followed, they are royally generous with their blessings."[314]

During the time of the deportations of German speaking persons living in Hungary she raised her voice on behalf of Románd village. [315] The German speaking, economically comfortable village was also on the list for deportation, even though they stood united against national socialism during the Nazi period. The Volksbundkalender remarked, "...with Románd we cannot do anything." Sister Margaret asked the authorities not to cause hopelessness among the minorities who are faithful to the nation. Her intervention was successful. The population of the village was not deported.[316]

During the debate on principles of law, freedom under law and law and order, Margaret Slachta spoke a second time when they discussed the right to vote. She pointed out that it is unlawful, anti-democratic and whimsy. "It creates protective walls around those in power by excluding several categories of persons from voting. The 6th paragraph of the law contradicts those who bring the law, implying that the citizens of the country want it that way. Otherwise it would not be necessary to exclude so many from voting. It is really

---

[314] Diary of the National Assembly, 1947, II. 25.
[315] See: Margaret Slachta's Christian Public Life: "Smaller Issues", p. 94.
[316] Diary of National Assembly, 1947. VI. 25

not good to shout out our weaknesses before the world..."[317]

The other issue she represented was to secure the collaboration of Church and State; it appears in nearly in all of her talks. She spoke of it during the debate to change the constitution. "...The form of state as a kingdom was based on a deeply religious vision...whoever bears authority, if carried by religious convictions and acts with responsibility before God, will hold authority differently than one who, without faith, sees the citizens only as instruments for power."

In 1946 she urged the restoration of diplomacy with the Vatican. "We are the orphan state of this earth; we cannot count on the assistance of our neighbors or any other royalty; but the Holy See stood by us until the last minute of the war and afterward helped us with soup kitchens, activities of charity and diplomatic steps. For this reason we must do everything to restore the diplomatic relationship." During the debate of the budget in 1947 she emphasized the cultural and public education portfolio that had the vocation to serve the nation's worldview, its ethics and spirituality. After several historical examples she referred to Hitlerism that brought to fruition the wild idea that there exist no dependence upon religion for morality. "It allowed that people of faith pray on Sunday but it was a great offence if, in the national

---

[317] Diary of the National Assembly, 1947, VI. 23.

arena, they wanted to realize what morality taught." She wanted to save the left from doing this. "It is not in the interest of the state that schools prepare such citizens from whom the strength flowing from religious education is missing. If moral strength and assets that can be developed through religious instructions are missing in human souls, then God save us from all that will happen in this frequently undermined, bankrupt nation."[318] Today we can add: Unfortunately this happened.

On 16 April 1947 Margaret Slachta gave her talk in the Parliament about the value of faith instruction. With this, she wanted to prevent the bill making religious instructions contingent upon special request.[319] She based her argument on the fact that people with religion - Catholics and Protestants - not only rejected but also acted against the Nazi ideology. She enumerated, in great detail, communication from Pope Pius XII to Apostolic Nuncio Angelo Rotta, who stood by the persecuted religious organizations and persons under threat of being killed. At this point, one of the independent representatives, Gyorgy Parragi, spoke out with a loud voice, "The only man in the Parliament!"[320]

She spoke up on behalf of rights of Hungar-

---

[318] Diary of the National Assembly, 1946. VIII. 23.
[319] See: Margaret Slachta's Christian Public Life, p. 128.
[320] Diary of the Nationa Assembly, 1947, June 16.

ians who left and could not return and for the rights of small nations.[321] In July 1946 Ferenc Nagy gave a report of his trip abroad on behalf of the peace-treaty. During the debate of this issue Margaret Slachta accused the peace-delegation that they went unprepared. Moreover she found fault in the fact that the Assembly did not get any information about the preparation. Worse than that, the documents that proved Hungary's responsibility for the war, as much less than the West, were left in the Ministry of Foreign Affairs. They should have been translated and submitted in advance to the competent authorities. She mentioned the 1936 British lower house talk of Lloyd George, who was one of those creating the peace-treaty in Trianon. He stated, "The treaty at Versailles is unjust. I must admit with sadness that we decided to give parts of Hungary to Czechoslovakia." Sister Margaret reported that the Christian Women Corp, under her leadership, submitted a memorandum to the United Nation asking that the peace-treaty debate be held by the principles expressed in the Charter of San Francisco.[322] "If the Charter works only with big slogans but does not act to make its aims a reality, our trust will die completely." At this point, Jeno Nemethy acclaimed in the assembly, "The only man in the Parliament!" Margaret Slachta modestly responded, "Thanks be to God, there are more of them."[323]

---

[321] See: <u>Margaret Slachta's Christian Public Life</u>. P. 122.
[322] The <u>Constitution of the United Nations</u> May, 1945.
[323] <u>Diary of the National Assembly</u> 1946, VII. 30.

The National Assembly discussed on 5 February 1947 the bill proposing authorization for the President of the Republic to ratify the peace-treaty. Margaret Slachta was the only speaker on the issue. She understood why the parties did not choose to speak to the issue. What could they say now? "Perhaps they could say that one needs preparation, skills and professional knowledge for creating laws, governing a nation or asking how a country that was dismembered into sixteen counties will be able to pay $2,000 million as restitution." "A population 600,000 depressed Hungarians who were annexed to Czechoslovakia[324] accompanied those who went to the treaty signing. They look at the bridge on the Hungarian side of the Danube to Bratislava also in Czechoslovak possession. The Western Carpathian Mountains will follow silently the delegation, from where cleansing of Hungarian nationals happened, of which no word was spoken. Weeping will follow them from Transylvania, the totally Hungarian speaking Nagyvárad, from Szatmár, from the Southern part of Hungary and Burgenland."[325]

Margaret Slachta spoke of the peace-treaty for the last time on 27 July 1947, after the national tragedy. It was a double tragedy because of the

---

[324] In addition 1.704.851 to Romania; 563.545 to Yugoslavia, and 64.646 to Austria. (Translator's note based on a contemporary map.)
[325] Diary of the National Assembly, 1947. II. 5.

terrible losses, but also because this treaty, contrary to that of Trianon (1921), did not guarantee the protection of minorities. She asked: "let us place on the agenda the question: to what degree are the government and the parties responsible for diverting the Hungarian nation away from its historical traditions, rejecting the basis of the nation's life inherited from Saint Stephan, and placing it on a materialistic foundation?" The presider interrupted, "Please, end your intervention! Do not abuse the patience of the National Assembly." Margaret continued: "...closing the chapter of our nation's third great tragedy...(sounding of the alarm bell). Presider, "I rebuke representative Margaret Slachta." (Alarm bell) Margaret Slachta, "Make the only honorable step toward the development of a better world." Presider, "I rebuke my colleague representative a second time. Please sit down." (Alarm bell) [326]

The protection of women's honor, family life and the nations' morality were Margaret Slachta's most favored ideas and perhaps the most out of sync with the times. Is it permissible at the door of the 21st century to give voice to such out of date thoughts? Yes, the one who gave a voice to such ideas, wanted to solve the greatest concerns of the century, of humanity and of Hungary - to give the mother back to the family. In the Parliament when the legislative bill Admission of Women to Higher Education and Universities was discussed, Marga-

---

[326] Diary of the National Assembly, 1947, VI. 27

ret Slachta asked the ministry to hinder the development of the negative impacts of this "very welcome law, namely that women's vocation in the family be taken into consideration, that she be the mother, the care-giver, educator of future generations. For this reason she talked again to introduce a system of family wage. She was afraid that women would embrace the possibility that all professions were open to them and would make use of this not out of vocation or because they were attracted to that specific work, but out of necessity, because it would not be possible to survive on one income. For this reason, she argued, it is in the interest of future generations, and of men themselves, that women should not become the breadwinner. It is desirable that men have enough income to support the entire family and women have a choice whether they want to remain in the family or embrace a job.[327]

She emphasized again the protection of children, women and family when the bill, Rights of Children Born Out-of-Wedlock, was discussed. She was opposed to the proposal, not to cause more suffering, but to protect the unity of the family. [...] According to the draft the aim of the law was to end the distinction between children born of legal marriage and those out-of-wedlock. Instead of the draft she proposed the following text: "The aim of this law is to ensure the legal standing of

---

[327] Diary of the National Assembly, 1946,VIII. 29. See: Margaret Slachta's Christian Public Life, p. 58.

the child born out-of-wedlock, together with up-holding the family as the basic unit that builds up the nation." She rejected vehemently the part of the law that said if the natural father could not be found, a male member of the mother's family would be selected to give a name to the child. That meant, false data would be inscribed official-ly; words would lose their believability. Everybody could choose whether to fulfill a promise or not, the truth told or not. At this point the presider silenced her because she did not stay with the subject. During the detailed discussion of the law she inter-vened several more times, here is one of her statements: "We may not tire in protesting against the deprivation of spirituality in our people, when the nation is left in misery, pillaged, and mutilated, by suggesting they free themselves from the voice of conscience, because they are sinless, their will is not free, and because being in love is so strong a passion it is impossible to resist it."[328]

There was only one instance when Marga-ret Slachta was successful. It was when she dealt with a book that was published under the approval of the Ministry of Information instructing 8-14 year old children how to abuse their body, including how to recognize symptoms of sexual illness. The book was written by Dr. Magda Ligati. "There have been and will be times in the future that porno-graphic books will be published, but to distribute it in schools and by a leading member of the ministry

---

[328] Diary of the National Assembly, 1946, XII.3-4.

with the promotion by the ministry, I believe there is no example. I cannot even imagine that a government exists on this earth that would embrace the role to murder its nation." She made a proposal for decision, that the House order the government to immediately recall the book of Dr. Ligeti and to begin without delay preparation for creating regulations regarding pornographic books. The House voted 62 to 43 in approval of the proposal. [329]

Against that book it was not only Margaret Slachta who spoke. The author of the book herself quoted one of her doctor colleagues who wrote in a medical journal: "It is a destructive, oppressive, trivial, irresponsible writing." One of the director's of a famous girls' gymnasium expressed, "I strongly reject this book and the solution it suggests on dealing with this delicate issue, because it spreads confusion and causes destruction in the souls of children." Magyar Nemzet on 31 December 1968 carried an article about the first book on sexual information in Hungary. In it, Dr. Ligeti said to the author of the article, "Margaret Slachta who became famous in her bigoted, false holiness, and prejudiced religiosity in the National Assembly among other things said the following, 'The author of such a book should be hanged!' " The editor of the newspaper article chose the following lead for the article: "In 1968 it was still possible to destroy ethical assets of others without consequences."

---

[329] Diary of the National Assembly, 1947, VII. 24.

One can question the professional responsibility of the editor, since he did not look into the <u>Diary of the National Assembly</u> whether the sentence is in it or not. Naturally he did not find it, because it was never said.

In 1947 new elections were announced. The National Committee allowed the following new parties to run: The Democratic People's Party (DNP), Hungarian Independent Party (MFP), Hungarian Democratic Party (MDP), Christian Women Corps (KNT) and the Catholic Peoples' Party, with the aim of preventing formation of an opposing coalition.[330] The infamous election, called Blue Paper, was held on 31 August. The KNT ran in the counties: Fejér-Komárom-Esztergom, Jász Nagykun-Szolnok, in the county of Pest and entire Budapest. The KNT received 69,536 votes in the above areas, in the area west of Danube it received 16% of votes, 57, and so in the new Parliament it was awarded four representatives: Dr. Joseph Groth, Mihály Kisházi, Margaret Slachta and Anna Veres (Sr. Mariann). Sándor Balogh remarked that the seemingly great number of the opposition (Coalition 274, opposition 140) was not united, actually only the MFP and KNT proved to be strong opposition.[331]

---

[330] Sándor Balogh: <u>Together or Alone</u>. = History, 1985/5-6, p.63 Zoltan Vas: About ourselves at that time, II. Budapest, 1982
[331] Sándor Balogh: <u>Together or Alone</u>... p. 64

Before the election of August 1947 the communist party announced the Three-Year Plan that "demanded the control of bourgeoisie and a new nationalization of properties." In the new Parliament on 28 October they debated a bill extending authorization of the government to create regulations and authorization to lead the nations' economic issues.[332] Sister Margaret spoke for protection of human rights. "The three-year plan places the measure of achievement too high, and still we must take it as natural if, among the many components, some are left out. For this reason we oppose calling it 'sabotage' if the plan's aim cannot be realized. The true aim of the three-year plan is political, it is not economic; in reality this plan means to greatly diminish citizens' freedom, their initiative, creation of enterprises, and minimize their sense of responsibility. Moreover for the sake of reaching the aim, the multiplication of bureaucracy causes concern. The basic idea of the three-year plan is that the most important dimension of production is the working human being. That means human beings are the means for production. The government wants to introduce the economy of workers, and this will lead to the economization of workers' energy." She started to talk about the fact that in the schools a new textbook was introduced that taught Darwinism. Margaret Slachta objected to considering human beings only as entities developed from animals.

---

[332] See: Margaret Slachta's Christian Public Life: "Negative Consequences of Economic Planning". p. 109.

"Those great burdens that oblige us to pay restitution contain many things, and these can be explained in different ways. If human beings are only material goods, will we perhaps be obliged to pay restitution with human beings?" The opposition applauded her with a loud: "Yes, yes" - on the side of the communist party negative noise. The presider chided the speaker, who voted against the proposal.[333]

On the following day the presider, Anna Kethly, announced in the Parliament, "Margaret Slachta, my representative colleague, has offended the honor of the nation and the interests of its foreign affairs. I propose to the Parliament to send her to the Committee of Immunity." On 30 October the decision of the Committee of Immunity was made and reported it to the Parliament. When they began to debate this question, the opposition stood up and left. Istvan Kossa, a communist representative remarked loudly, "Their action is an act of identification with the issue. They, too, affirm the case."[334] The Committee of Immunity stated her action and declared that her words hurt the nation's external affairs; "it seriously offends primarily Jugoslavia and the Soviet Union, even though

---

[333] Diary of the National Assembly, 1947. X. 28. During that time a rumor went around the Soviet Union demands human beings as restitution.

[334] Margaret Slachta's letter to Imre Kovács, 1950, X. 28, representative of the People's Party "...during my first expulsion you organized a beautiful protest in my behalf. The original letter is found in the archives of SSSA.

334

great gratitude is owed to these nations. Her statements are more destructive at a time when this government makes great efforts to lead the nation from its isolation after the war. On account of these offenses Margaret Slachta is excluded from this Parliament for sixty days."[335] The newspapers reported these happenings according to their party's view. Magyar Nemzet wrote, "The committee, as obliged, scolds Margaret Slachta because she offended, but speaking of a clerical reaction is an exaggeration." The paper reminded the readers of Margaret Slachta and the gray sisters' truly Christian and courageous actions during the terrible years of 1944 and found it sad that the judges of her talk are some who perhaps discerned with insufficient reflection whether it is right to express their opinion. It condemned one leading politician of the Small Landowner's Party, who sharply criticized Margaret Slachta's talk, but did not sign his name.[336]

What was Margaret Slachta's opinion of the case? On 29 October she spoke to the community of sisters.

I desire to speak with you tonight because I

---

[335] Diary of the National Assembly, 1947, X. 30. Magyar Nemzet X. 31 issue one can read Sándor Zold communist representative's talk: "Margaret Slachta is a common chatterer, a Pharisee, a slanderer who only is the medium of those who in the Parliament applaud those who slander the Soviet Union."
[336] Magyar Nemzet, 1947, X. 30., p. 3

know you worry about me. Unfortunately one cannot be entirely emotion free from the impact of happenings. However, if we fix our gaze firmly on the Lord, our nerves become quiet. We come to realize that God knows every happening that will befall us. Our good God does not sit far above the stars on his throne; our heavenly Father is present everywhere. We journey on our life's path holding his hand. Whoever stands on the place where God has placed her knows for certain that her vocation is there, on the very same spot, and finds herself to be secure there. She experiences how God gives her help. We may not think nor say, 'How terrible it would be to have to appear before the Commission on Political Immunity!' Whoever is in the place where God has assigned her to be, will consider the risks, the sufferings and trials related to her service differently than those who were not sent by God to be there. Do not therefore worry; nervousness does not help anything. Rather it will make things worse.

We, and each of us personally, have our specific mission. Only God knows in what form that specific mission will be manifested through each of us. Some are missions of great importance, highly acclaimed and admired. A personal mission may send me to but one person. My task may be very small; it may be one of very great importance and with a far-reaching impact. We may find our task to be easy, without any danger; but if God has given us a mission that by its nature is dangerous and burdensome, let us always remember: ours is the task to work; blessing it is God's. The outcome of the task or responsibility will be what God desires, how God arranges, and how God realizes. One needs to calm down one's natural anxiety with faith, and to remember, that in the given moment we shall have at our disposal all the graces necessary for the realization of the task. With this conviction difficult things will become easy, and self-evident. Grace from within will bring balance, fortify, anoint, and cause peace to dwell in the soul. Knowing that you are not worrying disproportionately for me will bring me great peace. I know you are accompanying me with love and prayers and are supporting me with your compassion. I know you will protect and nourish peace and good will, fidelity and union of spirit, and will preserve true sisterly love for each other. If you are trying to transcend whatever causes loss of peace, if you offer up difficulties that surround us - you will help and support me with your sacrifices. Regardless what the outcome of tomorrow's verdict, *let us understand and receive it in a supernatural manner.* [337]

With the expulsion her compensation for work was lost. She asked the Economic Committee to give benefit to those whom she helped so far. Her petition was rejected. Members of the Parliament continued to be outraged. The communist representatives expressed their criticism on 5, 12, and 18 November. In January 1948 the two months expulsion ended. "Margaret Slachta participated again in the session of the Parliament,"

---

[337] <u>Testver</u>, 1947, November.

wrote Magyar Nemzet on 9 January. "Her personality is very interesting and colorful in the Hungarian Parliament. Her political stance is the object of much criticism and attacks, but nobody can doubt her honesty, her convictions and moral force. A very mild atmosphere enfolds her. Her strongest opponents admit her non-violence and a Christ-like love."[338] During the "year of change" leading to Proletarian-dictatorship she spoke three more times in the Parliament, amid very ill omens. In January that year the communist party announced its slogan: "The nation is yours, you build it for yourself." In February they nationalized all the banks and 246 industrial and commercial enterprises. In the same month the Soviet Union and Hungary signed "a treaty of friendship and mutual help." In March two working peoples' parties, Social Democrat and Communist, announced their union and named it the Hungarian Workers' Party (MDP). After the first nationalization the Secretary of State stated that more nationalizations would not follow, but on 20 April they began the debate on the next bill, Taking Enterprises into State Ownership.[339] In her intervention Margaret Slachta stated, "...the bill on nationalizations expresses the communist ideology." Through it the state could take, according to its whim, possession of industrial companies, trademarks, and patents without the individual owners having right to compensation; earlier agreements lost their legality,

---

[338] Magyar Nemzet, 1948, I. 9. P 3.
[339] See: Margaret Slachta's Christian Public Life, p. 116.

and at the same time the state could demand the surrender of all those amounts that the company may have paid to several individuals over and above their salaries. This state-democracy, where the nationalized enterprises have no responsibility but the individual owners have lost all their rights, was an injustice on the part of the state that would undermine the sense of morality of the citizens. Therefore she asked to re-draft the bill in a way to manifest the values of private ownership, equity, and honor of the nation and justice.[340]

The next unjust bill came under debate in May. It proposed revoking citizenship and confiscating property of those who are in foreign countries.[341] Why was this bill necessary? In 1945 economic development began but very soon it stalled; many among the population did not agree with it, condemned the Soviet occupation and the curtailing of rights and, while it was possible, left the country for Austria. Some of the outstanding persons who emigrated were: Ferenc Nagy, Prime Minister, 1947. V. 14; Béla Varga the President of the National Assembly, VI. 2; Dezső Sulyok, President of the Liberty Party, 1948 VIII.14; Zoltán Pfeiffer, from the Independent Party; Károly Peyer, leader of the Social Democratic Party; Imre Kovács of the Working People's Party.[342] Many more ordinary or less well-known citizens of the country

---

[340] Diary of the National Assembly 1948 IV. I. 9. p. 3
[341] See: Margaret Slachta's Christian Public Life p. 122.
[342] Borbandi Gy. P. 135

left. During the debate Margaret Slachta tried, as much as she was able, to protect the rights of the émigrés' and their families. She objected to the fact that the law did not define precisely against whom proceedings would be started. Moreover, representation of those in absence was not secured. She objected that confiscating assets from minors would also be included in the law if "they followed the mentality of their parent." If a person who left had sold a property to another person, that legal arrangement would be invalid and fall under confiscation. Representative Slachta found fault with the law in that it punished but did not examine why the person or persons left the country. She attempted to protect those who left for reasons of conscience, for example, for being forced to join a party whose program was contrary to their convictions. She asked that those who wanted to leave for reason of conscience be given passport, because it is in no one's interest to hold back persons in conflict with their conscience and also are not able to find work.[343] "It is a contradiction to want someone to be in the country, who is, in spirit, already on the way out and at the same time not give opportunity to leave.[344]

Her last intervention took place on 16 June 1948 during the debate to nationalize all Catholic

---

[343] The nationalized workplaces would not employ them. (Translator's note.)
[344] Diary of the National Assembly, 1948. V. 4.

institutions.[345] "Against that bill only Margaret Slachta, the leader of the Christian Women Corps, and István Barankovics, the Democratic Peoples' Party, spoke up."[346] Only part of the intervention of Margaret Slachta is preserved in the Parliament's diary. She built her talk based on so-called "rumors" that in Hungary there is no democracy or freedom; there is terror, etc. "On my part, I would like to submit a proposal for decision connected with those (rumors) that, if accepted, the government will disclaim itself completely of these suppositions. This is important because our nation is in need of being looked at by those abroad that we are keepers of the peace-treaty. The second paragraph of the peace-treaty's second chapter assures the freedom of religion and makes assurance of democracy our obligation." Naturally during her talk there was continuous noise, the presider rang the alarm bell several times. Margaret Slachta continued her talk saying that before the plan became a law, the Minister of Foreign Affairs should be directed to contact the United – with a slip of tongue she continued – States' organization" – but immediately she corrected herself – the Organization of the United Nations to send a delegation to examine whether Hungary keeps the peace treaty. An indescribable noise began: "A common traitor!" "Send her to the Committee of Immunity!"

---

[345] See: Margaret Slachta's Christian Public Life p. 128   On Nationalization of Educational Institutions.
[346] Mindszenty: Memoirs, p, 207. Of Barankovics' intervention:UNIO 1991/2

The noise does not stop. Margaret Slachta tried to continue her talk. She showed the letters of protest against the nationalization of schools - someone shouted: "You wrote those;" "They are fake;" "Be ashamed of yourself!" She continued. In case her proposal for decision was not accepted, she planned to submit a petition to the United Nations' Organization that she read out loud. She proposed placing in the foreword of the United Nations' Constitution a paragraph according minorities in nations a right to place their grievances before them. It is important "that this paragraph be included in the Constitution of the United Nations Big noise. "An American agent!" In case it could not be included in the Constitution of the United Nations, then she proposed directing the Peace-Commission at The Hague to assure each oppressed nation a forum where they can submit their grievances and receive solution. After this she wanted to read her proposal for decision, but could speak only the first words. "National Assembly, stop the debate of the proposal..." Her following words could not be heard over the noise. "Sit down! Enough of your abuse!" Alarm bell. Later, when the presider closed the session, he signed the proposal that was not allowed to be read as: "gravely offensive to the national sovereignty and destructive to its honor" and ordered that the text of her petition be erased from the diary.[347] The text was the petition to the United Nations.

---

[347] Diary of the National Assembly 1948. VI. 16 column 556.

The bill was passed 230 to 63, and national-ization of schools became law. When the new law was proclaimed the members of the governing par-ty began singing the Hungarian anthem. Those who voted against stood up, but did not sing. Margaret Slachta remained seated. The presider condemned her for her double offenses - for her petition to the United Nations and for remaining seated - and referred her to the Committee of Im-munity. About the Committee of Immunity's ques-tion of the why she remained seated; Sister Mar-garet reported to the community, "I responded, I truly made a mistake. I was very deeply affected by the fact that those who started to sing 'God Bless Hungarians' at that moment deprived young people of God. I should have knelt down instead and prayed the Psalm: 'How could we sing the song of the Lord in a foreign land.' "

The Committee of Immunity expelled her from the Parliament for two six-month periods.[348] It was characteristic of the time that the 27 June 1948 issue of Magyar Nemzet wrote very circum-spectly of the debate of the law; it does not even mention the singing of the national anthem only that the bell was rung during the interventions of Margaret Slachta. The scribes of the Parliament's diary handed over to Margaret Slachta the com-plete text of her talk and it is preserved in the ar-

---

[348] Ilona Mona: Margaret Slachta and the "Nationalization of Schools" in: Outlines in Hungarian Church History III/ 3. 1991. P. 127-132.

chives of the Society of the Sisters of Social Service. Having been expelled from the Parliament the period of hiding began for Margaret Slachta. Of that there will be more.

The years beginning with 1945 had other happenings, primarily in community life. In 1946 atrocities began, not only against Margaret Slachta's public service, but also against the Society. One of the most serious was in Szegvár. The community received, in 1929, the house of Count Károlyi-Korniss for a foundation offering service for the people of the village, maintaining a kindergarten and caring for the village's elderly. The sisters did these services with the partial help of the novices who were housed there. On 7 March 1946, 100-150 women armed with sticks appeared at the door and demanded it be opened. They shouted, "Out with those who do not work, out with the nuns... ." They broke into the house yelling, "We conquered the fortress, the fortress is ours," as they expelled those who lived there. The noviitiate sought refuge on the surrounding farms for two months until they were able to reach the motherhouse. Margaret Slachta went to Mátyás Rákosi to report the actions of the members of the party in Szegvar. The communist party directed its rural organizations to end the atrocities and returned the house on 20 March. The community decided that sisters should not return and the noviitiate was moved to Budapest.[349]

---

[349] SZTTI 419. 1046-47

In 1947 the year of chapter followed with hope that the sisters from America could also participate. Letters went and came that the delegates from America and Canada received visas only to Vienna, and in Vienna the Soviet member of the Supervisory Commission denied signature for entry into Hungary. The sisters tried everything, even smuggling the delegates into the country. The correspondence took place through the American Military Mission because that was not censored.[350] In this way they told the sisters where and when they should be with the travel permit to Vienna; then they would smuggle them into Hungary. The American sisters did not go to the assigned place, for them such an illegal step was not imaginable. We read in a contemporary letter, "A more safe solution in Hungary today does not exist. Everybody here among the Americans knows this, but nobody talks of it."[351] There remained only one possibility for a meeting and that was to ask an entry visa to Czechoslovakia; but the Hungarian sisters did not receive an entry visa there. Sister Margaret with Sister Paula entered on foot, illegally through a cornfield on 7 July to Kosice. The American delegates could spend but two days there, enough only to inform them what happened at the chapter. The leadership of the community desired to postpone the chapter but church authorities in Esztergom would not allow it; so the chap-

---

[350] SZTTI 1195/18
[351] SZTTI 1195/21

ter was held without the delegates from the new world. This became the starting point for many problems, since the American delegates participated in a chapter for the last time in 1935. Sister Margaret spent eight days in Kosice and hurried home to prepare the election that was held, according to memory, on 31 August. The American sisters went home and, in September, the information arrived that the Californian sisters made a foundation in Shanghai and ask for help of sisters from Hungary. Two assigned sisters left during in the fall and by Christmas the foundation in Shanghai was opened. Sister Margaret started her own visa petition in January 1948.

A co-worker during her travel abroad was allowed to go to Switzerland. She reported that the love and honor with which Sister Margaret is mentioned abroad is very touching. In Einsiedeln she was led to the statue of Mary, and lifting up her mantle saw Sister Margaret's picture cut out from a newspaper.[352]

1948 was the year of Jubilee of the Society's birthday and a year of change in the country. The jubilee was celebrated only in a closed circle. Cardinal Mindszenty participated with only the closest co-workers and the sisters. The Cardinal congratulated the community in a letter. He compared 1871 France with Hungary.

---

[352] Testver, August, 1948 p.28.

In the national mourning Bishop Bougaud Laval consoled the French, that the Daughters of Charity, the true glory of that country, were born and continued, ... We, too, had sadness earlier, and more recently greater than the French. Let us seek the consoling moments when from a fiery supernaturally focused Hungarian spirituality the Society of the Sisters of Social Service sprung up. They were born from our hearts; all nations invite them. I visited some of their houses in Canada and in the United States; I heard the opinion of their competent bishops: late arrival of feminine knights; unshakeable warriors of justice; in historical wars against the spirit of Rome and Hungary in the midst of ridicule, rudeness, tricks, slander and violence. In difficult wars the demand is not a quick victory, but that truth not be silent, not be hindered and forced underground. See, this is the face and the spirituality of the past 25 years. This is the ecclesial and national importance of Society of the Sisters of Social Service, as its general superior serves with all her soul and self-giving.

Sister Margaret greeted the small attendance of the meeting, first the Prince Primate, "...who stands here without compromise... is not afraid, makes no compromises, does not look for benefits, only the Christ-like truth and morality. Many whisper that his stance will lead to confrontations and will result in war. We already know from experience that these struggles will see loss of blood from which the Church will win."

Regarding the history of the Society, Sister

Margaret took the occasion to express her gratitude to Edith Farkas, "Our birth was in 1923, however our vocation did not start then but in 1908 in the Social Mission Society. We have no reason, my dear sisters, to spread a veil over that year, when - of God's grace - our Society was born. When we return to the cradle of our Society, our grateful reverence flows back to Edith Farkas and our Bishop Prohaszka. The past 25 years confirm the fact that their decision was the will of the Providence of our good God."[353]

The closed meeting of the Assembly occurred on 19 May 1948. In a month Margaret Slachta was deprived of her political immunity and the thirteen-month long hiding and illegality began. She never thought to leave and go abroad because the conditions at home were difficult. In her teaching on 8 December she told of a letter she received with the message, "We watch your efforts from abroad. Discern if it is worthwhile to continue this, since these days such work means martyrdom or, at least, suffering of soul. Of martyr's these days there is an over-production. Leave for abroad, from there you can help your country better." She responded that this could not be the motive for travel abroad. However she wanted as soon as possible to make a visitation to the community abroad. That desire was long held, but since 1936 there was no possibility. It was not possible to travel to neighboring countries either, only illegally,

---

[353] Testver: Pentecost, 1948. P. 2-3.

as she had done in 1947. On 18 January 1948 she submitted her petition for a passport in order to visit the districts abroad. In a particular way her visit was very much needed in China, for the situation in connection with Sister Alice.[354] In Sister Margaret's letter to Sister Alice on 30 September, the petition of passport is mentioned. She writes, "It seems hopeless for me to ever get a passport."

Having become free from her civic duties, Sister Margaret began to revise the constitution according to the decisions of the 1947 chapter and submitted it on 15 July to Esztergom. It received approval on 20 August. The decree to nationalize all educational institutions applied to the *Social Liceum*, but not to the School of Social Work; the former was lost. She worked to change the structure of the School of Social Work in such a way that it would become a catechetical school as well. Its students however could be only the novices of the Society, or only such who wanted to become catechists. She planned four preparatory years for the school and thought of opening a 'small seminary' for girls of fourteen who sensed a vocation.[355] This became a reality, but not until 1950.

Civic life became darker and darker. The personal safety of Sister Margaret became endangered. During the fall of 1948, a sister assigned as

---

[354] This question will be discussed in the history of the Society, to be written in the future. I.M.
[355] SZTTI 533/20

cook in Buda was stopped on the street by a middle age man inquiring about Sister Margaret. She is not here, the sister replied. No problem, said the gentleman, but please give her a message that she must leave as soon as possible to go abroad. He also told where the road is free and she could get across the border. As soon the sister got home she told what happened. On the same evening Sister Margaret called the sister and asked about the message. She asked her to repeat the message several times. Sister Margaret understood that this was a provocation. On 19 November a caricature appeared in Ludas Matyi entitled "Slachta at a Fortuneteller." The fortuneteller sits before Margaret Slachta and between them a card is laid out with the pictures of Szakasits, Rákosi, Péter Veres, Révai, Marosán and Rajk who was the Minister of Interior at that time. The fortuneteller places her finger on the last and says: "This young man with brown hair thinks of you often."[356] On another page a well cared-for garden was drawn and in it, as gardener, Gábor Péter is working. Before him stands László Rajk who points to a hen with the face of Margaret Slachta scratching the soil, and says, "Chase out this forever croaking old hen from the garden of democracy before she can harm it."[357] By that

---

[356] History, 1983/5-6. Those enumerated were the president of that time and the members of the government.
[357] Jokes During Elections, Cleopatra, Budapest 1990 p.29. Gábor Péter was the head of National Security office between 1945-53 Rajk the Minister of Interior between 1946-48.

time Sister Margaret did not live in the mother-house, but in a not well-known local community house of some friends. In her letters she made references to the situation. e.g. "...the happenings are like a never stopping mill... The situation here is such that we ask of you remembrances of prayers from your community... we are overwhelmed, concerned and very sad."[358] Also the push against the Prince Primate was getting worse. On 3 December on the front page of Ludas Matyi appeared a big Nicolas with the title "Nicholas's Workshop in Esztergom" and pictures of little ones, "On Saint Nicholas day ordinary shoes are placed before the door, but this year they won't."   Sister Margaret spent Christmas at the motherhouse. Before the midnight Mass, standing on a chair, she taught a new Christmas song to the sisters. She seemed to be so relaxed and joyful, as if she had no concern whatsoever. On 26 December Cardinal Mindszenty was taken captive with the accusation "for actions to overthrow the republic, spying and illegally handling foreign money." On 4 January 1949, the Hungarian bishops held discussion on the situation and whether to send a statement right away to the believers. It was urged by Michalovics, a representative, and Margaret Slachta; but the bishops felt it was not yet timely.[359]

On 15 January when Sister Margaret was at

---

[358] STTI 533.1948, letters of November and December.
[359] Gábor Szalacz: The 17 Years of the Hungarian Catholic Church (1948-1964), Munchen, 1988, p. 32, 35.

the home of her sister, Borbála, a sister, came there telling that detectives were looking for her at the place she used to be. On the following day she asked permission of Bertalan Badalik, Dominican Provincial and later Bishop of Veszprém, to be allowed to go to the convent of the Dominican sisters. She wore their habit and stayed with them for one month. That habit had a closed neck, like habits do. One of her companions asked whether she feels hot in the habit? She responded, "Yes, but it has an advantage you will come to realize when you too will have a wrinkled neck. I am thinking that we ought to do something for our sisters' clothing for old age." On 25 January the following letter - with a hidden meaning - was sent abroad. "Our no good sons see that their mother likes to play with them, recently they want to play hide and seek with her."[360]

Despite all this endangerment to her security she wrote a letter on 21 January to József Révai, who on 9 January 1949 publicized an article with the title "Pharisees" against the flood of protests from abroad after the arrest of the cardinal. In Hungary on account of terror there was silence. The Conference of Bishops dared to state only: "The members of the bishops conference are bound by ecclesial laws. Based on those over bishops we may not criticize, especially over a cardinal. For this reason we may not make a

---

[360] SZTTI 1190/29. With this kind of letter she wanted the sisters know that she must hide from Homeland Security.

judgment-like statement."[361]   Margaret Slachta's letter says,

> ... I want to reflect in a short way on the 'Pharisees.' Do you truly believe that there is freedom in Hungary? Are you not inclined to think about the phenomenon that whoever can leaves the nation, even from among your own people - or if they are already abroad, they do not return? People perhaps do not feel comfortable with the more than 35,000 police who make freedom more difficult.

After this she mentioned the accusation that the cardinal wants to take away the lands from the farmers.

> But he, while he was a bishop of Veszprém asked the permission of the Ministry of Culture to be allowed to parcel 6,000 hold [362] from the lands of the bishopric and distribute to poor people. Not even the people can accept your statement because not long time ago Rákosi said, that in our country the small farms system did not work, therefore it needs to be changed, that the people may enjoy the benefits of large-scale farming productions. The peasantry, after the recent threshing, understands this very well...according to my view of life my greatest question is always, what happens to their soul. In this situation I feel mostly pained, that you act

---

[361] Salacz: i.m. p 34.
[362] "Hold" was a measure in Hungary at that time. 1 hold = 1.200 square meters. (Translator's note.)

against your best convictions. Your article leaves the impression that you wanted to show through your style and statements that you are a good communist. This is not done well, as so many other things; for example what you do and have done against the Cardinal. Since society has no stratum that has not been embittered, there is tension everywhere. If you continue this way, at one point, the strings will break. Since everybody knows who is the *spiritus rector*, and who are among the leaders' puppets in the storefronts. If order would collapse, the bitterness will be expressed in violence. *There is only one man in Hungary who has power over masses of people without forcing them - the Cardinal!* You have knocked down the only dike. I hope, you do not take this as a threat; it would be bitterly comical if a mouse would threaten an elephant! Moreover, this is not my stance. I only want to beg you, think of something more beautiful, something better, more noble, more intelligent than the great violence that characterizes your paths.[363]

It is characteristic that the leader of the People's Democratic Party and ten of its politicians left the country in February. Margaret Slachta remained. The power of state did not halt on the path it had begun. On 3 February 1949 it sent the cardinal before the people's tribunal and on 5 February made the verdict for life-long imprison-

---

[363] SZTTI 1190/20. Jozsef Révai, politician, (1898-1059, director of the communist party's ideology, between 1949-1953 minister of education.

ment.[364] In a letter Sister Margaret wrote, "We are in an indescribable mourning on account of the latest happenings. This is a completely mystical event. God accepted the sacrifice of his life, of which he always prepared himself for the country. The situation was made worse when they destroyed his good name; they put him in a false light and we are pained over this more than the terrible verdict."[365]

Margaret Slachta left the refuge at the Dominican Sisters at the end of January and went to another convent. From some references it can be presumed it was a community of sisters who maintained an orphanage. In the meantime a book was published with the title: The Cardinal's Criminal Case Record. (The Yellow Book) In it there was a mention of Sister Margaret. She moved into the community with the orphanage on 20 February. From there, on the 25th a message arrived that she, at the age of 65, was in bed with scarlet fever! From the correspondence that survived, it seems that she was quite sick for a short time. At the beginning of March, she sent letters regarding different critical issues. In these there was always some reference to the situation: "...we are concerned, our situation is difficult ... we are not at home, because of my health the city atmosphere is harmful. We are deeply concerned and live in uncertainty ... sadness is great ... I work at this time

---

[364] Of the verdict see: Szalacz, i.m. p. 32-53.
[365] SZTTI 533/35

behind the scenes ... I am not at home. It is better for me to be in a wild forest."[366] This is how she tried to express her hiding. However there were two occasions when she endangered herself. Even though the <u>Yellow Book</u> on the cardinal was published in January, it seems it got into the hands of Margaret Slachta later. Having read it, she wrote a confession and sent it immediately to Kálmán Kiczko, the assigned Defense Counsel.

Regarding the accusations contained against me in the <u>Yellow Book</u>, I state the following:

1. It states that the Cardinal made provisions through the Small Landowner's Party that trustful representatives be elected into parliament who represent the form of state as a kingdom during the elections of 1945 and for this they enumerate Ferenc Kovács, Pál Zeoke and me. Contrary to this, the reality was that I entered the Parliament on the list of the People's Democratic Party, and because events happened so fast, I missed doing what a person of the church would have been obliged to do - asking His Eminence's approval. Ferenc Kovács had no role whatsoever in issues of constitutional law; Dr. Pál Zeoke was never in the Parliament. Therefore this accusation that His Eminence initiated organization for re-establishing a kingdom, does not hold up.

2. According to the <u>Yellow Book</u> His Eminence

---

[366] SZTTI533/36-37

upon his return from Canada held a 'secret meeting' ard discussion with me and with some kingcom party persons. Contrary to this, neither with others nor alone was I invited for a discussion with His Eminence in connection with his trip to Canada.

3. The Yellow Book states the accusation that the Cardinal gave me financial assistance on the occasion of the election of 1947.

First of all, I protest against this as something that could be a reason for accusation. The head of the Catholic church, and someone who carries the honor of constitutional law, has the right to assist a party that stands on a pure Catholic and moral basis, a party that primarily has no real-political program but before anything else wants to realize in politics the church's and Catholicism's Christ-like worldview in the Parliament. It is completely misguided to characterize the role of Christian Women Corps, as if it would be the Cardinal's arm. The Christian Women Corps was founded during the fall of 1918 and since then it functioned without interruption. It always followed its pure convictions. The basis of the Yellow Book's accusation is the following: In 1947, before the elections I asked from him assistance, but he answered that he has no money for election propaganda. I got from him 20,000 Forint in several installments to help those in need. We made a study of those in need, and distributed the funds. For the amount they received, we asked a receipt from them. I made the accounts to His Eminence during the fall of 1948 attaching the receipts.

4. The <u>Yellow Book</u> testifies that the Cardinal was a sympathizer with the Arrow Cross. In 1944 he went to prison not because he opposed them, but purely because he got into a disagreement with the local chief bailiff who wanted to make a home in the bishop's palace.   In those days the household tasks, porters and service in the offices were done by women who were bombed out from their homes, because the male employees were drafted one after another. With these women I was in close contact; in this way I knew there were two Jewish girls among them.[367] In the same way, I know from a cleaning woman that taking lodging in the bishop's palace for some members of the government was the reason of his arrest, and not the struggle with the bailiff. In fact persons, by the name Szálasi, Lászlo Endre and other government members moved in. The bishop was arrested because he refused to allow them entry. I also know, flowing from our social vocation that the bishop was not against little people but the contrary. It is hard to believe how much he

---

[367] These women were the novices from Oradea, because the novitiate building was destroyed during bombing.

did while he was a parish priest in Zalaeger-szeg; how the poorest families and students received his greatest attention and care.

In the same way I know that, during the few months he was bishop in Veszprém, among his activities the first was to ask from the Minister of Culture agreement for more than the half of the land - a benefit for the diocese - to divide into parcels and to sell to poor families at a very low price and to use the income for establishing charitable institutions.[368]

Before the election of 1949 Margaret Slachta endangered her safety again. Even though the elections of 1947 were for four years, new elections were announced. In the beginning of 1949 the creation of the Hungarian Independent People's Front was announced; the parties and organization united under it ran together as one with a combined list for the election of 15 May. This actually meant dissolving all the democratic parties and was the first step in establishing the proletariat dictatorship. Margaret Slachta submitted to the central leadership of the People's Front that the Christian Women Corps wanted to enter the race for the elections as a Christian opposition. Naturally she was denied. On the day of election she appeared at the place of voting and voted. This was the first time when those who voted for the Peo-

---

[368] SZTTI 1187.

ple's Front did not have to enter the voting booth; they had only to fold the ballot and place it into the urn. Those who did not want to vote for the People's Front could mark the no vote only in the booth; courage was needed to do this.

Pentecost 1949 was on 5 June. Vows were pronounced on this greatest feast day of the Society. Sister Margaret spent the day with the community, and the teaching she offered was preserved. In it, she spoke of her most loved topic: supernatural life in new colors. "...The well developed Christian adores God in spirit and in truth; in her personal life she belongs completely to God, her morality is ordered to God's will; her worldview is supernatural; she sees God at the center of existence, and knows that she receives from God her natural rights. Her life is vigorous and rich. She knows consciously what her obligations are: humility and high aims to become a child of God. The systems of new paganism break human life into pieces."

Realizing more and more the greatness of the Hungarian tragedy, she dedicated the past five years to public issues and left aside her community responsibilities. Therefore she decided to leave without a passport to make the obligatory visitation of the houses overseas. Her friends at the embassy obtained for her and for two companions identification certificates with different names and with the signature and stamps of the four occupying powers. She says good-bye to the community through a letter.

Budapest, June 20, 1949

My dear Sister Paula! Dear Sisters!
I did not tell you where I travel in order that you have no difficulty from it. But if you look at the envelope you could have read that I traveled abroad to visit the foundations that I have not visited for 12 years. You know that I never wanted to leave. Even now I am not leaving for the reason to flee. However, since the Center of the People's Front did not allow participation in the elections on the 15th, my possibility to serve the country as a Christian opposition has ended. Abroad, I can respond to the community responsibilities that I set aside while serving the country during the siege and for the common good. As soon as I am done with my work abroad, I shall hurry back, trusting in Divine Providence to help me return because a pure intention takes me abroad and a pure intention will bring me back.

I am sad that I leave illegally, but I have asked from all forums of authority permission to leave last year when I was expelled from the Parliament for one year. Then I would have had time to make my trip all around. However, all the forums I have turned to, none was willing to receive me, not the Minister of Interior, the Prime Minister, nor the President. Minister Ortutay, to whom I submitted such petition, received me cordially the first time and seemed to be willing to help. He asked me whether I intend to return. I assured him that I would. Later he avoided facilitating my trip abroad. Since no government has the God-given right to place obstacles without reason to the fulfillment of the obligations of its citizens, but shuts them within borders, my departure without permission is morally justified.

You shall not hear from me because I want to return most decidedly to my regular place of work. I am asking for your prayers that I may not lack the help of our merciful God, and I ask you, if my temporary absence would come to light, please prove the truth of my absence. You know the best that I did not want to leave my country, nor do I want to do it, but my responsibility obliges me - and it will bring me back. My dear Sister Paula and my dear Sisters, let us pray for each other until the hoped-for seeing each other.

I embrace each of you with all my soul in the unity of our vocation.

Sister Margaret[369]

She left with two other sisters: Sister Klementin and Sister Natalia with the help of a farmer who had land both in Hungary and Austria. They were hidden within the hay-wagon under the hay, during the night of 22-23 June 1949. They arrived in Detschjahrendorf, Austria. When they could leave that Russian supervised zone Sister Margaret used the name Etelka Toth. She wanted

---

[369] SZTTI 1186/40.

to remain incogrito until the end. From Vienna she wrote to her sister in America on 30 June: "I hope you received my telegram sent yesterday. I ask you do not tell anybody that I came, since after I complete my job I want to return..."[370]

---

[370] SSSAB, N.Y. Letter to Dr. Iren Slachta.

Emigration

"...after I complete my work, I want to return..."

This was her life goal for close to four years. What was this work? There were three great tasks: first to attend to her community responsibilities; secondly, she wanted to do something on behalf of the imprisoned Cardinal Mindszenty and for her country suffering under communist dictatorship; thirdly, to help those homeless Hungarian nationals who fled to the West. She wanted to help the sisters living scattered under suppression in Eastern Europe, Slovakia, Romania and Hungary.

For this reason, she kept using the cover name of Sister Etelka and her closest sisters used it. Unfortunately not everybody took this seriously, as is evident from one of her letters: "...you rolled a millstone onto me, my dear sister, by giving in writing to someone that I am here. My God, perhaps the other sisters realize even less what will happen to me, if my presence here will become known, preserved in written words." [371] "...I got into the U.S. not with the thought of remaining here, but because for the past twelve years I did not respond to this obligation to visit the local communities. At home all possibility ended for me to do anything at all for my unfortunate homeland. Since I

---

[371] SSSA-B, N.Y. to Sister Clara Brosz, 1949, X.11.

want to return, it is for me a question of life and death that my presence here not be known. I ask you not to mention me to anybody. One does not know what might get to be known by whom. I have come to visit all the local communities I have not visited for a long time. Unfortunately what two persons know is no longer a secret." [372]

The news had already spread that Margaret Slachta left her country, but because she left without permission, and because she used a different name, it could not be known where she was. For this, different presuppositions started. The most interesting among them was a Swiss newspaper article. It showed the picture of Sister Margaret in the uniform, which read as follows:

Behold a modern saint. She does not suffer behind closed convent walls embracing sacrifices, but suffers the pains of a present day concentration camp. She did not live far from the world, but was in the middle of political fights; she organized a Christian Women's party, and regardless of diplomacy, she threw herself into political struggles. She fought alone, isolated in the Parliament, for Christ and the Church. She did not distribute 'soup for the poor' at the gate of the cloister, but in her country she fought with her total energy for the people deprived of their rights in all areas, to save them from a terrifying death. This is the Hungarian Margaret Slachta, who is the foundress

---

[372] SSSA-B. N.Y. To Sr. Alice Slachta, 1949, X. 4.

and superior of the Sisters of Social Service, who now disappeared and is in an unknown concentration camp. Many persons suffer with her the same fate. And we have no possibility to help! But we can do one thing, and we must do it: we may not keep silent. We must raise our voice repeatedly, to express our objection, and awaken the conscience of the world.[373]

Based on the text, the editors of Die Schweizerin presumed that Sister Margaret was in one of the Hungarian internment camps. The Hungarian politicians who were already in the west sent letters to the American houses of the community inviting Sister Margaret to their different organizations.

We know that Sister Margaret did not want until now to have an active role in public life. To discern whether she wants to embrace or not to enter into public life, we shall leave it always to Sister Margaret. A leadership position and distinctive reverence will always be reserved for her among us....[374]

...I searched for your address for months now... we must get organized... regarding a leading personality here in the United States now only one person can be considered: You! - And you have to embrace this.[375]

---

[373] Die Schweizerin, 1952/6,SzTTI 1188/59
[374] SSA-B, N.Y.The letter of István Kray, 1950. Jan.-Febr.
[375] SSA-B, N.Y. Letter of Lajos Rosta, previous representative of Szeged, 1950. August 8.

...At last I got the address from Lajos Rosta. The aim of my letter is to express my respect to you. I ask you now to kindly let me know whether you want to keep your political incognito forever. I beg you give up your reserved attitude and become active again...[376]

Dear Sister Margaret! I have known for a long time that you are here in the U.S. I wanted to visit you several times but received the response that you want to remain incognito. Today I shall visit you... I would like to convince you to end your incognito.[377]

Sister Margaret did not end her disguise. She persevered in her decision to return to Hungary after she finished her work.

Sister Margaret remained in Vienna until 5 September 1949. She received news of the suppression of the Romanian religious. Sisters from Cluj were taken to a concentration camp, where the imprisoned were housed twenty-two into a single room with a dirt floor. The superior of the group, Sister Augusta, wrote on a card, "My name is Rachel, my city is Bethlehem." In Czechoslovakia, the deportation occurred on 8 November. These happenings only increased her conviction that she expressed in her proposal in the Parliament on 16 June 1948, to turn to the United Na-

---

[376] SSA-B, N.Y. The letter of Dezső" Sulyok, 1951. I.30
[377] SSA-B, N.Y. the letter of Dr. Béla Fábián, 1951 X. 5.

tions and to the Justice of Peace at the Hague, that these organizations examine in the communist countries the situation of those forced into minority status and take steps for their protection. In that talk she spoke also that the U.N. create an international legal forum so that those who were deprived of their rights would have someplace to turn. She submitted this proposal to the United Nations and she wanted to urge the realization of her proposal.[378] She stated with bitterness: "If one views closely the function of the United Nations, one becomes sad; they know everything, but are helpless!"[379] Regardless she kept on working. She wrote a memorandum to President Truman [380] and the Chair of the American Bishops Conference on behalf of the religious behind the Iron Curtain.[381] On 6 September she left for Rome, where she tried to have an audience with the Pope, but on account of the shortness of time, she got only to the Vatican's Secretary of State, Msgr. Barbetta and his substitute, G. B. Montini. With their mediation she could give her report to Pope Pius XII, and received a significant amount of money for the School of Social Work in Budapest. In her letter of thanks to Msgr. Barbetta she gave a detailed account of Cardinal Mindszenty, based on the news received from home. "A few days ago I received a letter dated 27 October in which I was let know

---

[378] See: Margaret Slachta's Christian Public Life, p. 130 -131.
[379] SSA-B- N.Y. Her letter to Béla Varga, 1953. V. 28
[380] SZTTI 1106-7

that his aged mother was allowed to visit her son in August and September. She could only stay with him for a few minutes while the guard was also present. The condition of his Eminence is fairly good, but he has aged twenty years - this is the opinion of his mother. The Cardinal said that with the exception of 20 days he could celebrate Mass and he prays daily six rosaries. The mother found that her son is intellectually free. He also said not to pray for him, but for the great cause. The mother got permission to visit him in October, but later the permission was withdrawn without giving any reason. She was not allowed to give him the fruit she brought, even though he would have a very great need of it. Now nobody knows in which prison he is kept."[382]

Because she had to leave for America, Sister Margaret spent only 10 days in Rome but she still met Vilmos Juhasz, from whom she learned that during the Holy Year of 1950 an exhibition was being planned. "We plan to create an exhibition of the persecution of the Church behind the Iron Curtain. It would embrace the entire region behind the Iron Curtain because it would be viewed by great number of visitors, but the main emphasis will be on Cardinal Mindszenty." Sister Margaret was still in Hungary when the attacks against the Cardinal began, and she had watched the press. She submitted 3,000 attacking newspaper clippings for the exhibition, including the car-

---

[382] SZTTI 1104. The author translated this from French.

icatures of <u>Ludas Matyi</u>. From these 200 were published between January and November 1948, and from December 1948 to January and February 1949, 2,500 were printed. The government undoubtedly supported these attacks; considering the smallness of the country this was an incomprehensibly great and shocking number. This is an example of how the secret forces, together with their political organizations behind the communist government, exerted influence to suppress a single person, the Cardinal.[383] Since Sister Margaret was already in America by 16 September 1949, she mailed the newspaper clippings to Vilmos Juhász. He thanked her very gratefully. However he wrote sadly that the Italian exhibition committee would use only a limited amount of material since they wanted to create an optimistic exhibition; therefore they would limit those regarding the Church's persecution. Later, letters report that the material of the exhibition, among them the newspaper clippings, got lost.[384] Vilmos Juhász received a visa to America, and with closing the Holy Year, all the material of the exhibition disappeared.

I shall give an account of one more activity regarding the legal proceedings of Cardinal Mindszenty. Áron Márton, bishop of Transylvania was incarcerated on 3 October 1949. According to their method several months were needed to pull

---

[383] SSSA-B N.Y. Sister Margaret's letter to István Deér, 1950. I. 11.
[384] SZTTI 1189/20

together the accusation. Sister Margaret wrote a letter on 8 March 1950 to the Vatican, "Is it known in the Vatican the news that trickled out from Romania that they want to morally destroy Bishop Marton, by connecting him with three nuns? They dug out carcasses of babies as 'proof' of indisputable evidence. Would it not be advisable that a competent person or forum put news of this in the *Osservatore*? It still hurts me that in January (1949) I sent information – still in time – to Rome and indicated, that injections or pills will follow – to communicate in newspapers, that in His Eminence, Cardinal Mindszenty, a strange (drugged) man will talk in his name and the results achieved by the Russian method are morally not valid. O, if this would have been communicated before!!! If only Bishop Marton would have been protected!"[385]

Sister Margaret arrived in New York on 16 September 1949. She did not start her work with the community right away and she gave the reason for it to the sisters in a letter. First, she emphasized her incognito – "for the reason that my presence here will not come to light. I asked from Washington official permission for not using my own name. The Department of State knew what a hell exist at home, especially what it would mean if I return to Hungary. They permitted it – so call me only Etelka. My papers were made out in this way." Following she explained that she had not

---

[385] SZTTI 1189/20

begun her official visitation because the United Nations is now holding a conference at Lake Success. Its theme is Safeguarding Human Rights. She is working on this and she will speak more of it.

Sister Margaret left Washington DC on 19 December 1949. On 4 January 1950 she held a Small Chapter in Buffalo, to discuss with the American superiors:
1. Where the Generalate in America should be? (The Generalate normally would be in Hungary, but the suppression would begin at the end of June)
2. How they could help the European homeless priests and seminarians?
3. The difficulties of the various local communities
4. Fulfillment of the 1947 Chapter decisions.[386]

However, she felt that her energy was diminishing. On 11 January 1950 she wrote in a letter "...compared to my energies I carry too many tasks, therefore whatever I am doing takes much longer."[387] During the early days of January another trial occurred. Two sisters from Hungary tried to cross the Iron Curtain, but only one got through; the other was taken captive and sent to prison. She was incarcerated for seven months.[388]

---

[386] SZTTI 1189/23
[387] SZTTI 1197/5a
[388] Sister Laura Pankotai gets through; Sister Kriszta Szendrői was imprisoned. (Translator's remark)

The days of the Chinese foundation were also numbered since, on 1 October 1949, the Chinese People's Republic was founded. Sister Margaret gave freedom to the sisters to decide whether they wanted to stay or use the still existing option to leave. In the meantime more and more depressing news came from behind the Iron Curtain from the people languishing in various European refugee camps, who begged her to obtain visas to the United States for them. For a visa to be given, the U.S. wanted a statement of acceptance from persons ready to support or vouch for them. It was surprising that, while the conditions of those living under Soviet influence were well known, the refugees were handled as if they were against the democratic values. A citizen of the United States who gave a statement of acceptance must also provide support, and pay $10 for the 'affidavit'. The help sent for the European sisters was already beyond the ability of the Society. "...I cannot do more," wrote Sister Margaret, "I have too much financial burden. We already pick up on the street paper, clips, and strings."[389] "You can imagine how difficult it is to find a citizen of the USA who is willing to give an affidavit," she wrote to Maria Blasko, who was earlier a co-worker and friend, and who wanted to enter the States from Vienna. Sister Margaret wrote on 3 May 1950, "We have a quite long list of DPs, (displaced persons) under our work and many other responsibilities...." She

---

[389] SSA-B N.Y. A letter from Buffalo, 1950. III. 14

wrote sadly, "A happy person here has great difficulty understanding how deep the wounds of those DP's who have lost everything, are separated from their families and are thrown into an unknown dark night."[390] Of the many letters asking her help some examples:

> Dear Sister! I heard how many of my fellow citizens you helped with emigration; this is why I dare to interrupt you with my petition. I have known Sister Margaret Slachta well in Budapest, I ask her to please take me in your protection.

(The letter is addressed to Etelka Tóth; there are more that mention Sister Margaret.)

> We left Budapest in 1944. In 1945 we left from Sopron. We fled to Upper Austria, where my good husband was taken captive and was returned in November to the Hungarian government. Now we got of him the worst news. In 1950 we went to Dublin with my son. We do the meanest and most difficult jobs just for food and lodging. I cannot bear for long being a housemaid; I am 60 years old. In 1951 we submitted our petition to enter the USA, but the consulate here does not know anything about us. I ask you to please to support our case in Washington and please ask to take our case into consideration.
>
> Mrs. Bálint Homan[391]

---

[390] SSSA-L 1950.IV. 19, letter
[391] SZTTI 1197/9 She was the wife of the previous Minister of Education in Hungary.

Similar letters streamed to her from all sides.

They asked help in their personal difficulties e.g. for establishing a new newspaper for émigrés. On this Sister Margaret's advice was that tit would be better to have fewer papers - instead unite energies. "It is a problem that everyone wants to start his own paper, bring great sacrifices for it and after a while they have to close it down. Instead, if you would unite the papers that serve the same goal, the readers would not become over whelmed and the editors would also profit."[392]

Others asked money as a loan for publishing a book or sent a copy and asked for payment. This is what Dezső Sulyok did with his book, The Hungarian Tragedy that he recommended to Sister Margaret with reverence. Sister Margaret apologized that she forgot amid her many tasks to respond to him and to send payment.[393] There is one émigré who thought that Margaret Slachta held fortunes and asked her to give to his relatives in Hungary $1,000 monthly. The many small petitions are not enumerated here. This is enough to illustrate how many petitions came because of the opinion the community of émigrés had of Sister Margaret Slachta.

On 31 March 1950 Sister Margaret gave a talk at Fordham University on international rela-

---

[392] SSSA-B N. 1953. N.Y. XI. 11 the letter to Katona Korodi
[393] SZTTI 1197/1c

tionships, ethics, and of political themes connected to this.[394] At the age of 66 she began experiencing the burdens of age, "...The problem with me is that I am beginning to lose my hearing. A heart attack happened last night. It was not strong but still it is a serious warning. I am getting over it now, but very slowly."[395] Still, she had need of her strength because the news of the next tragic happenings soon arrived. During the night of 18-19 June 1950 the Hungarian sisters were placed into an internment camp, as were all Hungarian religious.[396] With this, the existence of the Society behind the Iron Curtain ended. Now the question came from Hungary: what should happen with the elderly and ill sisters and they ask again and again for economic help. The letters are cryptically written so it is difficult to decipher. "...The arriving letters are puzzles. I beg you have mercy on me. I am not used to complaining, but my nerves cannot bear any longer the many stresses, the uncertainty, fear for you, and the months passing without being able to help."[397]

Sister Margaret began her visitations with the local communities, starting in Western Canada, then down to California. Since her flexibility was no longer as before, she had difficulty orienting herself to the new situations, to the American

---

[394] SZTTI, 1187/2
[395] SZTTI 1189/35
[396] Salacz i. m. p. 68
[397] SSSA-B N.Y. 1952. V. 21

and Canadian life-styles to which the new generation was accustomed. They did not receive gladly the physically broken superior who spoke with an accent; they did not understand why she was so preoccupied with the suppressed sisters in Europe. In a nation where most people live well, it seemed a virtue to waste. They could not understand why their superior was among them with a name, not her own, and why she would find fault with their use of water, food, and clothing. The greatest difficulty was verbalized by her two co-foundresses, the superiors of California and Canada (both Hungarians) – who saw that Sister Margaret and those who came with her occupy themselves not with the problems here, but only with what happens in Europe, where everything was destroyed. They also felt that she did not value sufficiently their achievements, and they did not feel the uniting efforts of the Generalate.[398] Sister Margaret felt that she had finished her visitation role, and according to her previous decision, planned her return to Hungary.

In spring 1951 the Cuban foundation came into existence; it also seemed that sisters could work at Radio Free Europe and this work fell to the sisters in America. In November 1951 Sister Margaret returned to Europe; she hoped that in Vienna she would find a man who would smuggle her back into Hungary. Later on she wrote of this.

---

[398] SZTTI 1188/44

This is actually a very complicated thing. One cannot truly comprehend how complicated, and if one looks back she cannot believe herself the many complications of escape, the labirynths, the hunger for money, difficulities with post, transportation, etc, etc., and baseness of the smugglers, who are not led by love for human beings but for money. This is like a swamp, where persons stumble, yet want to run forward and are attracted by the light reflected by water. When one wants to take hold of what one sees, it turns out to be a phantom. There was a situation when I went with a companion close to the border, thinking I am close to realization, yet today I am where I have been for six months before. Naturally I am told from both sides (before and behind the Iron Curtain) not to return.[399]

I felt hurt realizing that when you became frightened that I go back you found a way to send five letters to protest my return. It would be shameful for me to doubt that your motive was your concern for me. But it was also self-protection on your part. They asked P. Pio, the stigmatized Capuchin, on my behalf; he too opposed the return.[400]

In the end Sister Margaret gave up her plan.

At the same time she wanted to bring out those sisters whom she thought could help in the work in America. Naturally this idea was also unsuccessful given the conditions. In December

---

[399] SZTTI 1188/64
[400] A Sziv, 1976/8.p.347.

1952 three sisters started out to get through the Czechoslovak-Austrian border. "I am in very great spiritual stress connected with my work here. I now am expecting every day, whether my sisters will arrive, and I am worried how they will get through; also for the cold weather, that thanks be to God is now mild, but still it is neither summer nor fall." [401] From among the three, one succeeded to get through; one was shot and killed by a bullet from the border-guard; the other was taken captive at the border and imprisoned partly in Czechoslovakia and partly in Hungary. In the beginning there was a belief that both were in prison. Sister Margaret "was deeply broken by this happening, and she was trying to turn every stone to gain contacts for freeing the two sisters. She grieves very much, spends sleepless nights, I truly fear for her."[402] After all this, Sister Margaret realized that it made no sense to stay in Europe; she must return to the United States with lessened physical and intellectual energies. In February, 1952 she had undergone a hysterectomy, this is the reason she wrote on 11 October: "...I feel fairly well; I still feel a little of the surgery and doubly a little of my age..."[403]

Yet there was a very great need that she be in good physical and intellectual condition because

---

[401] SSSA-B N.Y. 1952. XII. 23

[402] SSSA-B. N.Y. Letter to Edith Weiss, (who financed the smuggling. Translator's addition.)

[403] SSSA -B, N.Y. 1952 1953, VIII. 1. To Dr. Iren Slachta.

in the American districts the situation deteriorated. The leadership elected at the 1947 Chapter now uprooted from their earlier soil, including Sister Alice, was without information and experience needed to face the new environment. Sister Alice, who as leader of the Chinese mission for the community in Shanghai, caused many irresolvable problems with her rigidity. Sister Margaret wrote innumerable letters, all with the request, "...don't be rigid, don't be attached to the letter of the law. You made mistakes by excess."[404] Unfortunately Sister Alice disturbed the peace in the American district as well. She made arrangements lacking discernment, flowing from not knowing the situation, and naturally in the name of Sister Margaret. She overlooked the sisters and superiors working there for 25 years. Everybody was expecting the Chapter of 1953 to finally heal the wounds and elect a superior who would be able to work with total energy and, with the knowledge of the situation, resolve the existing problems. Sister Margaret arrived in New York, under her own name on 5 May 1953 with the sister who fled from Hungary. Sister Margaret gave an account of herself to her confidante in August this way, "My ability to remember diminishes frightfully. I have difficulty concentrating; work is always too much; I hardly can cope. I never get any rest...if only I could sleep more."

Since 1935 this was the first Chapter in which those in the West could participate, but sis-

---

[404] SZTTI 533.

ters from Slovakia and Romania could not. Those who earlier had arrived in the States represented Hungarians. Members of the General Council were present. The Californian and Canadian sisters wanted, before anything else, to repeal the modifications made in the constitution by the chapter of 1947. (The canon lawyer in Esztergom had obliged the community to have the superiors appointed instead of elected. The chapter delegates had agreed to it only at the request of Cardinal Mindszenty, who told them that the final approval must come from Rome, and there, they can place back the original text into the constitution.)

The Californian and Canadian sisters brought a number of such proposals that related to their specific situation. Before anything else they wanted to elect a new superior general. By that time it had become clear to them that Sister Margaret, considering her age and the burdens of the previous more than ten years, was no longer able to respond to the tasks of a superior general. Added to this was the fact that for more than ten years Sister Margaret lived for public issues; all the care and concerns relating to community life and the issues of sisters was handled by her substitute, Sister Paula. In the new world Sister Margaret was no longer able to establish personal relationships with the sisters, who in reality had a great need for it. The Californian and Canadian sisters' superiors were each founding members, and they felt that neither Sister Margaret nor the sisters coming with her understood them. The sisters who fled from Eastern Europe suffered homesickness. From not being able to speak English in an acceptable measure (some could never speak it) they found themselves in a totally different culture among people of different background and that, in America it was not possible to do things that they were accustomed to do in Hungary. In small Hungary, Sister Margaret and the Society was an important asset, recognized even by the American diplomats present there. Here, in contrast, the immigrants every-day was begun where, in the land of Free America, everybody carves out a future and happiness according to their abilities. In the refugee community, Sister Margaret could no longer offer the earlier basis of security; her energies were all spent; there was no one to lean on. The natural reaction of the Hungarian sisters was attachment to their memories; they found to be good only those things that were the same as they were accustomed to at home. In the American sisters a resistance developed and some sad expressions began to be used such as 'Canada belongs to the Canadians' referring it to religious life. It happened that they spoke of the general superior as 'she' or 'they', while they spoke of the local superiors as 'I or 'we'.[405] Sister Alice, who was the substitute of Sister Margaret while she was in Vienna, had a sad role in all that developed.

While Sister Alice was still in China, Sister Margaret wrote to her from Vienna, "My little Alice,

---

[405] SZTTI 1189/89, p.4.

I am truly grateful with all my heart that you struggle to keep the rule. Only let us not swing so far out, as to arrive where 'the letter of the law kills.' Foerster says it is the greatest injustice to apply the law to unequal situations in a uniform manner. In the same way it is a mistake to force a regular schedule into very difficult situations just to be faithful." These admonitions had no effect, and Sister Alice's direction was made in the name of Sister Margaret.

The chapter began in 1953 in Hamilton with the Hungarian representatives in majority. In voting they rejected the American and Canadian proposals. At the time of elections the majority, based on the decision of the 1947 chapter, held that Sister Margaret be the lifelong superior general. During the first discussion, Sister Margaret spoke in favor of this. Whoever had known Sister Margaret would know that, for her, the law was sacred. Characteristically she shared once that during the parliamentary cycle of 1945-48 she asked something of Rákosi regarding a law. He responded, "You spoke against it, why are you interested?" Sister Margaret responded, "It has become a law and I respect the law." [406] Sister Margaret spoke this kind of reverence for the law. The condition of the letter killing the spirit happened! The sisters from California asked to interrupt the Chapter for a few days, because they wanted to go home to consult the community. They left. During the re-

---

[406] The author's remembrance of the happening.

cess Sister Margaret reflected on the situation, decided that she would step down, and give her place to the one whom the chapter elected.[407] However, on 25 August 1953 a telegram arrived from California. They had decided to separate from the original group.[408] They planned to keep the spirit, modify their constitution; and retain the name Sisters of Social Service. Canada did not follow them immediately, but within a short while the process of their separation took place. By the fall of 1955 the Decree of the Sacred Congregation of Religious arrived from Rome, recognizing the independence of the California-Canadian sisters. However, they ordered preservation of unity through a Federation. The Federation became a reality in 1972 and has functioned since then.[409]

After the very difficult year of 1953, Sister Margaret allowed herself some rest. "After some years of interruption, I am resting here because the old horse can no longer pull."[410] Saint Francis called his body 'brother ass' Sister Margaret called hers 'old horse.' Unfortunately she did not spend her vacation just resting, she worked on corre-

---

[407] Having read the minutes of the Chapter of 1953, this fact is stated there. Sister Jean Marie states the same thing in her History of the Federation. (Translator's note.)
[408] SZTTI1188/7
[409] By 1993, 110 members gathered in Buffalo. From Europe 28 members were received and paid for their travel. (from Hungary 12, Romania 7 and Slovakia 9.)
[410] SSSA-B, N.Y. Her letter to Zsigmond Michalovics, 1954, III. 16.

spondence that needed response. "...You have no idea how overworked I am. I am thinking always of our survival, of helping our sisters, how to bring them out from under suppression; of a million kinds of details, arranging things without stopping, writing letters. My abused head frequently denies my memory to function. Please do not forget, I am 70 years old. Never in my life did I sit on a sofa trimming my nails, but particularly not during the past 10 years."[411] In July 1954 the Kersten Committee asked her to testify about the communist system and how it is abusing human rights.[412]

Little by little the situation within the community began to be regulated. From Rome a new regulation arrived to organize the Federation in a manner that allowed members to be assigned from one organization to the other.[413] Since Sister Margaret ended living incognito, she accepted the invitation of the Actio Hungarica organization and in January 1956 she was elected honorary member; in March she was asked to give the festive address. "She gave an inspiring talk about the love of nation," wrote the Magyarság.[414] The editor of

---

[411] SSSA-B. N.Y. 1954. III. 29. Letter to Dr. Iren Slachta.

[412] Select Committee on Communist Aggression. It was under the leadership of Charles Kersten since July 1953.

[413] SZTTI 11 1192/43. In this document one can read: that Cardinal Larraone a high official in the Sacred Congregation, having received the information on the happenings oversees said "I know her (Sister Margaret). What happened is a tragedy."

[414] SZTTI 1100, 1956, III. 23, p. 8

the Kronika asked her to edit an article with the title, "Message from Margaret Slachta." On this she responded, "If I would not be such a beggar for time, I would gladly embrace this idea, since I desire deeply to serve the public, but our small numbers, our concerns for survival and rooting the community makes this impossible for me."[415]

During the month of October 1956 hope arose for a short time, but soon came the tragic happenings of November. Among the 200,000 who fled Hungary nine young women came to join the group under the leadership of Sister Margaret, together with five professed sisters. They were a great joy but also a concern when they arrived because they did not speak English and housing and supporting them was a great burden. Beyond that "the task to help those at home, to care for the ill and elderly, and dealing with begging letters from unknown fellow Hungarians" used up the resources.[416] Letters asking for help arrived in droves; the people thought that resources of Sister Margaret were inexhaustible; they could not imagine that she lived in such a meager situation as she did. What made the situation even more difficult was that her intellectual endowments and physical energies rapidly declined. Two letters bear witness to this fact, one was written by a young Hungarian sister. "...I heard that you cannot sleep well and that you suffer from stomach

---

[415] SZTTI 1197/20b
[416] SZTTI1204/6.

pain. I beg you kindly, please rest some alone and please do not work day and night on unresolved issues. I see what a difference of quality in your work, if you are rested or not. In a rested condition you are alert beyond your age but not when you are tired. Truly, it is not important that you write a whole lot of letters, but that good decisions be made; that you recognize difficult situations for what they are; that understanding for sisters and novices be born from Sister Margaret."[417] This letter touches gently on the fact that Sister Margaret no longer is able to meet her responsibilities as a superior. From Hungary one of the co-founding sister writes more clearly: "...From your letter I presume that your nerves are not in order. I wrote to you in several letters my new address, but you do not respond to them. Reflecting on all this I suggest you dedicate yourself completely to rest." The writer of the letter suggested clearly that she disengage herself completely and hand over her office to someone else.[418] This decision however was delayed; she did not notice her own decline. In January 1961 she received the notice of the serious illness of her younger sister Barbara who remained in Hungary. Sister Margaret wanted to return to Hungary. Those around her opposed the plan; Sister Margaret asked advice from Béla Varga[419] who most decidedly spoke against it. "I un-

---

[417] SZTTI 1193/2

[419] Bála Varga 1903-1996, Catholic priest, representative in the Independent Small Landowners party, who for his activities during the war was made an honorable Polish citizen

derstand completely what it means when a relative of ours is sick to death at home. For the whole world do not attempt to return home."[420] Her sister Barbara died during the year, and this affected Sister Margaret very painfully.

Sister Margaret used up all her energies working on behalf of others and, even being in shreds, she wanted to help. Her abused physique affected her intellect.

About her earlier public service the paper, American-Hungarian People's Voice, wrote 11 March 1962 that in the Yorkville Casino hall the American-Hungarian Association of New York held a freedom celebration. "Following a decade and half silence, Margaret Slachta gave the festive talk at the March celebration." The paper recognized particularly her work during the Nazi times. "When men cowardly hid, the whispering persecuted spread the news that Margaret Slachta helped everybody; truly it is admirable how many hundreds of persons were saved by her. Though her nerve-wracking heroic acts are fit for novels she never received any public recognition..."[421] The broken, aged 78 year old speaker no longer resembled the once inspiring public speaker. She no longer took a public role, and one year later, in

---

and an officer in the French Legion of Honor. Leading figure of the émigré's' politics.
[420] SZTTI 1204/17f
[421] SZTTI 1193/3ab The American Hungarian Voice of People, 1962. III 6. 8.

1963, she resigned her office as superior general. From that time on she lived like a simple sister.

In 1969 Sister Margaret celebrated her Diamond Jubilee and the groups that had become independent sent her festive greetings signed by all sisters. Among the many English greetings we find some Hungarian as well. The two co-founding Hungarian sisters greeted her in their mother tongue: "With love and gratitude, Sister Maria." (Schwartz); "With deep love and gratitude, Sister Frederica." The latter wrote an extra greeting. "Well, life is a great mystery. How differently we see life, the happenings when the head becomes gray. I think of you and yours with very great love. I give thanks with you for when I was your joy, and I ask you to leave for God's grace when I caused you pain, and please know, we always had a high respect for your person. With respectful and great love, Sister Frederica."[422]

In 1971 Dr. Iren Slachta died. For Sister Margaret three more years were given. From December of 1973 she became so weak that she could get up and get dressed only with help, but she still could go to the chapel by leaning on sisters. On 4 January 1974 she was found next to her bed at daybreak. "I slipped down," she whispered. A priest was called and she received, with total consciousness, the sacrament of the sick and received a Papal blessing. On the following day

---

[422] SZTTI 1193/69-70

her fever rose very high and the doctor took her to the hospital, but the process could not be halted. She had a cerebral stroke and pneumonia in the right lobe of the lung. The Buffalo community surrounded her bed praying and singing until she stopped breathing.[423] To Hungary the news was sent, "Grandmother was called to God on 6 January 1974."[424]

Her death did not remain a personal matter of the Society. The Associated Press sent the news of her death to 6200 American newspapers. This happened with very few Hungarians in a foreign country, wrote the <u>Hungarian Catholic Sunday</u>. In this way those received information of her initiatives and fruitful activities but had no idea that such an outstanding personality got refuge in the New World.[425] For her burial the whole community gathered. From California three sisters came; Canada was represented with fifteen sisters. From Puerto Rico, from Cuba, and from the American district all, except the ill, were present.

On 9 January the Bishop of Buffalo with 30 priests celebrated the Eucharist at the burial Mass. The burial took place in the Holy Cross Cemetery. During the Mass the Bishop spoke of her merits, at the grave a Hungarian Jesuit and émigré, ex-

---

[423] The community sang her favorite hymn to the Holy Spirit: "Spirit of Fire, Come to Us."
[424] SZTTI 1193/101
[425] SZTTI 1198, 1974II.3.

pressed appreciation for her services and historic activities.[426]

The sisters and those who knew well of Sister Margaret's activities found it very significant that she was called home to God on 6 January, a day so much loved by Sister Margaret, as it was always the day that she gave the yearly program for the Christian Women's Corps. The talks she gave on that day strengthened her hearers in the values and principles of the Gospel. Regarding the feast day, one of her admirers said, "Her soul was gold, her life was frankincense, her illness the myrrh. Therefore, the Lord received her as a feast-day gift." [427]

The 90 years of Sister Margaret Slachta's life was rich in happenings during the new era and its changes. She was born in a happy and peaceful time in a middle-class family, she grew up in comfortable circumstances and earned a teacher's degree. She became acquainted with the Christian women's movement. After working as a teacher and a patroness, she entered the Social Mission Society, where she became the director of their apostolate at the age 26, lived through World War I; witnessed the loss and collapse of her country, the revolution, the People's Council. She

---

[426] SZTTI 1193/101

[427] The letter of Dr. Georg Kis, pastor, the pioneer of Christian Jewish Dialogue in Hungary, and a collaborator of Sr. Margaret in the Ghettoes.

recognized what needed to be done, organized an agricultural association to keep the Social Mission Society alive. With the rise of women's movement she stepped into political activity. In 1920, at the age of 36, she becomes the first female representative in the Hungarian Parliament, and as the defender and promoter of the Social Mission Society's original vision she left behind all her previous achievements. In the midst of incredible difficulties she founded the Society of the Sisters of Social Service, not guessing that she was laying down the foundations of an international organization. In 1923 she began building the community's spirit; she formed the new community; and after innumerable difficulties the fruitful ministries were begun. Soon World War II arrived and, in it, a new paganism, the theory of race rose up. She opposed it with her entire being and inspired others to a spiritual and active resistance.

After 1945 she opposed the theory and practice of historical materialism without compromise. At the age of 65 she left her country with the intention of returning, but she could no longer return. She crossed the ocean, but this change was beyond her intellectual and physical ability to adjust. It seemed that her life's failure had arrived; the fruits of her life were destroyed beyond the Iron Curtain and in the America.

For twenty years she lived with Alzheimer disease. She died poor, having returned to God all she had received, like Christ on the Cross. Her

life, full of contradictions, was a series of successes and losses. Success did not daze her; losses
did not break her. What kept her going? A basic
vision that she proclaimed, spoke of, acted on, and
applied in all circumstances: a supernatural stance
that became natural for her. For this reason the
life of Margaret Slachta cannot be characterized
as failure. "One of the great miracles of grace is
that everything here on earth receives a different
meaning and value than what, on a natural level it
means."[428] "Our faith recognizes the One who directs unseen life and history and notices His plans.
We are able to perceive that which, from the outside, looks like shame but from within, by the light
of eternity, is immeasurable glory. This is the consolation of the just: 'You will forget your sufferings;
your life, more radiant than the noon-day, will
make a dawn of darkness." (Job: 11: 16-17.)

---

[428] From the "Mission of God's Sanctifying Love." Manuscript, Cluj, Romania, 1944. P.42.

Margaret Slachta, the Person

Perhaps there is no need for this chapter, since the reader has found rich information on which to base an opinion. However, it might not be superfluous to add some things to what has been written. It might still be possible to highlight some characteristics, adding some color to the picture. [...]

Examining the personality of Margaret Slachta one sees how the religious and the public servant roles became one. This was an inseparable combination. In her public actions she argued on the basis of the Ten Commandments; when she offered spiritual instruction to sisters she used national or international politics, or some comparisons in natural science. In 1947 she expressed her disappointment that sisters did not reflect and work well enough with the spiritual material offered to them. "I know how difficult the times we will have to face, yet on the spiritual front-line we are to be able to stand our post. The present happenings are in some way like the conditions in 1918, when in the leaders of the ruling party consciousness of their vocation and the grace, the light and the strength of being sent was missing... and those who are missing this, are not able to fulfill their vocation, to lead the people to God."[429] In 1941 at

_____

[429] Her teaching on June 2. "Who does not work with the received material on the Gospel, will remain on the surface and will not be able to stand firm on principles."

the time of the deportations at Korosmezo she wrote the following to Mrs. Horthy, "I dare to bring the case to your High Honor for the sake of rights, justice and Christianity..."[430] After 1945 she spoke in the Parliament, "...let us turn to divine help, to heavenly power. Human help cannot save us, our own humanity is no protection against the selfishness of our weak beings."[431] This is the reason that her colleagues in the Parliament said - even those with good will toward her - that her stance and ideas were 'naive'. Zoltán K. Kovács recalled smiling 16 June 1948 when Margaret Slachta gave her grand talk against the nationalization of schools that resulted in being expelled from the Parliament, "she thought that she would convince the communists." On each occasion she expressed this living conviction. Her naiveté is like that of prophets, when Israel had to politicize prudently in the midst of two great powers in conflict with each other (Egypt and Babylonia). The prophets proclaimed, "return to the Lord, he will have mercy on you." Her naivety however was built on reality. She saw precisely and clearly the situations and conditions. In 1944 she placed the house, where Jewish people were hidden, under the Swedish and Vatican protection; but she hoped the real protection from God. For her, God was the only true reality. "God's actions never miss their goals. He does not take back from human beings their freedom of will once given, and

---

[430] SZTTI 1132
[431] Diary of the National Assembly, 1946 VIII. 23.

with which human beings can damage God's plans. But at the ultimate development God's majestic ideas will get realized, regardless that evasions, interruptions, even destructions marked the direction of the road. In the end no one can achieve victory against God, only with him."[432]

She did not forget that here on earth matter carries the spirit. At the same time, she was not a slave of material goods. For building the motherhouse and the Holy Spirit church she received permission to collect money. As soon as she received some she offered 20% of it for poor churches. She held on to the principle to accept only such favors that everyone is granted. In 1926-27 a good friend in high position arranged an extraordinary tax reduction for the Society. Margaret Slachta did not accept it and paid the total amount of taxes. Between the two wars, Budapest had its own customs area. At the train stations and on the roads leading to the city, people had to pay customs on some articles. The farmers from the villages could deliver food to Budapest only after having paid customs. There was a particularly strict control during World War II. One sister succeeded in bringing a great amount of foodstuff without paying customs. She bragged about it in the community. Sister Margaret heard it and ordered the sister to return, pay the taxes and, only then, bring the food home.

---

[432] Voice of the Spirit, 1940/5 cover page

The democratic posture of Margaret Slachta belonged to her sense of reality. Before Vatican II there was a marked difference in clothing and in manner of address between the educated and non-educated sisters. Among the Sisters of Social Service everybody wore the same clothing and everyone was addressed in the same way. The Rev. Dr. George Kis once told that he "tried to call her Very Reverend Sister Superior." Each time he received the reply, "only Sister Margaret."

We need to speak of her stance that favored kingdom as a national form; public opinion held that it was her political stance. It was only in a small manner. We remember that in October of 1918 the <u>Hungarian Woman</u> affirmed unanimously the National Council, and after the abdication of King Charles IV, she said good-by to the royal couple with very warm words adding, "whoever steps into the hall of new historical developments without closing the door of the old one with reverence is already a betrayer of the new vision." Unfortunately, the October revolution of 1918 resulted in the Hungarian-Soviet Republic in 1919. The country was robbed of its many parts, impoverished and in turmoil. The parties for Horthy became louder and louder, and the legitimists, siding with kingdom, were considered against Horthy. Sister Margaret was committed to the national vision inherited from Saint Stephen, a kingdom. Today this is called being European and she emphasized this not only between 1920-22, but also between 1927-1944 in her speeches in the Parliament and even after 1945. Those who were her co-organizers and even sisters called it erroneously of being for the king. In actuality she spoke several times, "it is not a question of the king, but of the nation's constitutional form of kingdom from the great spiritual heritage left by our first king." This great spiritual heritage was Margaret Slachta legitimism, that is, "...if the people and those who carry the highest power know and profess that they carry power with responsibility and that they owe responsibility to God."[433]

She held the question of women as her great and favored task. She understood well the stance of Edith Farkas: "The Social Mission Society wants to develop and secure the Women's' Movement on the basis of Christian ethics"[434] and "...let us work fervently to develop public opinion on women's education, on citizenship... Let us inform Catholic women that yes, we take into our hands the problems of womanhood; that their just rights will find protection and promotion among us... We shall do everything in our power for the political recognition of women as Hungarian citizens, so that the value and interests of individual women and, through it, the entire women's movement will develop ethically and economically.[435]

Contrary to the turn of the century's liberal

---

[433] Diary of the National Assembly, 1946. I. 31.
[434] Christian Women, 1915/5.
[435] Christian Women, 1917/7, p. 5-7

women's movements - and that of the present - which demanded equal rights, Margaret Slachta did not emphasize the rights but, rather, women's specific values. These specific values - to which she witnessed - she recognized through her own vocation and understood it from fathoming its depth. A woman's vocation is to be the partner of man, because their interest is the same. She saw that on earth all energy by itself is one-sided, and, if it gets isolated, it fails on account of its one-sidedness. Against this there is one protection: to recognize our co-dependence and to search for a complement. The two sexes think differently. Men include in their thinking their own specific mental functions; so do women. Only the two together make one whole. Men's way of thinking is abstract. Women see beyond the abstraction those who will be affected in a good or an unfavorable way by the abstraction. Therefore she spoke in the Parliament of protecting women's economic energies. The bread-winning woman carries a three or fourfold burden. The consequence of the manifold burden is infant mortality and early death of men because their mothers could not give sufficient life force to the baby in ; she could not offer adequate care for the infant and the small child. The woman receives on earth the greatest role: she can give life, persons for the nation and for humanity.[436] "A nation will die only if its morality is destroyed. When women fight for morality they

---

[436] From the talks of Margaret Slachta in the Parliament, 1920-22.

fight for the life of their nation...the existence or destruction of a nation is in the hands of women... How sad that women are so little aware of this vocation! It is for this reason that Margaret Slachta and the Sisters of Social Service worked in various women's movements and Margaret Slachta established the Christian Women's Corps in November of 1918.

If we ask sisters to speak, we receive a multi-colored characterization. In the SZTTI[437] we shall find many similar memories, most of them from the years of suppression. They were written usually in a 'flowery language': 'aunt' 'mother' and always without date; many times the happenings circumscribed are not clearly stated. "When my aunt was abroad..." or "Once she sent me to a house marked with star."[438]

Her basic stance, love for human beings, was noted by those who shared their remembrances. One sister wore a torn vest. Sister Margaret noticed it; she took it from her, mended it and gave it back to her. For another she touched her winter coat and found it too thin; that it is not warm enough. Immediately she gave her a knitted sweater that could be worn under the coat. In the Society there was a custom to hold a 'family day'

---

[437] The Archives of the Sisters of Social Service in Budapest.(translator's note.)

[438] Jewish people had to wear a yellow star. (Translators' note.)

when the relatives of sisters and novices would be invited. The young sisters would provide a program and afterwards there was an agape with some sandwiches. At one such family day, when the guests were sitting at tables, Sister Margaret walked among them. She overheard one of the guests remark that instead of lemon some rum would be good for the tea. Sister Margaret went immediately and brought rum - the guest spoke for years about who made her tea very tasteful. Even though she was the superior, she did not accept personal service. If she came home late, the sister cook would have set her food aside in the oven. She took it out, ate and washed the dishes, put them in their place and, only afterward, went to bed. One sister in 1948 came home late; there was still light in the dining room. Sister Margaret was there with some older sisters. The young sister greeted and started to a small table to eat. Sister Margaret asked her, "Are you eating supper, my little sister?" At her affirmative response Sister Margaret said, "Come, sit at my place, I am already finished" and she served the supper to the young sister.

Sister Margaret had great concern for the sisters' health. Daily exercise and washing the body was obligatory.[439] During summer she rented a pool for the sisters. At first, each sister dressed in her cabin into swimsuits, but did not

---

[439] Showers at that time did not exist in Hungary. (Translator's note)

dare to come out. Seeing this, Sister Margaret came out first in her swimsuit - then the sisters, too, dared to come out. Afterward Sister Margaret scolded the community saying, "our body is the creation of God, we may not be ashamed of it." Of another pool experience a tall sister gave an account: there were two of them with Sister Margaret, who was of medium stature, and she suggested a swimming contest. The tall sister hesitated; it was quite clear that she would win. Sister Margaret understood the reason of her hesitation and said, "Do you think I shall not be able to bear it if I lose?"

Did she have any faults? Most certainly, since no human being is without them. We already have read she knew of herself that she was hard headed. In some way she wanted to realize her ideas beyond her abilities and possibilities. This could be perhaps expressed: if she received an apple seed, she would think how many years will pass before it will bring fruit; she however saw already the developed apples in all their beauty, and started to plan accordingly. Her co-workers, primarily those in the community, she did not chose; she accepted them. Most of them did precisely and gladly what she asked of them. Congenial with her were perhaps two among the leading sisters; both of them lived distant from her. One was Sister Augusta Ikrich, the foundress and superior of the Transylvanian district. She was absolutely necessary in planting the seeds of the Society in that country. The second was the foundress of the Californian district, Sister Frederica Horvath, who was to establish the Society in the United States that flourished with American members. These two understood, identified with and, in their particular situation, further developed the ideas of Sister Margaret. The other, very good, and committed sisters all leaned on her and, therefore, it was impossible for Sister Margaret to decide between two vocations: that of the Society or of public service. She carried this double responsibility, of which one is quite enough for a person. Of the picture she had of herself, we know very little; only two of her personal descriptions remain. In 1926 she alone led a retreat. Of this she wrote to her confidante, "I could dedicate time to myself in silence...I had a painful insight into myself and my life...it is still difficult for me to bear myself...truly I would like to be better with all my heart, but I do not succeed. I feel deep pain knowing that my faults and failings... burden you spiritually, just as the sisters failings and faults burden me...."[440] She confided similarly to a young sister, who saw her putting a little bug in a safe place and the sister asked why she was doing it. "Frequently when I become sad over my miseries, I think, perhaps God will be merciful to me, as I am merciful to this little bug."[441] After this it is not surprising that the motto chosen by her at the time of taking vows is "My Jesus, mercy." The self-image pictured here perfectly fits a ripe personality defined

---

[440] 1157/59
[441] 1158/3

by Erich Fromm, "who does not want for herself more than for what she worked hard, who let go...of her narcissist dreams, who became humble through an interior strength, which is the only source of productive activities."[442]

This was the reason why she had courage to take a stance, to speak up, to act in hopeless situations for causes of God and human sisters and brothers. Of herself, she expected nothing but she was certain that with God's help she would overcome all obstacles.

---

[442] Erich Fromm: The Art of Loving. P.45

APPENDIX

The Christian Women Corps Now

The talk Margaret Slachta gave at the
25th anniversary of the founding of the
Christian Women Corps on 28 November 1943, [443]

The Corps' chief work since 1939 has been to make conscious in society Christian truths to increase the ability to resist contemporary public opinion and to lead back to Christ those whom the new ideology has already misled.

The Corps began working in 1918 in the midst of storm. Even today we fight against the direction of the wind. Those against whom we fought in 1918 knew they were enemies of Christianity. When we work now against public opinion, we oppose those who think they are Christian but their actions at every step are not. This has the consequence that those who want to be uncompromised Christians are in the eyes of the "race-Christians" heretics and betrayers. For this reason to be faithful to Christian doctrine demands a much deeper consciousness in faith, a much stronger character than what we needed at the beginning of

---

[443] Two prints of this talk are known: <u>Hungarian Sion</u>, a Catholic political weekly (25 January 1943) and the <u>Sun</u>, in Cluj (1 January 1944). The <u>Sun</u> copy did not give the subtitle.

our service. The Christian Women Corps wants in its present efforts, a just stance, and it objects to any means that rejects Christianity. It draws the attention of public opinion always to the fact that to end injustice through injustice, denying rights by rights denied is not possible. Ethical wrongdoing cannot be remedied by ethically wrong actions; doing so is the greatest error. Let the public know that all violence is a boomerang that hits back with a double force. Injustice done to others destroys the basis of rights for oneself. Gaining momentary success with unchristian means is sacrificing the nation's deeper understood future interests. And every sin hinders God's blessings.

This conviction is expressed in the memo-randum of the Christian Women Corps, in which they protested against the race-ideology arisen during the past years and against proposals of laws that rejected Christian tenets. During the 6 January 1940 talk each participant of the Corps signed and submitted to the Prime Minister the statement of protest against the law-proposal to deprive people (Jews) of their jobs. In 1942 the Christian Women Corps submitted circular letters to each representative and to the members of the upper house, explaining that the law-proposal of nationalization of each landowners' property can be justified only by objective reasons, and not by racial considerations. That means only from those may the land be taken who do not cultivate it for the common good; or who do not secure for their workers adequate sustenance and environment for a dignified life.

On another issue of the 40's, but inspired by the same spirit, the Christian Women Corps approached the Minister of Defense, asking to end the atrocities and revenge on the Hungarian front that do not correspond to the laws of Christian warfare and which may bring greater danger for soldiers who are taken captive.

The Christian Women Corps proclaimed Christian vision through the "movie-front'. To the films that were shown, a highlighting of Christian vision was attached to make the viewers conscious of Christian ideas that underscored the movie's story.

The truths of Christianity and their demands on society and on political life were also given voice in the pages of the Voice of the Spirit, published during the middle of each month. This served as the organ of the Christian Women Corps from 1943 on. Its various articles try, with many different methods, to help the readers understand that Christianity is the summary of laws upholding both individual's and society's life. It is none other than God's revelation by Christ to the deeper self of human beings and of their goals as children of God. Whoever separates self from this degrades self and sacrifices the basis of one's own happiness.

I had to say all this. Life is always uncertain, today more than other times. Who knows when will be the last occasion when I may speak of these serious truths to the community! I feel a vocation to this era. I do have a message for it and without any other consideration I would like to say some more things of the unchangeable and eternal truths. I ask my sisters to stand in the radiation of these eternal truths, rather than under the nightmarish attraction of swamps. Only these truths can bring blessings to the nation and the homeland. In this sense I would like to mention how much we miss, in public life, the recognition that God is the Lord of society and of nations. We are ashamed to speak in the name of our Lord, our heavenly Father, to protest in God's name, even though we could prevent so much injustice, so much violence with it! How many persons could retain their homes, their family, or their happiness if we would speak up in this way. I mention here a small nation in the West, where the Catholics and all the leaders of the other denominations submitted a protest to their nation's commissioner when the authorities brought a regulation ordering sterilization in marriages of mixed races. This memorandum begins in this way:

> We submit to you in the name of our Lord our request; ...since the time of being occupied, more such laws were brought that are contrary to the laws of Christ, yet we, and our government always strove to live like Christians. You have a responsibility to end the regulation of sterilization, and to do eve-

rything because it is against the law of God. You stand under God's law, and actually more so, because you carry a great power and, on account of this, you carry a greater responsibility...

When shall we speak in this kind of mother tongue, in our community, before the public and even in the Parliament? What we also miss is a moral courage. The war fronts are only concrete expressions of that war that exist between the two fronts: the materialist and the transcendent worldview. A coward army never on earth won a victory. We cannot win a spiritual victory for our vision if we lack courage to stand up and fight for those values we represent. A new phenomenon is that young woman who entered into the office of the factory, having in hand the Working Woman where the officer saw on the front page the picture of the Pope. He began right away to demean her. The girl objected, but the man continued. She slapped his face. The case was submitted to the leadership of the factory and, in honor of the leadership, the officer was punished.

Or let us take another example from the West that happened in a Protestant church gathering. The believers went to participate in the Lord's Supper. In the line, their nation's highest office-holder approached. The pastor walked around, avoiding him and said, "For traitors there is no Supper of the Lord." It is true that the pastor was led out of the church with hands tied together, but he protected the moral point of view.

This is how I respond to the gentleman who read my letter to municipal commission of Pest and remarked that he too would write such a letter for 10,000 Hungarian Forint. Perhaps he would, but not the girl mentioned before, nor the Protestant pastor, nor the Christian Women Corps. They and we do not ask what shall we get if we write a letter, or give a speech, but we would ask in what manner shall we start to fight for an attacked value of truth. We not only do not expect to receive something, but discern what shall we give for this step: perhaps a job, perhaps a mandate, perhaps something more. We do not build our nation with what we receive for our services, but with the sacrifices we must make doing our job.

Now only one more thing! In our activities we must express more this truth: work is the part for human beings; blessing is God's! If God does not work with us, the best plan and the most assured undertaking will fall apart like a house of cards. If we think that we can create happiness for ourselves against God, perhaps not immediately but God will most certainly show us that only with Him is happiness to be found. There is no happiness against him. If God warns, drought and floods, frost and heat, bacteria and landslides will fight against us rebellious human beings; or even persons who lost their humanity will fight us. In that case God will tear apart - a wild beast with a wild beast.

I pointed out this truth in my letter of January[444] when so many were trembling for their sons and husbands on the front. I asked our Hungarian sisters to send to those who fight on the front heavenly help in the manner to be as compassionate to others as they hope from God compassion for their sons and husbands. Out of this viewpoint I have recommended into their good will the non-Christians as well. Is there anyone who could witness that my writing was not according to the teachings of Christ? Still, uproar came from many directions, even though everybody knows that the January letter had objective reasons and basis in the many happenings in our nation.

I asked to resist the temptations of contemporary worldview that is made easier. Though we were burdened with national sins our nation could distance itself from those excesses that will remain the shame of the 20th century's history. There still happened many such personal actions that call for the wrath of God and hinder his help.

The situation of our nation, humanly speaking, is not resolvable. We are dependent on Divine strength to be freed from our situation. How much we would have to do; and how much we may not do that the irresolvable situation by human effort may be resolved by Divine Providence! Christ our Lord told us the secret for this, "Seek

---

[444] See: Margaret Slachta's Christian Public Life p. 139.

first the reign of God and its justice, and the rest will be added to it" with God's help. Beyond all diplomacy, all human wisdom and all the force of arms, God can do immeasurably more. As a result, only those people who, being conscious of their souls' responsibility and their dignity as children of God, know the mysterious depth of existence and work on earth with undying aspirations to build a happy society on firm basis. Yes. Only they are accepted as co-workers by God!

The Christian Women Corps, all who are here, myself included, we all want to serve our nation in this way so that we may call it as ours by God's Providence.

Recognitions After Death

1985. September 20 Margaret Slachta receives from the State of Israel the distinction of "Righteous Gentile" and a tree is planted in her memory at Yad Vashem.

1990 The believing Socialists hold a memorial meeting in her honor in Budapest.

1995. March 15. Margaret Slachta and the Society of the Sisters of Social Service receive a memorial medal from the Hungarian Government.

On May 7 Margaret Slachta received from the Hungarian Republic the "Courage" medal of merit.

1996. On September 8 a memorial plaque was placed on Thökölyi St. 69, (the first motherhouse) and the Hungarian Holocaust Committee held a meeting in memory of Margaret Slachta.

On October 16: The "Righteous" academy memorial meeting held and organized by the Christian-Jewish Dialogue

1997 February 10: Ágnes Tölgyesi shows the film titled "Credo", a portrayal of Margaret Slachta.

2017   The district of Zuglo in Budapest authorized erection of a statue of Margaret Slachta recognizing "her life as a model for all Hungarians."

Chronology

1884	September 18, Born in Kassa, Hungary (now Kosice, Slovakia)
1890 - 1895	Grade school
1895 - 1901	Girls' high school
1900	Pilgrimage to Rome with her mother
1901 - 1903	Teachers' college in Kosice
1903 - 1906	College for teaching in high schools
1905	Her narrative, The Secret. published
1906	Edith Farkas' presentation in Kalocsa
1906	20 March the "Patronage"[445] is founded, and Margaret becomes the assistant superior.
1906 - 1907	Teacher in High school, Györ, Hungary nominee for Patronage
1907	Margaret's study on: "What Are the Requirements of Founding and Maintaining a Patronage" is published in the Yearbook of Patronage.
1907	September - December Educator in the teachers' college, on Csalogány Street, Budapest;
1908	January - February in Berlin, taking a course for Administrative Secretaries of Working Women's organizations; in March gives presentation in the Patronage's social study course; on 19 November she enters the Social Mission Society
1909	Vows pronounced at Pentecost: in Szikszo
1910	At the Catholic Congress in Szeged she gives a presentation on the protection of workingwomen; her presentation is published with the title: "Protection of Working Women"

---

[445] A protective organization for women. (Translator's note)

1911	Named Superior of the Seminary (the novitiate) in Budapest and the Vice President of the Social Mission;[446]
1913	Her article, "Women's Right to Vote," is published in the: Értesitő[447]; in September the first committee meeting of the Catholic Women's Council
1913	The second committee meeting of the Catholic Women's Council; 12 December began a lecture tour in Transylvania;
1914	15 - 19 April she offers a description of the Social Mission Society at the Austrian Catholic Women's Day; in July she lectures on a course of the Social Mission Society on social work; informs that the Catholic Women's Council will not be founded
1915	The School of Social Work of the Social Mission Society is opened; in March The Christian Woman, a Catholic periodical starts publication; Margaret Slachta is the editor; after Pentecost she develops with four others the plan for the National Organization of Social Mission; from 1 September she is assigned to Szikszo for one year. She begins her tour in Transylvania on behalf of the national organization
1916	In January she organizes the Social Study Club of the Catholic Women in Temesvár (now Timisoara); she travels each month to lecture there; in February she lectures in Gyula, and comes to know the young Wilhelm Apor[448]; on 27 August the Romanian army invades Transylvania; in November

---

[446] An organization to involve volunteers empowering the poor. Eventually it became a nation-wide organization. (Translator's note.)

[447] A periodical

[448] Later a famous Bishop. (Translator's note.)

	she visits, with Sister Paula, the destroyed areas to organize help for the people.
1917	September 18 - 21: The Transylvanian section of Social Mission is founded; on 10 - 11 November the national organization is realized; Margaret is the acting manager.
1918	Beginning in March the name of the periodical Christian Woman is changed to Hungarian Woman; it is the periodical of the Christian Feminism and the newsletter of the Social Mission Society's national organization. Editor: Margaret Slachta;
	In May Sister Margaret describes the organizational work of the Social Mission Society and the Christian Feminism in Vienna; in September the first Social Work Guide is published.
1918	17 October István Tisza announces in the Parliament: Hungary lost the war. On 28 October the Christian Women's Corps is founded and submits to the Ministry of Interior a bill for women's right to vote. 30-31 October "The Fall Revolution"; on 16 November the National Council[449] gives women the right to vote!
1919	21 March: Hungarian Soviet Republic; Sister Margaret submits to the Republic a petition to cultivate non-used areas in Budapest to raise food and in April the no. XI. Agricultural Co-Operative is organized; The Social Mission Society, co-workers, other religious community members began working in it. In August the Romanian army occupies Budapest; in violation of the prohibition of gathering the Christian Women's Corps holds a Club-meeting each Tuesday; 24 October Sir George Clark, the representative of

---

[449] The transition government in Hungary

the Council of Five of the Entent[450] arrives in Budapest; Sister Margaret organizes 35,000 women for a silent march before the Entent's representative[451]; on 16 November the Romanian army leaves Budapest; on 17 November the Hungarian National Army enters Budapest; Constitutional life begins; preparations start for national election.

1920   Károly Huszár, prime minister, initiates social action to ease hunger in Budapest. His co-workers are the Sisters of Social Mission Society and the members of the Christian Women's Corps.

In the elections of Januray István Haller received three mandates, and returns the mandate for the first district of Budapest. A second election for district I is announced. On 11 February a delegation of 100 women ask the nomination of Margaret Slachta. On 26 February the presidency of the National Unity Party's committee selects Margaret Slachta with absolute majority to be the party's nominee.

On 3 March Margaret holds her first talk on her program; on 9 March the second; on 16 March the third talk on her program only for women and on the 21 March a third talk on her program only for men. On 25 March the First District of Budapest elects Margaret Slachta as the representative in the Parliament.

She accepts her mandate on 28 March; and enters Parliament for the first time on 29

---

[450] The representative of the victorious Western powers (Translator's note)

[451] I learned each woman held a rose in her hand (Translator's note)

March. She gives her first talk in the Parliament on 23 April. On 15 July she is elected as a Councilwoman. From August to October she is on a tour abroad.

27 October she organizes a congress for women on behalf of women's right to vote.

1921   6 January: the first review of the Christian Women's Corps. 28 January: Before the beginning of debates Margaret Slachta placed on the table of the House the protests of 170 social and cultural organizations against truncating the law regarding women's right to vote;

14 May: The International Standing Committee of Suffrage asks Margaret Slachta to be a corresponding member; 28 December: Her talk on behalf of women's right to vote is published with the title: "Why Do We Have a Need for the Right of Women to Vote?"

1922   14 February: Her second talk on behalf of women's right to vote; 16 February: The first session of the Parliament ended.

22 March: The Christian Women's Corps approaches the Episcopal conference to support their petition that Margaret Slachta be allowed to enter the process for election to the Parliament; On 2 April 2 an article is published in the Nemzeti Ujság.[452] The Christian Women's Corps publishes the article on the political service of the first woman representative.

During summer she travels to London and from there to America; 1 September: She writes a letter (from London) to Edith Farkas in the case of the latter's plan to unite the Social Mission Society with that of the People's Daughters. She asks permission to re-

---

[452] A daily paper. (Translator's note)

	turn to Hungary. She returns. She makes great efforts to hold Social Mission Society together; 10 December: The yearly meeting of Social Mission (the national organization.) is held and Margaret Slachta submits the work-plan for the following year.
1923	On 5 May she is dismissed from the Social Mission Society with her companions (35). 12 May: Founding the Society of the Sisters of Social Service (SSS); The "Sister Alliance"[453] is created; During summer in Tömös (Transylvania) discussions regarding the Constitution; 15 July: Margaret Slachta is elected as superior; in November in the hospital and surgery for gall bladder problems
1924	Early in Spring: Seeking employment for Sisters in Switzerland and France;
1924 - 1925	She works in the United States and Canada
1926	22 December: Sister Margaret returns to Budapest
1927	8 February: A highly successful meeting and report on her activities; Captured Sunbeams is published. In September the novitiate is opened with 32 asking admission. In November a surgery for gall stones; In December the candles of the Everybody's Christmas Tree are lit in 15 places in Budapest;
1928	From the Desert to the Center of Life is published;[454] From November until April 1929 once more in America.

---

[453] The Sister Alliance was the economic arm of the SSS, as it refused to own institutions. (Translator's note.)

[454] A book explaining the mission – vision of the SSS. (Translator's note.)

1930	Sister Margaret resigns as Superior General; during summer she participates in the meeting of modern feminine communities in Goldenstein, Austria; in December she is elected as a Councilwoman in Angyalföld;[455]
1931	Organizing Workingwomen begins[456] The Wolff party impedes the Christian Women's Corps from running during the election;
1932	Pentecost: Sister Margaret is re-elected as Superior General
1933	The Holy Spirit Association is established
1934	Publishing of the <u>Voice of the Spirit</u> is begun[457]
1935	In September she travels to America. On the 7 October her sister dies.
1936	16 January her mother dies and on the 30th her father dies; Sister Margaret returns to Budapest on 30 September.
1937	On the 3 November the school of Women's Catholic Social Service is opened; leaflets describing its program are published. (In 1938 a second, and in 1943 a third edition is disseminated.)
1938	In May the International Eucharistic Congress is held in Hungary; November the first Vienna Decision; parts of the Northern section of historical Hungary is re-annexed.[458]

---

[455] A very poor section of Budapest. (Tranlator's note.)

[456] It was called into existence on the model of the Belgian Cardinal Cardejn: "Jeuness Ouvrier Chretienne."

[457] A monthly periodical sharing the vision of Christian national and public life. (Translator's note.)

[458] Hitler's policy.

1939	6 January: Christian Women's Corps meeting "Against Nazism" as a theme.
1940	September: the Second Vienna Decision. Parts of Transylvania are re-annexed to Hungary; November 8: Deportation of Jews from Csikszereda (now Miercurea-Ciuc); December the Christian Women's Corps submits a petition on behalf of the Jewish Labor Camp workers;
1941	6 January: Christian Women's Corps meeting; During summer: Chapter; Deportation of Jews at Kőrösmező; (now Ukraine) Sister Margaret travels there to observe and to bring help; 21 September: the Russian Command orders police surveillance of Sister Margaret.
1942	6 January: On account of Sister Margaret's talk to the Christian Women's Corps meeting the German Ambassador submits a protest against her through the Minister of Foreign Affairs; accusation is made against Margaret Slachta. She is condemned on the lower court; however, the King's Table acquits her. In February the first Worldview Course is begun in Budapest; it is later followed nationwide; in March information is received of the deportations in Slovakia; after 25 March she travels there.
1943	6 January: In the <u>Voice of the Spirit</u> the "New Year's Letter" is published regarding the workers in the forced labor camps[459]; on the 7 February the authorities of Pest County condemn the "New Year's Letter." Margaret Slachta addresses an open letter to them;

---

[459] They were Jews. (Translator's note.)

8 February: Slovakia announces the deportation of all Jewish people from its territory. 20,000 lives are in danger;

3 March: Margaret Slachta's travels to Rome; she confers with Cardinal Spellman, the Archbishop of New York;

11 March: Audience with Pope Pius XII; Margaret Slachta drafts the "Worldview Creed" in Rome;

Initiates the Movie Front[460];

12 May the 20th Jubilee of the Sisters of Social Service.

1944 January 6: on 19 March the German army occupies Hungary; in the month of April the Voice of the Spirit is suppressed; saving Jewish lives begins.

During summer the Fire of Pentecost[461] is published;

On 24 December Margaret Slachta accompanies the only Everybody Christmas Tree in the city of Budapest surrounded by the Russian army;

27 December: Sister Sara Salkaházi is executed by the Arrow Cross soldiers:

1945 7 January: The Arrow Cross is searching for Margaret Slachta in the Motherhouse

13 February: The siege of Budapest is ended; in March the American Military Mission moves into part of the Motherhouse;

The Budapest National Committee does not allow the Christian Women's Corps to run as a party; The Voice of the Spirit is suppressed;

---

[460] People were invited to watch an appropriate movie and its ethical dimension was highlighted that raised consciousness on a contemporary ethical issue. (Translator's note

[461] A periodical

	7 October: Local election. Margaret Slachta is elected as City Councilwoman on the ticket of the Small Landowner's Party; November : Elections for the Parliament, Marçaret Slachta is a representative on the Citizen's Democratic Party's list; November: Sister Margaret's peptic ulcer surgery;
1946	31 January: Margret Slachta's talk in the Parliament in favor of the form of state by the vision of Saint Stephen; 7 March: An instigated mass of people occupy the novitiate house in Szegvár;
1947	Talks in the Parliament: 6 January; 5 February; 12 February; 25 February; 13 March; 16 April; (for the freedom of religious education) June 1 - 29: Chapter. In Kosice (Crossing the border illegally) 7-15 July meeting with the American delegates; Talks n the Parliament 27 June 27, 23-24 July; National elections 31 August; The Christian Womens' Corps enters as a party, and sends four representatives into the Parlieament 28 October: talk in the Parliament that sends her to the Committee of Immunity; 30 October: The Committee of Immunity expels her for 2 months from the Parliament; September: Foundation in Shanghai, China
1948	Talks in the Parliament: 29 April; 4 May; 16 May, Pentecost; The Silver Jubilee of the Society of the Sisters of Social Service; 16 June: Margaret Slachta's great talk against Nationalization of Schools. The Committee of Immunity expels her from the Parliament 2x6 months. She loses her political immunity.

1949	From January she hides in the convent of the Dominican Sisters, dressed in their habit; In February she goes to a different convent; on the 25 February she becomes ill with scarlet fever; 15 May: National elections; she goes to vote 20 June Margaret Slachta writes her letter of farewell; 22-23 June she crosses the border to Austria; from that time on she uses the name of Etelka Toth; June: Religious in Romania are taken into detention; September: Margaret Slachta travels from Vienna to Rome and on 16 September arrives in America. 1 October: The Chinese Republic is established; the foundation in Shanghai is ended. November: Religious in Slovakia are taken in detention
1950	A "Small Chapter" with the American superiors; Margaret Slachta begins her visitation in the U.S.A and in Canada; she experiences more and more signs of decline caused by age; 19 June: Religious in Hungary are taken into detention;
1951:	Foundation in Cuba; in November Sister Margaret returns to Vienna with the hope of returning to Hungary;
1952:	A gynocological surgery in Vienna;
1953:	May 5: Margaret Slachta arrives in America under her own name; August 10: Chapter begins, held in Hamilton Canada. California becomes independent;
1955:	Canada also becomes independent; Rome orders the creation of a Federation.
1961:	Sister Margaret's sister Barbara dies;

1963:	Chapter during summer: Sister Margaret resigns as superior general;
1969:	Pentecost: Diamond Jubilee celebration of Sister Margaret;
1971:	Sister Margaret's sister Dr. Iren Slachta dies;
1974:	January 6: Sister Margaret Slachta returns her life to God.
1985:	September 20: The State of Israel confers on Margaret Slacht the award: "Righteous Gentile" and plants a tree is in her honor in Yad Washem.
1990:	The Believing Socialists hold a meeting in honor Margaret Slachta in Budapest;
1995:	March 15: Margaret Slachta and the Society of the Sisters of Social Service receives a memorial medal from the Hungarian Government; May 7: Margaret Slachta receives the distiction "Brave" from the Hungarian Republic
1996:	September 8: A memorial plaque is placed on the wall of Thökölyi u. 69 Street house (the former motherhouse) and a Margaret Slachta Memorial Meeting is held by the Hungarian Holocaust Committee . October 16: The Righteous Scientific Memorial meeting is held organized by the Christian Jewish Dialogue;
1997:	February 10: Ágnes Tölgyesi presents "Credo," the documentary film portraying Sister Margaret Slachta.
2017	Zuglo City Council authorizes erection of a statue of Sister Margaret Slachta recogniz - ing her as a model for all Hungarians.[462]

---

[462] Added by editor

About the Author

Ilona Mona (Anicia) SSS

Ilona Mona was born in 1921 in the village of Tápiósüly in Hungary. She was the oldest of three children. The family moved to Budapest when she was seven years old; she attended grade school and high school in Budapest where she studied German and French languages.

She was nine years old when she received her religious vocation. After first communion, inspired by a book about the Little Flower the thought was born in her heart: "God chose me for himself the way he called Saint Therese." But she searched the how and the where for a long time.

After graduation from high school she worked in the Center of Food Stamps; this place was close to the parish church dedicated to the Visitation of Mary. She spent the lunch breaks in the church, in adoration, while searching where the Lord was calling her. In 1941, after an outburst in prayer ("Lord, do something, I cannot go on like this!") she found a flyer about the School of Social Work. Right away she applied to the School of the SSS. During the two years of study she encountered sisters but they did not make a positive impression on her.

She asked permission to participate in a Holy Hour in the chapel of the sisters; there, gazing at the Blessed Sacrament she experienced an inner impulse that she had to enter to this community. On 19 March

1942 she applied to the SSS as a non-conventual, i.e.as a secret sister.

After graduating from the School of Social Work she became a social worker in the city of Mosonmagyaróvár (Northwest Hungary). She worked there until the bombing of Budapest started in 1944. As she was very much concerned about her family, she contacted her sister Veronika and then traveled home and asked the National Office of Social Affairs to transfer her to Budapest. She was reassigned to Pestszenterzsébet. She survived the siege of Budapest living with her family in a basement. With her sisters she worked as a Red Cross nurse. In January 1945 during a bombing raid she and her father were injured. Her father died of his injuries.

At Sister Paula's request she continued her novitiate as a conventual sister. Her four years of non-conventual novitiate was counted as one year of conventual preparation. In 1946 she asked for a religious name: Anicia - derived from the family name Anicius of St. Benedict. Her motto was: "abyssuss Abyssum invocat" (in English: "deep calls onto Deep" Ps 42,8). She made her first vows at Pentecost 1948. At the time of her final vows she added to her motto: "Amen, Alleluia." In 1948 she was assigned to the National Association of the Catholic Working Girls (DL).

In 1950 sisters throughout Soviet controlled countries "were scattered." The Constitutions of the SSS enabled the sisters to continue their consecrated life even though the religious orders were dispersed. The sisters could follow the goals of the SSS even in secret; they had weekly meetings in small groups in apartments. However, after 1950 the livelihood and

housing of the sisters was not simple. Since the DL (Catholic Working Girls) house was closed, sister Anicia lived in rented rooms. She arrived at the apartment of Mrs. Margit Hetenyi to the Gellerthegy Street in 1954. Mrs. Hetenyi had asked Sister Paula to send her sisters as tenants. A year later Sister Ilona Borsai (Picuri:"Little One") moved in to the same apartment. During the course of years many sisters found home in this flat. The door was always open for sisters coming from abroad, from Transylvania, for any who needed help, both sisters and friends. Sister Anicia has lived in this same place ever since.

During Communism the life of a non-conventual sister was not lacking dangers: monitoring (being spied upon), interrogations, and prison. Sisters were arrested and imptisoned throughout Eastern Europe. Sister Anicia was interrogated at one of the holding centers as well.

Beginning in 1951 Sister Anicia worked in a machine factory as unskilled labor; in 1953 she received a disability pension because of her heart condition. Later she was employed in the "cottage industry" (it gave work like handicraft, sewing, etc. mostly for former runs). After some years, with the help of Sister Ilona Borsai she was employed as a part time typist in the Institution of Public Education. With the support of the Institute she was accepted to ELTE (Eotvos Lorand University of Sciences) to the faculty of Hungarian-library. She earned her degree in 1961. In 1961-62 she was a music lexicon editorial corrector and from 1962 to 1976 she was the librarian, then the chief librarian of the Bartók Béla Musical Vocational Secondary School (formerly National Music School).

Her scientific work is outstanding. Her special field of research is the history of Hungarian music publications. Her work was published by the Music Institute of MTA (National Academy of Sciences). In 2002, for her merit in the field of scientific, pedagogical and librarian work she was awarded the Golden Merit Cross of the Hungarian Republic.

She became the historian of the SSS, collector of SSS documents, and the biographer of Sister Sara and later of Sister Margaret. From as early as 1964 she was continually preoccupied by the question, "Who was Sister Margaret?" In 1964, with the help of her family, she visited Buffalo, New York for the first time. (Her blood sister left Hungary in 1956 and settled in the USA). She met Sister Margaret, who by then was already sick - and this stimulated inspiration. After long prayers she understood that the Society was God's idea - spelled out by Sister Margaret, and that she (Anicia) had to serve this same idea. Beginning in 1976, the time of her retirement, she started to collect the historical documents of the SSS stored in the National Archives, the National Szechenyi Library, the Archives of the Archbishopric in Esztergom, the Archives of the Capital and of the Parliament. (The archives of the community were either lost or scattered due to the communist persecution). In addition, for a while she was working with the bequests of the sisters. This is how she came across Sister Sara's diary. As a researcher she did very precise work. Researchers, university students and many more used the archives she created; they referred to it as SZTTTI (Historical Archives of the SSS). She was regularly invited to give lectures at the Society of the Hungarian Church History; the lectures were published in the Schemes of Hungarian Church History. She appeared several times on

television as they broadcast her talks about Sister Margaret. When any documentary related to the Society was created Sister Anicia provided the material. Series of articles and studies published in journals are the hallmark of her work.

Sister Anicia also served as councilor in the Hungarian District; three times she was chapter delegate (1976, 1991 and 1997) and she was elected several times as a local moderator of the sisters. She intermittently taught the history of the SSS for young sisters throughout the 1980s and 1990s. She gave retreats to the sisters. Between 1991 and 1995 she published a series of articles about Sister Margaret. Her book on Sister Sara was published in 1990; and the one on Sister Margaret in 1997.

According to Sister Anicia nothing happened in her life the way she had thought and planned it to happen. Everything turned out better and had a happier ending than what she had expected or hoped.

Sister Anicia died 2 July 2019.

●●●

The five Slachta sisters, from left to right: Iren, Borbala, Maria, Margaret, Elizabeth

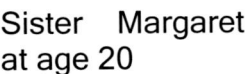

Sister Margaret at age 20

Sister Margaret, when she was a member of the Social Mission Society.

Above: Sister Margaret receiving her mandate to become the first woman member of the Hungarian Parliament on March 28, 1920.

Sister Margaret on January 6, 1924

Clockwise from top:
Sisters Frederica (left),
Hedvig Vozary (right),
Petra Ronai,
Paula Ronai,
Gertrud Horvath,
Mechtild Kun,
Mary Schwartz,
Yolanda Horvath

Sister Margaret with group of sisters in Buffalo in 1925

Sister Margaret with Sister Frederica in Los Angeles in 1936

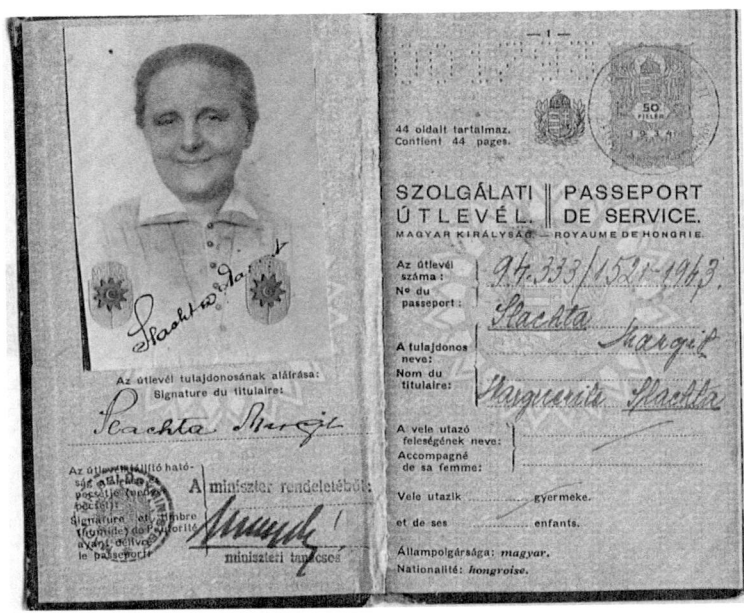

Sister Margaret's passport, which she used when traveling to Italy to meet Pope Pius XII. She requested his help to save Jewish people in Slovakia. Because of her intervention the pope ordered the Bishops of Slovakia to protest the deportations, which were then temporarily suspended.

Sister Margaret in the corridor of the Hungarian Parliament in 1948 holding letters of protest against the nationalization of schools.

Sister   Margaret
during her last years

Sister Margaret's grave in the Holy Cross Cemetery in Lackawanna, NY

Yas Vashem certificate and medal,
which she received posthumously in 1986.

441

Margaret Slachta

by
Ilona Mona, SSS

Translated by Anne E. Lehner, SSS
Edited by Damaris Bradish, Ph. D.

Sisters of Social Service
296 Summit Avenue
Buffalo, NY 14214

ISBN: 978-164633202-1